Bizarre Britain

Bizarre Britain
A Calendar of Eccentricity

Roy Kerridge

Basil Blackwell

© Roy Kerridge 1985

First published 1985
Reprinted 1986

Basil Blackwell Ltd
108 Cowley Road, Oxford OX4 1JF, UK

Basil Blackwell Inc.
432 Park Avenue South, Suite 1505,
New York, NY 10016, USA

British Library Cataloguing in Publication Data

Kerridge, Roy
    Bizarre Britain: a calendar of eccentricity.
    1. Great Britain – Social life and customs – 1945 –
    I. Title
    941.085'8 DA588
    ISBN 0–631–13741–6

Library of Congress Cataloging in Publication Data

Kerridge, Roy.
    Bizarre Britain.
    Includes index.
    1. England – Social life and customs – 1945 –
    2. Folklore – England. I. Title.
    DA589.4.K47 1985 941.085 85–6165
    ISBN 0–631–13741–6

Typeset by Alan Sutton Publishing Ltd, Gloucester
Printed in Great Britain by Billing & Sons Ltd, Worcester

Contents

CONTENTS

Acknowledgements

Fourteen of the articles in this book appeared, in a slightly different form, in the *Spectator*. A few paragraphs have appeared in the *Field*, the *Daily Telegraph* and the *Salisbury Review*. I thank all the editors for giving permission for this work to be reproduced here. Thanks must go also to the following individuals who have helped and encouraged me in various ways: Mark Cronshaw, Nisa Khan, Lionel D'Rozario, Roger Scruton, Caroline Yeates, Jessica Gwynne, Mark Foot, Mike Strong, Dr Ian and Mrs Eileen Paisley, Mr and Mrs Price and Tim of the Bridge Street Stores, Knighton; Tim Edye, Nicholas and Anne Bagnall and family, Michael Wharton, Mr and Mrs Irving of the Narrows Bookshop, Knighton; David Beech, Ted Dugan, Steve and Julie Winnard and family, Tess Buckland and Derek Schofield, the Haxey Chip Shop lady, the Knighton Chip Shop people, Ros Hoy and Agnes Graburn, Geoffrey Messer, the Secretary of the Victoria Working Men's Club, Bacup; the Haxey postmaster, Mrs Farmer and family, Mr and Mrs Hughes, Martin, Angela and Edward of Caernarvon, the staff of the White Lion Free School, Islington; and last but not least, my two Sussex typists, Celia Barrett of Littlehampton and Christine Talbot of Lancing.

Author's Note

The following names used in this book are fictitious: John Bickle and his family, Mr and Mrs Price of Pembrokeshire and all their family, friends and acquaintances, Lula, Edwin Gospatrick, Mrs Logan, Barry of the Preachers, Mr and Mrs Davey and family and Major Blank.

Introduction

Leaving the warm, friendly atmosphere of primary school for the homework-ridden rough-house of secondary school was a terrible shock for me, back in the nineteen fifties. 'It's not the work he objects to, it's the discipline,' my mother explained to a friend.

'On the contrary,' I piped up at once, 'it's not the discipline I mind, but the work! Anyone can obey orders, and the discipline's dead soothing. It's the work I don't like, 'cos it's too hard to understand.'

Even so, my memories of Holloway Comprehensive are happy ones, thanks to two subjects that redeemed the rest, English and History. Mr McIlwain, my old history teacher, thought I had a flair for the subject. He was wrong, for I only enjoyed history while the Middle Ages were being taught. Never able to remember the names of kings, or dates or battles, I delighted in the ideal of the medieval village, huts grouped around a castle and a monastery not too far away. The peasants interested me more than the priests and barons, and I drew a picture of them ploughing their strip fields with stunted oxen, a windmill standing on a grassy knoll nearby. Along the horizon stretched a dark line of oak forest, full of wolves and deer. On my visits to Brighton, the train would cross a viaduct outside Haywards Heath and I would revel in the sight of the forest of my dreams, an oak wood that loomed over the fields, brooding and filled with ancient magic.

My idea of a 'normal' English way of life seems derived from the Middle Ages. At the back of most people's minds are the fairy-tales they learned as children, most of which are set in the same medieval dreamworld. So the way of feeling, and sometimes thinking, that appears to be natural is one which places a king on the throne, and the throne not far from a window. As the palace is on a hill, the monarch can look out and see tiled roofs far below, huddled above cobbled alley-ways that give way to dusty paths leading to thatched villages and the homes of the lesser nobility. Music of church bells fills the air, and everyone has the chance of going to Heaven when they die. Nobody questions this way of life. If they did, the dream would become a nightmare. Heretics and traitors would appear and either destroy the Church–state or be themselves destroyed, horribly tortured in dungeons. Fortunately, God looks down from the clouds all the time, and prevents any such catastrophe.

This England never quite existed, yet it survives to this day, the foundation of a healthy mind. It can be felt in our institutions, in the popularity of the Royal Family, in the terraced streets that yet remain as villages in our cities, in the county families who run fêtes and try to look after 'their' people, and in the Anglican ghost of the medieval Church, now a ghost of a ghost but still faintly visible. Being aware of such an England is a tonic in itself. Belonging to it is a matter of luck, of being born in the right place, to the right people and with a tranquil, easy-going mind.

But the false sciences of the day have led many minds away from fairy-tales. Sensing that something is wrong, these lost souls try to find their way back, but fairyland is an elusive place. Rejecting the torturous world of sociology and computers, people seek solace in cults, communes and crankiness. Thus they place themselves further and further away from the cosy 'ordinary' world they seek. To *try* to be a natural is a contradiction in terms.

As stranger and stranger new customs are introduced to Britain by searchers for self-fulfilment, our old customs, deriving from the Middle Ages and beyond, struggle along somehow, as best they can. Often they are preserved by village families who have 'always' sung, danced, dressed up or acted in a certain way. 'Always' is a long time. One of the reasons why I preferred peasants to noblemen when I was a boy was because they held to pagan ways in secret. History for me led backwards to the cave and the leaping shaman in the firelight. And now I have found that not only the medieval peasant felt the stirrings of something far older than he could understand moving in his soul. We all do so.

Recorded history – that of the last few thousand years – is only the tip of a gigantic, strangely shaped iceberg, when compared with the previous million years of unlettered humanity. Unwritten thoughts, deeds and customs, spoken about and deeply felt in days long before the Bible was written or the pyramids were built, can still affect us all. Chips from the submerged ice surfaced when the Reptile House was opened at London Zoo and the public at once began throwing pennies into the crocodile pool, their sacrifices to the water dragon. To take another example from our hidden past – why should it, evidently, be so laughable or shocking for a Briton to eat horseflesh? Saxons ate it on their pagan holy days, and to shun such meat was once the sign of a Christian. Our *old* customs, which now seem merely bizarre, usually hint at a prehistoric explanation.

But what of the *new* customs, the other strand in Bizarre Britain's weird tapestry? Many of them, by an absurd paradox, are old customs in the wrong hands! Thanks to the Welfare State, people are no longer driven to every means imaginable to earn an honest penny. Humble folk who may once have been Punch and Judy showmen, street clowns, tumblers and ballad singers now draw the dole. Today's clown, folk-singer or Punch and Judy man has been to technical college, has read about folk customs in books and is probably paid by the local council for his services. The unsophisticated know all too little folklore, while the educated know too much, all jumbled together from every nation under the sun! It is as if someone has been playing pea-and-thimble with brains and heads – the right thoughts are in the wrong people!

A feeling of estrangement from peasant life has resulted in the boom for Folklore. Complex minds which once may have reached towards high art now absorb little else but a variety of folk customs torn from their native settings. This Irish stew of peasant notions bubbling in the mind of an art student or computer operator, each ingredient affecting the taste of the next, helps to Keep Britain Bizarre.

Brooding deeply on the folklore of an alien people does not turn you into one of those people. It simply changes you in unpredictable ways. This is what happened to the youngsters who first listened to rock-and-roll, itself a hybrid of Negro blues and Southern hillbilly music. Instead of becoming Negroes or hillbillies – a delightful prospect – they became Teddy Boys, hippies, Mods and Rockers.

Any Scotsman who knows his Scotch can tell you that something good can be bad for you. The enormous impact of traditional American blues music on the young English middle class in the 1960s is a case in point.

In 1912, E.V. Lucas wrote in his novel *London Lavender* of the perils involved when folk-songs are popularised: 'It might be dangerous. These songs are too fascinating. Mayfair would be decimated.' Prophecy, inspired prophecy! Strange things happen, realms can be overthrown, when the heirs to a literary tradition inherit somebody else's oral tradition instead! That which is age-old seems to strangers to be exciting and new. McCarthyite investigators in America were quite right when they declared folk music to be Communism's fifth column. The folk-singing German *Wandervogel* paved the way for the Hitler Youth. The difference between

INTRODUCTION

'wild' or unselfconscious folklore and 'tame' or collected folklore, is that tame folklore, by a paradox, is passed on through books, often written by 'progressive' authors. My own descriptions of Bizarre Britain include both the natural and the would-be natural.

Some have tried to return to Christendom by becoming 'born again' Christians, a separated people. But I believe that Christendom itself remains, gleaming here and there through gaps in the piles of accumulated scientific rubbish. A mixture of old ways and new, Bizarre Britain awaits our exploration. Let our journey begin – a quest that strangely resembles the wanderings I have made between 1980 and 1984, crammed neatly into one year. We shall begin with January, a month named after the god of endings and beginnings.

for Christopher Booker

The Haxey Hood, and Winter on a Welsh Farm

With a sense of mounting excitement, I hurried towards the village of Haxey. My route was a disused railway line that made its way through scrubby woodland among the flat fields of the Isle of Axholme in Lincolnshire. Despite the efforts of the Dutchman Vermuyden, who drained the fens in the seventeenth century, the Islanders still claim to be surrounded by water – in a ditch, dyke, canal and river. Talking of ditches, it was rather awkward the way the railway people had removed the iron bridges, so that I had to climb down and up steep embankments every mile or so. As I neared Haxey, I saw a strange, tall, four-legged animal standing in the middle of the path, far ahead of me. Now and again it moved uncertainly to and fro. I had just made up my mind that it was a baby elephant when it split into two and proved to be a pair of sweethearts, who had been hugging one another. Averting my eyes in embarrassment, I opened a gate and stepped into Haxey village.

Here, every January 6th, on Old Christmas Day, is played a curious game known as Haxey Hood. The Hood itself resembles a large German sausage, brown and shiny and about two feet long – a thick strip of rope encased in leather. According to legend, a certain Lady Mowbray was crossing a hill outside Haxey one day in the thirteenth century, when her hood blew away across the fields. Thirteen peasants rushed after it like mad, and despite the strong wind, one brought it back, to be awarded the title of Lord Boggin. The grateful lady granted them the land they had raced over, and the men of Haxey were asked the re-enact the event every year. So far they have always done so, and the main players and organisers are still called Boggins. Scholars claim to have

1

found a pagan origin in the Hood game, and some trace it back to the fertility rites of the ancient Celts.

Haxey village seemed to be built up and down a long street, with a church at one end and a pub, the King's Arms, at the other. 'No matter which pub holds the Hood, the King's Arms or the Carpenter's, the biggest celebration is always at the King's,' the postmaster, a keen fan, told me. So to the King's Arms I went, where I found the Boggins in red jerseys, looking very like rugby players. Sturdy young men with short curly hair, they gave the lie to one of Orwell's prophecies, that very soon no one would say 'I were cooming oop street,' any more.

'. . . So I took a look mysen, and there was 'ood staring me int face, laik, sort of thing, laik,' one of them remarked. This proved to be prophecy of a more inspired order, for at that moment the door flew open and in strode the Lord Boggin holding the sausage-like Hood, followed by the Chief Boggin and the Fool. They made an impressive entrance, for both Lord and Chief wore huntsmen's jackets and boots, together with hats covered in plastic flowers and ornaments, topped by two pheasant tails sticking up in the air. Middle-aged men, they did not let their head-dresses interfere with their natural dignity. As staff of office, the Lord held a rod of bound willows. The Fool's hat was of green velvet, covered in badges and he wore baggy white trousers with red patches.

I introduced myself, and found that all three men took the Hood game very seriously. It was by no means a frolic, for local feeling ran high, and King's Arms and 'Carps' supporters were as fervent as football fans. The object of the game was to push the Hood against the opposing crowd into your pub doorway, and the winning pub held the Hood for a year. As the 'Carps' was at Westwoodside, a mile or so out of Haxey village, there was a strong feeling of rivalry. A third pub, halfway between the two, was now closed on Hood night, as the landlady feared for her carpet and curtains. If that landlady could have heard what some of the young men were saying about her, she would have turned as red as a Boggin. Several older people in the village saw her point of view, and one later told me: 'No one leaves cars out on Hood night. Sometimes the lads turn them over or dance on the roofs in their great boots.'

Just now, however, all was peaceful, as the Fool had his face ceremonially made up with streaks and splotches of black and red. Then the younger Boggins lined up behind the three leaders and gave us a deep, rousing chorus of 'To be a Farmer's boy'. Many of the drinkers present worked on the land, and looked down into their glasses modestly. Local newspapermen crowded around Stan Borr, the Lord

Boggin, oldest of the team, who had held his post for many a year. Arthur Clark, the Chief, was a shrewd, horsey, Flurry Knox of a man, well suited to his huntsman's jacket. After a few more drinks, the Boggins gave us a hearty version of 'John Barleycorn'.

> He'll make a man into a fool
> And a fool into an ass!

sang the Fool in a booming voice. Inspired by good Sir John Barleycorn, Bt., they finished their concert with a curious ditty called 'Drink Old England Dry'. This appeared to be about the Napoleonic wars, but had been updated to include later heroes and enemies:

> Supposing we should meet with the Germans by the way,
> Ten thousand to one we will show them British play!
> With our swords and our cutlasses we'll fight until we die, we die,
> Before that they shall come and drink old England dry!

> [Chorus] Aye dry, aye dry my boys, aye dry!
> They say that they will come and drink old England dry.

> Then up spake Lord Roberts of fame and renown,
> He swears he'll be true to his country and his crown!
> For the cannons they shall rattle and the bullets they shall fly, shall fly,
> Before that they shall come and drink old England dry!

One more drink and the Boggins were away, leaping into the back of a lorry that was to take them to the Carpenter's Arms. No more was seen of them for an hour, by which time a large crowd had assembled around a flat stone outside the churchyard, formerly the village cross. Mothers, children and tweedy couples with dogs looked on. Having whizzed right round the parish, a line of scarlet Boggins could now be seen striding up the village street. When they reached the stone, the Fool suddenly made a dash for it. With a roar the young men set off in pursuit and carried him back, kicking and struggling. Holding the Hood aloft in his right hand, he climbed on to the stone, and made a welcoming speech, apparently unaware that a sack of straw had been tipped out behind him and set on fire.

'Matches? Do you want a light for a cigarette?' he asked innocently. Flames shot up within an inch of his posterior. Named Peter Bee, the

Fool was known to his friends as Buzzbum. Despite his uncomfortable position, he gave a serious talk to the young men present, for anybody could join in the game, and all had to know the rules.

'Now remember, this isn't a Running Hood, it's a Sway Hood!' he warned. 'If anyone's caught running with the Hood he'll be sent back and the Hood will be thrown again. And I'm not joking!'

'Neither's that fire,' a housewife observed as a tongue of flame flew pantwards. Hastily, the Fool ended his speech with the ritual words:

> Hoose against Hoose,
> Toon against Toon!
> If thou meets a man
> Knock'im doon!
> (But don't 'urt 'im.)

With that, he jumped down before he could prove the folklorists right and become a human sacrifice. The fire was put out, the Lord took the Hood and the Fool waved a stick and bladder at the crowds. What appeared to be all the Islanders of Axholme surged in one great mass after the Boggins onto a bare, windy hill outside town, supposedly the spot where Lady Mowbray had lost her hood. We all clumped across the ploughed hillside and gathered round the Lord, who planted his willow staff into a furrow.

'The farmer always ploughs this field so you don't get hurt when you fall down on the soft earth,' a Hood-follower told me. However, this did not explain why the field was covered in sprouting green wheat. Perhaps a good trampling from a Hood game does wonders for the crops.

False hoods, made of sacking, were piled around the Lord's feet. Members of the crowd, usually pretty girls, were invited to throw these for the local boys to fight over. If a player could reach a pub doorway with his trophy, he would receive a prize of 'ten bob'; the sturdy Islanders would as soon say 'fifty pence' as declare that they came from 'Humberside'. If anyone pronounced 'hoose' as 'house' they were sternly corrected, for the rhyme had to be repeated each time a hood was thrown.

As soon as a hood went up in the air, the young men rushed towards it, knocking down anyone in their way. Rugby tackles sent the rich earth flying, and bruised young men, some dressed in baggy overalls, sat nursing their injuries ruefully. The hood could be thrown from one man to the next, but the Boggins usually caught it and it was then

4

taken back to the Lord for a re-throw. No one was allowed to tackle a Boggin, and every time a hood was lost in this way, the loser shouted, 'Boggined!' One visiting youth from Scunthorpe who *did* fell a Boggin received an awful ticking-off from his mates. 'Why hadn't nobody *told* me!' he howled at the top of his voice.

To my alarm, a hood flew over my head and I feared I would go down with the scrum. Memories of total despair and bewilderment on the school football field flooded back. 'But what is the *object* of all this?' I remembered asking myself, as I avoided the stampeding hordes at my first game. Those early primary school lessons in avoiding sportsmen now stood me in good stead, and I escaped the Revenge of the Hood.

After these skirmishes the game grew serious, as the real leather Hood was held aloft by the Lord, and the 'hoose' incantation was chanted for the last time. Through the twilight the mighty sausage spun, and where it landed was transformed into a Sway: fifty youths, heads down, arms locked together, struggled to and fro like a monstrous headless beast with rows of muddy knees. Everything had to be done together in a mass, in the midst of which somebody clutched the Hood. The Hood-holder, whoever he was – a brave, desperate man who had possibly been disappointed in love – had to push towards the pub of his choice. He could not break free and run; 'running Hoods' were forbidden, for the Hood must stay in the Sway.

As each pub was over a mile away, the game lasted several hours. Youths leaped into the Sway and were swallowed up alive. No one was ever killed, as every time someone fell over, they was a cry of 'Man down!' and he was dragged out by the legs. When the Sway crashed blindly into Haxey or Westwoodside, stone walls could topple and cars be overturned. It was all too much for me, and I adjourned for a newspaperful of chips. When I came back, a large, restless crowd stood talking in the middle of the road that ran beside the field. By now it was dark, but that was not the reason why the Sway could not be seen. It had broken up into puzzled individuals, for the Hood had vanished! Just when the Sway was at its hottest and most furious, someone had asked where the Hood was. Nobody knew, and after a search, the Lord and the Chief had driven into the village to make enquiries.

'It's the first time this has happened in living memory.' a young man told me. An ugly mood seemed to seize the crowd. No one moved out of the way to let cars go by. The startled motorists, staring at the surly Boggins in amazement, must have thought that a Red Revolution had begun. A youth began beating on the side of a car, and a hefty Boggin restored order by butting him in the face. Blood had now been shed, but before worse could happen, the Lord, pale faced and trembling, drove up and told his story.

Stunned, Boggins and others listened as their Lord spoke. *The Hood was at the King's Arms!* In the height of the Sway, someone had stuffed it up his jumper and sneaked out between the forest of legs. With four others, the minimum allowed for a breakaway Sway, he had slipped down to the King's Arms, leaving the others pushing and groaning. It was an outrage! The Lord and Chief had demanded the Hood be returned, but the landlord and others had refused to let it go. His explanation over, the Lord drove off and left us standing there. Four youngsters began a Hoodless Sway, struggling across the furrows like stags with locked antlers, but I decided to go down to the King's Arms to see what was happening. On the way, I met two youths searching for a lost ten-bob bit. I found it for them, and we walked down the hill together.

'Every year the game's fixed! Someone bribes the Boggins,' my new friends told me, yet both agreed that a Hoodnapping of this kind had never happened before. Later, I learned that back in 1943 the Hood had been smuggled from the field by some visiting soldiers, who hid it in their jeep.

I told the young men that I was a writer.

'Do you think you ought to phone Fleet Street?' one of them enquired anxiously. When they learned that I was not a sports reporter, they were slightly disappointed, as they longed for the Hood game to be treated as seriously as football in the outside world.

Sure enough, in the King's Arms, there hung the Hood, above a picture of the Mona Lisa, who now looked more enigmatic than ever. 'It were a breakaway Sway fair and square,' the landlord insisted. Nevertheless, an Indian schoolmaster from Doncaster, a most erudite man, was scandalised. 'Normally if the King's Arms had won the Hood there'd be such a crush of men grabbing the free pints that you'd drink out of your neighbour's glass,' he explained. 'Tonight even the staunchest King's Arms men wish the Hood had not been taken this way. No one is singing, although I believe somebody struck up a verse of 'Robbin' Hood'. But it was not considered in good taste.'

Together we trudged over the hill to the Carpenter's. With their consciences clear, the 'Carps' crowd were making merry, stamping their feet to Scottish fiddle music from the juke-box. The floor was awash with mud and broken glasses. Also broken was the Fool's bladder, which had snapped off its stick on someone's head.

'As far as I'm concerned, the Hood is null and void,' the Fool pronounced with bitterness. Bitter of a different kind soon weaned him from his 'mighty mood'. Before long he had joined in the banter between Islanders and visitors, as cheerful shouts of 'Fisherman's filly!' and 'Country bumpkin!' filled the air. The former insult, I was told, plumbed depths of obscenity seldom known to man. An irrepressible young man, fat, and glassy-eyed, fearlessly chaffed a craggy-faced country Teddy Boy: 'You ought to pay me for talking to you, 'cos you're *sooch* a coontry boompkin!'

The Fool had donned a curly wig by now, and the red streaks on his nose were emerging with a more natural hue. 'Two pints of dandelion and burdock and he's away!' someone shouted.

Outside, the word 'Hood' seemed to be on everybody's lips. 'In two weeks' time this will be all forgotten,' whispered the schoolmaster from Doncaster.

Months later when I passed through Haxey, I found the Hood field luxuriant with wheat. By then I had been to Abingdon, in Oxfordshire, where each year a mock Mayor is elected and chaired around the town, accompanied by a stout man in a floral hat. This worthy carries a pole on which is fixed the head of a gigantic black ox carved out of elm wood. Garlanded with flowers, the head has the date '1700' painted on its forehead, above its large white and red eyes. Enormous curved aurochs-like horns painted black seem to be a part of the carving, but are actually those of a real ox who had met his fate in the year written on his brow. Apparently, in 1700 there had been great rivalry in Abingdon between the young men of Ock Street and those of a vanished district near the ruined abbey, known as the Vineyard. After an ox-roast, the men had formed into two teams to fight over the animal's head, which was scrummaged to and fro in a rough Haxey-like game. Ock Street won the contest, and the horns, soon afterwards fixed on to the mask, have been preserved by the family of one of the original contestants, Hemmings.

Pagan overtones in the story suggest that tussles over an ox-head had occurred more than once, before the eighteenth century. Garlands of flowers adorned most animal sacrifices in classical times, and still do in modern India. In Dorset, villagers once paraded with an ox–devil head on a stick, called the Ooser, perhaps a remnant of a Stone Age 'horned-god' cult. Real horns fixed to a wooden mask suggest the Neanderthal custom of fastening a real bear's skull to a model body, as found by Alpine cave-explorers. The Haxey Hood may once have been

7

the Haxey Head, for draught oxen were sometimes known as 'plough boggins' in the old days.

According to a pamphlet written by a former vicar of Haxey, the church bells used to ring as the Boggins made their rounds of the pubs before the game, and the Fool's burning was a more harmless affair, with damp straw used to make more smoke than fire. On my visit the church was locked, no bells rang and no clergyman was in sight. Where vicars abdicate, paganism creeps back, and something faintly brutal and alarming can overtake the most merry and harmless country festival. Stan Borr, the Lord Boggin, is soon due to retire, and I hope he may preside over a more successful Hood game before he hands his staff of office to a younger Boggin.

'Not far from yere, in the Gwaun Valley, they still celebrate Christmas on Old Christmas Day,' my Welsh friend Mrs Price told me. 'They do some funny things there, mind. When they die, they stuff each other up the chimneys, so people tell me.'

We were sitting around the fire in the Prices' seventeenth-century farmhouse, where I was a self-invited guest. The farm was in the middle of a wood among the Pembrokeshire hills, and in the distance the white-capped Prescelly Mountains could be seen. Slabs of slate, on which Mrs Price baked her Welsh cakes, enclosed the huge stone fireplace where logs blazed merrily. Above the mantelpiece hung a whaler's harpoon. Mr Price had once been a ship's carpenter, and ships in bottles he had made, with waves of painted putty, stood in slate-lined nooks built into the fireplace. Mr Price was busy in the workshop he had converted from a stable, and his son and Tim the apprentice-cum-farmhand were somewhere out in the cold, looking after the animals. I made myself comfortable in Mr Price's chair, which he had bought from a dentist, and gratefully accepted another cup of tea.

Years before, I had met the Prices at the home of a country squire who wanted Mr Price to make him some wooden stocks to complete some antique guns he owned. Mr Price, too, was an enthusiastic gun-collector, and while the two men drank whisky and discussed weaponry, Mrs Price had told me of the farm they had just moved into, far from their native Merthyr Tydfil. Then and there I decided that Mr and Mrs Price were my kind of people. Mrs Price, a little, pink-faced bustling woman whose mission in life was to make others happy, always seemed pleased to see me. Her husband, a genial giant of a man with grey whiskers, seemed more amused than anything else whenever I bobbed up again.

I would share a bedroom with Tim and a fearsome black coke stove known as 'the bogey'. This room still resembled the stable it once had been, with a half-door then another door inside leading to a similar room that contained a pile of coke and a freezer, and several hens, a cock and a cat who all roosted on the rafters. My bed was low on the ground, and snug with an enormous patchwork quilt. This quilt, together with the Prices' way of life and that of their neighbours, reminded me a great deal of books I had read on Appalachian log-cabin life in America. All the neighbours seemed to be small farmers, and most of them helped each other out at hay-making and harvest time by lending machines and working in rotation. This was a new peasantry that had arisen from the break-up of great estates. Mouldering nearby in the woods was a great white mansion, cracked and peeling, to which the Prices' farm and stable had once belonged.

In the morning I would wake a long time after the hard-working Tim, dress and hurry out into the farmyard. To reach the snug kitchen and front room, and the oak-beamed tranquillity of the old house, I had to cross the cobbled yard, which formed an imperfect square, framed by stone cattle sheds and stables, painted white, and broken at one end by a Dutch barn and an iron gate. I would hurry through groups of self-important, easily irritated ducks and chickens. One side of the square was completed by the long, sturdy two-storey farmhouse, the walls bright pink beneath the slate roof.

'I wanted the place to stand out, so I used white lime mixed with red oxide for the painting,' Mr Price told me, fingering his beard. 'The old Welsh way was to use real ox-blood, but I had to make do.'

Whether in the gloom of a January morning or on a spring day when swallows swooped into the stalls where their mud nests hung on beams in the semi-darkness, the farmyard seemed a strange, haunted place. The outhouses gave me a feeling of having slipped back into a bygone age, for the sagging slate roofs were plastered with ancient 'concrete' whose chief ingredient seemed to be mud. Inside the farmhouse, the long room where I sat by the fire was used for eating, reading and doing the accounts. It was dominated by an immense oak table with vines and fruit carved around the legs. Visitors assumed the table had come with the house, but in fact Mr Price had made it himself. Easy chairs, bookshelves and guns filled the rest of the room, with a television for John Wayne films and a black Welsh dresser hung with china. Near the dresser was a small window with slanting wooden slats, that intrigued me. Mr Price had long ago fitted a pane over them, but the slats remained, acting as a net curtain, for those inside could see out but not vice versa. Before glass came into general use, such windows must have been common. Some of the Prices' neighbours on remote hill farms still had no electricity, and the nearest town, St David's, had a shop with a window full of oil lamps.

Everyone in the Price family worked very hard, which made me feel faintly uneasy. Not only am I lazy, but I'm also very helpless – the fear of doing something wrong and causing havoc acting as a spur to greater laziness. When washing-up was spoken of, I buried my face in a book. Mr Price was fond of gripping adventure yarns, and his library contained sea stories, scientific works, classics, Conrad, an American gun almanac he called 'the shooter's Bible' and, above all, collected volumes of *Strand* magazine, my favourite.

Tim, a big, curly-headed, gawky young man with an enormous grin, and Davey, the Price boy, never read anything except paperback westerns.

'That was a rotten school you went to, that Comprehensive', Mr Price observed to his son. 'They didn't teach you *anything* there, not a damn thing! All you did was play football.'

'No, it was a really good school, Dad,' the young man said, his eyes shining as he recollected his Golden Age. 'What's wrong with football? It's better than *reading* any day.'

Settling himself in the dentist's chair, which I had now hastily vacated, Mr Price stretched his boots towards the fire and filled his pipe meditatively. His great black thumb rose up and down like a steam hammer, pressing the tobacco into place. Noticing my admiration for his thumb, my host began one of his true-life sea stories – this one about the time when he had been working on a ship with a madman on board, during the war.

'This fellow had gone doolally, and he was being shipped home from India. When one of the crew offered him a lit cigarette, he bit the man's thumb off! Straight away the madman jumped over the side, perhaps in remorse, broke through a net placed there for safety and vanished into the sea. We had an African sailor on board, and when he saw this, *he* jumped straight into the sea to rescue the mad fellow. He had just time to raise one arm above the surface and then the sharks closed in. If a shark swims straight behind a ship, it always means death. If it overtakes the ship, then all's well. There's lots of sayings and proverbs at sea. It's bad luck to whistle on board, that kind of thing. I used to take a rise out of passengers when we crossed the Line.'

'"Did you feel the bump in the night when we went over the equator," I'd ask.

"Oh, that's what it was!" some of them would say, quite seriously. I put a hair over the end of a telescope and told them to look through it to see the equator.'

'"If you listen, you can hear the dogfish barking and the catfish miaowing down there in the sea," I'd tell them. They'd believe *that* but when I told them about flying fish, they wouldn't believe it!'

At that moment, Mrs Price took down the hunting horn from the shelf in the kitchen, stepped out into the yard and gave a long, loud blast. Through the window I could see Tim, who had been mending a roof, hurry down so fast that the ladder shook. Wiping his hands on his overalls, he rushed to the bathroom for a quick wash, before leaping into his seat at table. I was there before him. Mrs Price was a famous cook, and the meal began with soup, or 'cawl', then an immense roast meal and finally a fruit pie with cream, as well as never-ending supplies of tea and bread and butter. On this occasion the table was crowded, as a young couple, Ted and Yvonne, had accompanied the Prices from their village just outside Merthyr and were staying with them until the derelict farmhouse they'd bought was made habitable. Their daughter Sharon, and Rosie the Prices' milkmaid, made up the party.

Rosie was a little round goblin of a woman, very merry, her wizened face breaking into earthy, gap-toothed grins with something cheerfully malevolent about them, a spirit from the wood smoke. In repose her hairy chin nearly met her nose; she had dark, lank hair and her body seemed to be all bottom. Devoted to the cows, she rose at dawn and waded through the muck to milk them by hand into a bucket. The more modern-minded Tim took care to wipe the teats with an antiseptic rag when he milked, sitting on a stool with his head down, pulling first at the front two, then at the back. Mrs Price's rich golden butter came from the Jersey cow.

Old Mrs Edwards, the previous owner of the farm, had gone to an orphanage near Oxford, some time in the 1920s, to find herself a milkmaid. She happened to pick Rosie, then aged thirteen, and took the child back to Pembrokeshire with her. From then on, Rosie looked after the cows, sleeping in the kitchen with her clothes on, and learning nothing of the outside world. Her mistress had neglected to tell her about wages, so Rosie worked for nothing until Mrs Edwards' death. Then, to her bemusement, she received thousands of pounds from the strange old lady's will, as if her wages had been made up in a lump. Too simple for any company save that of cows, she insisted on staying on when the Prices arrived. They showed her how to draw her money, and Rosie's life now began to look rosy indeed.

So when the dinner horn sounded at the Prices', the board was full. Everyone joked and laughed except Mr Price and his son, who ate seriously. Tim, who hoped for his carpentry City and Guilds, was most respectful. Seating himself below the salt, he addressed Mrs Price as 'Mrs. P.'.

'Could you pass a little more bread and butter over yere, Mrs P?' he would ask. 'Can I trouble you for the salt, Mrs. P.?'

Fascinated, I listened to the ebb and flow of the conversation.

'It cost fifteen pounds now to have a bull slaughtered, they were telling me, mind. And I met old Mr Evans, he was raving mad because he lost a cow over a cliff now, did you hear about that? "And they say it's not a mountain farm!" he was shouting, quite excited, really. You see, he couldn't get the subsidy, as the government said he didn't qualify for being on a mountain, even though he's on a precipice.'

Talk of social events could be confusing, as everyone seemed to be called Jones. 'Australia Jones is coming along, and Jones the Clog will be there.'

Jones the Clog, was, of course, a clog-dancer, but Australia Jones took some working out. Far from being a lager-swilling convict-bred bush-ranger with corks dangling from his hat, he proved to be a true Welshman who had been born in the Australia public house in Portmadoc, North Wales. This well-known hostelry on the quay used to boast a sign-painting of three seafarers looking at a map and presumably deciding to discover Australia. Two of them were dressed in Elizabethan style, with ruffs, the other as an Edwardian motorist in cape and bowler.

After the meal I settled down by the fire with *The Pilgrim's Progress*. Some earlier member of the Price family had written a message in it for me.

> Now slowly read and often pause,
> Think much, the book keep clean.
> And when returned to me
> Let not folded leaves be seen.

Mr Price announced that he was going back to his bench, and I said I would hitch-hike into town and do some shopping. My host did not approve of hitch-hiking 'cadgers', and said as much, but unless public transport is restored, we who suffer proudly from mechanical blindness will have to hitch. In Pembrokeshire, male hitch-hikers should wear suits and ties, whatever the weather, so they can be mistaken for chapel ministers. It was by such an imposture that I reached St David's that day.

I was picked up on my return by a jovial Northern Irishman with an accordion lying in the back seat of his old car. He was amused to hear where I was going, for Tim was an old friend of his. He tore around bends in the high-banked lanes, frightening me into fits, then came into the house to see Tim. At once, Mrs Price invited him to stay for a meal, after which home-made parsley wine and Scotch were brought out, and we all had a sing-song. Ted and Yvonne danced with everyone, Sharon and Rosie clapped and jogged and the Irishman's fingers flew over the buttons of the accordion. Polkas, reels and hornpipes swirled around the roof beams. My benefactor could even play calypsos and make up verses about members of the company. This was the best bit of hitch-hiking I had ever done.

'Look at the time, it's after one!' I exclaimed at last.

'Terrible, isn't it?' said Mrs Price with a giggle.

FEBRUARY

UFOs, the Church,
and Old Haunts

Waves crash across the promenade and seagulls wheel above a lead-grey ocean, as hardy souls in mackintoshes bend their heads and totter along the Front. There is something poignant about a holiday resort in February, and Brighton, where I spent my teenage years, is no exception. I often return and relive those strange times at the beginning of the 1960s.

I still feel a pang when I walk past my favourite coffee bar. Well I remember the pride of being known in a place supposed to many to be the toughest in town, and the comradeship of having pointed shoes and being able to slump against the coffee bar wall staring up through a dirty window at the steps leading down to our basement. I looked at peoples' feet as they ventured tentatively down. If any wore round-toed shoes I would swell with superiority, and get ready to put on my 'more working-class than thou' act that sometimes fooled them and sometimes didn't. Round-toed shoes represented the world I had escaped from. Sometimes I wondered if I would be willing to die for my coffee bar.

In the event, someone else died, and after the manslaughter case, the place was closed down. Once, long before, it had been the scullery of a private house, and the fireplace and other homely touches were still to be seen. Glancing down at it the other day, I was surprised to see it apparently inhabited. Curtains had been put up, and a sign on the door read 'UFO Society'.

I knocked, hoping for a chance to see again the dingy room that had once given a meaning to my life. A stout rheumy-eyed man with a droopy moustache let me in. Saying that I was interested in UFOs, I asked if I could come in and see his library.

14

Soon I was drinking coffee, looking at pictures of flying saucers and admiring my host's diabolical machines for tracking alien space creatures in flight. He had two such contraptions, arrayed with light-bulbs, taps, wires, levers and dials, rather like electronic brains crossed with pop group amplifiers. I could imagine them switched on, lights flashing and needles whirring with ominous 'boylk-boylk' noises.

'There's NO WAY, right? that these little beauties, right? won't show up any UFO, within six or seven miles of here, NO WAY, right? We do night watches here, and there's NO WAY a UFO could go unnoticed. But we're only ordinary blokes, right? We need the universities and their money, right? and we're trying to get them interested.'

Trumphantly he showed me a photo of a small white blob which might have been a UFO, but my attention wandered. I was surprised to see that the basement was also his home, and that amid the UFO trappings and the old coffee bar decor, a very congested household was managing to exist. A stove had been fitted into the pin-table alcove, and a drudge of a wife in jeans and lank hair was bending over it. The sink remained, left over from the scullery days, and a mattress lay on the dance floor doing duty as a bed. Pictures of flying saucers graced the walls, and as we spoke, a dog and three cats ran round and round the room, which also contained a cocktail cabinet and a modernistic divan. Library shelves had been fitted, and I thumbed through a pamphlet taken from the piles of UFO literature.

This showed pictures, clumsily drawn, of the sort of creatures observed to have come out of UFOs for a quick look at our planet. I was surprised how traditional they were – gods and goddesses, gnomes, devils and angels. The only one of these creatures, in flowing robes or with bats' wings, that could not have been seen on an ancient manuscript was an abominable snowman. I questioned the snowman's ability to drive a flying saucer, but was ponderously assured that it could handle the simpler models.

So have the gods returned, and the break from Christianity to scientism has now led back to paganism. My host appeared to have found a more satisfactory meaning to life than I had known on the same premises – a spiritual meaning, however absurd. Nor was he alone, for thousands and thousands of the young to middle-aged believe they are being watched by benevolent beings from Above, with powers far greater than those any mortal can possess. Sometimes, in Bermuda triangles, or through black holes, these gods snatch us away to dwell in a chromium-gleaming paradise, and perhaps tell us who we really are.

How is the Church coping with this new interest in the unseen? To find out, I walked up the hill from Brighton clock tower to the agreeable district known as Seven Dials. Nearby, there used to be a private girls' school full of very jolly young misses in berets and purple and white-banded scarves. Later, the school changed hands and became a record-breaking abortion clinic, while keeping the same name. Not far away, with a tall goblin-cap spire, is an Anglican church that has enjoyed a great vogue with the students from the University of Sussex.

Evensong was in full cry when I entered and found the dark Victorian building packed with young people. The white-haired vicar, a big man with a booming voice, shouted a coarse sermon on Samson, and then advertised the 'book of the week', a brightly coloured evangelical paperback. I will say, he looked rather ashamed as he did this, but the youngsters, who held their arms in the air, saw nothing strange about it. Instead of shaking the vicar's hand as they walked out afterwards, they put money in it and collected a copy of the book. The few old people present went home, and the rest crowded into the elegant vicarage for coffee and a sing-song.

I followed suit, and found myself in a comfortable old-world home that would have done credit to any Georgian clergyman. Rows of books lined the walls. Flushed with excitement, the youngsters sat on the carpet, their legs crossed under them. They looked so lively that I feared for the many ornaments, but no damage was done. Enter the vicar, who appeared to have once been a cultured, well read man, and now could scarcely believe his luck at attracting so many young people to his services. Any desecration of old ways was worth it, he seemed to be feeling, in exchange for this honour. As his smiling wife entered with a tray of coffee, someone twanged a folk-guitar and the whole lot launched into endless folk choruses. A young man banged at the piano as if demented, and everyone started to sway, arms up again. After twenty minutes or so they were beginning to feel highly emotional, and a glassy-eyed youth with wild brown hair, a dark smear of moustache and rimless spectacles, began to leap up and down, singing away with a fatuous expression on his face that I shan't forget in a hurry. Whatever had happened to the English middle class? Behaviour that would have seemed natural in a Pentecostal church seemed eerie in a Jane Austen vicarage.

A fair-haired young man, who had appointed himself cheerleader, urged his audience to wave their arms in different directions. The joy of togetherness overcame the students, who writhed wildly to and fro.

One girl suddenly broke into loud sobs and embraced another. I said goodnight to the vicar and left.

Some memories of my school leaving days in Brighton might now not be amiss. My very first job, found for me by a vengeful careers officer, was at a wire-weaving firm in the backstreets of Hove. Here wire birdcage fronts, wastepaper baskets and fireguards were all made by hand, mostly by fifteen-year-old boys. At the age of eighteen, I resembled an immature fifteen-year-old, and few could believe that I was older. There was a difference between myself and the other boys, however. I couldn't do the work.

This was one of the greatest shocks of my life. At school it was often said that if you couldn't pass the exams you would have to work in a factory. So I felt that failing exams, in a sense, qualified you for factory work. It was implied that lack of intelligence was needed in such work – a drastic mistake, for quick-wittedness and a bright, instinctive feel for tools and machinery are essential. 'This is the end!' I thought. 'I can't do school work and now I'm in a factory and I can't do factory work! Whatever am I going to write books about now?'

My greatest difficulty lay in the most elementary job of all – snapping a length of wire off a roll with a pair of tweezers. Another boy would have to do this for me. The wire-weaving lads, an affable bunch, were not very different from schoolboys. They bore me no ill will, and one brush-haired boy would tell me elaborate stories of his sex life, which even I could see were untrue. A time-and-motion man appeared on the scene when I had worked there for a week, and stood disapprovingly behind me with a watch in his hand while I nervously fumbled the wires, under, over, under, over.

The few older workers there treated me as an unusually green greenhorn, and sent me out for striped paint and straight hooks. Only in the corner shop, when I stammered out my request, did I realise that I had been tricked. The hardware salesman was very kind about it. Are such traditional jokes still played on industrial tenderfeet today?

I attempted a stark working-class novel, which emerged as a kind of diary in which my ineptitude at wire-weaving was glossed over as inexplicable. Reading it today reminds me of that grim fortnight that seemed an age, with, as my only consolation, the songs 'Only Sixteen' and 'A Teenager in Love' repeated again and again on the radio. I fail to understand how today's students manage to work cheerfully in factories for six weeks at a time or more, and then return to academic work. My life had been so sheltered that I could not understand the speech of the older workers at all. I remember a confused conversation about 'parties': I had not realised that to the older men a 'party' meant a girl.

There's only one window, so the lights have to be on all day [I wrote.] The workshop consists of three benches, the jig, several wheels for hauling wire off, a sink and most important of all, a radio. It's a dark, grimy building, with cold brick walls and a wooden beamed ceiling, with wire everywhere. The floor's littered inches deep with rejected snippets of it, and the walls are festooned with uncompleted weaves, dangling from hooks. I'd run out of wire for my weave, so I rummaged under the bench till I found a new roll and checked it on the gauge – yes, gauge thirteen! I heaved the roll on to the wheel, cut through the wire knot holding it together and grabbed the sticking-up bit of wire with the 'starting end' label on. Carefully, I wheeled it through the two cogs that put the crimp in it. . . .

After a great deal more of this technical stuff, in which I weaved wires in and out, pulled the ends up, tossed the whole mess to Harry who bent it over the iron frame and flicked it to Lenny on the jig for soldering (was ever a writer more out of his depth), it was lunchtime.

Everyone downed tools and made for the sink. The jelly like skin cleanser was scraped out of the tin and smeared on vigorously, then washed off and soap used. After I'd emerged from the fight for the bit of black rag serving as towel and dishcloth, I pushed some wires out of the way, hopped up on to the bench, as there are no chairs, and pulled the paste sandwiches out of my pocket. Soon the benches were crowded with us swinging our feet to 'Workers Playtime' and munching away.

Before lunch was over, a rowdy but innocent game of circuses was started by an older worker, who played a lion-tamer, and a boy who acted a roaring lion, much to everybody's enjoyment.

After the midday break, the rest of the day went like a song; the weaving became automatic, the mind ceased to function and I just saw the gleam of the wires through a sort of mental fog. The only conversation was when what we in the trade call

18

'mistakes' were made. This is when you weave two consecutive unders or overs and you have to pull the wire out and start again. A harsh swearword is heard when this happens.

'Mistake?' a nearby worker grunts questioningly. 'Mistake,' you grunt back confirmingly. Sometimes someone sings the first line of a pop song, then dries up; Harry always sings 'Daisy, Daisy, Give Me Your Answer Do' in a high-pitched idiotic whine, and Lenny whistles 'Living Doll'.

In this way, five-thirty was soon reached, and I thankfully washed my hands for the last time and wished the guv'nor goodnight. He nodded at me, and broke into a frenzied argument with some species of rodent inspector.

If I were to fill in a census form accurately today, I would have to state that I belonged to the fake working class, along with thousands of my generation. We in the fake working class are so accustomed to being ill at ease in workmen's cafés that we would not feel at ease anywhere else. Many of us are active in trade unions as we are far more at home in the world of ideas (mostly rotten ones), voting and wheeling and dealing, than real workers are.

My brother Martin, to his honour, glory and credit, saved me from becoming the president of the TUC. He once asked me to do his English composition homework for him, 'Why I Like Living in Brighton'. When I showed him the result, he refused to take it to school, and wrote his own essay instead. Proud of my creative effort, I sent it to my grandfather's favourite weekly, *The New Statesman*, which published it at once. I received fifteen pounds, a lot of money in 1960, and an invitation to go on writing for them. If I remember rightly, they retitled my composition 'The Voice of the Yob'. For some time after that, the Voice of the Yob was heard in the land. When I received the letter of acceptance, I grew too excited to work and told the puzzled wire-weavers that I had a headache. Reluctantly, they allowed me to go home. Now to return to the present.

Roaming around the streets of Hove one day recently, I listened to the children singing as they played, almost on the edge of a very dangerous road.

> I am a chicken with its head cut off,
> Doing the Gypsy Ping Pang Pong!

19

Fond of collecting street and playground songs, I reminded a friend's ten year old boy of the rhyme he had taught me when he was seven.

> Teacher, teacher over there,
> I can see your underwear!
> Is it black or is it white?
> Oh my God, it's dynamite!

'That's brilliant!' he said. 'Do you know any more?' Having passed the right age for that song, it had gone completely from his mind.

Outside Brighton, in a downland village, the children of my friend Mr Bickle the pigman have a lovely song, which they chant as they play.

> Duke he came-a-riding, riding, riding,
> Duke he came a-riding, Y.O.U.
> Whatcha coming here for, here for, here for,
> Whatcha coming here for? Y.O.U.
> Coming for to marry, [the boy says].
> Who you gonna marry [ask the girls]?
> Gonna marry red dress.
> Who is red dress?
> Sasha [or Tracey, Nicole or whoever] is red dress.

Paired off at last, the tiny couple are greeted with a well-known rhyme: 'Now they're married we wish them joy – first a girl and then a boy!'

A big man with crinkly black hair and a rich local accent, John Bickle keeps his pigs in a row of sties some way from his council cottage, in the middle of a field surrounded by woods. The sties' indoor shelters are not in the old stone style, but resemble an aviary, with a corridor, and he locks the pigs in at night. Nevertheless, he told me that a thief had broken in, one moist winter evening.

'Saw the lock were forced like, went in an' found my best pig gorn! Outside I saw a *wheelbarrer* track, one long line through the mud. The thief must o' took my pig an' wheeled 'im off in a barrer! I followed the track up through the woods and down on to the road, where it joined with tyre tracks on the mud. So he must ha' wheeled the pig up into a van an' drove *off* with 'im! Forty quid's worth of pig there.'

I commiserated, though reminded rather of Tom, Tom, the piper's son. These were Mr Bickle's own pigs. He looked after another lot of pigs on the Home Farm of the local estate, and these animals wandered freely in the woods for much of the year, kept from straying by electric fences strung from tree to tree. When not looking after pigs or eating enormous meals cooked by Mrs Bickle, the pigman liked to go shooting rabbits, accompanied by his three lively Jack Russell terriers. With gun and dogs, he would drive over the Downs in his Landrover, until he reached the rabbit place, a field with a long hedge, and a bank honeycombed with rabbit holes.

One cold day, I sat on the hillside above and watched John Bickle and his three white terriers work their way along the hedge. Not being well versed in gunmanship, I kept out of his way on these occasions. Although I regard the rabbit as my totem, and couldn't entirely approve, I had to admire John Bickle's sporting-print turnout of white breeches, black boots, brown jacket and a woolly bobble-cap. As he walked, with gun pointed at the ground, he spoke to the dogs in an odd barking language – 'Heh heh heh!' Now and again he would grow as excited as the terriers, and hop and skip his way down the tussocky slopes. The sky was slate-blue, and the downland scene illuminated, with Pre-Raphaelite clarity, by a sun that would soon vanish. There was a squeal as a dog nipped a rabbit, which nevertheless reached its hole and dived inside.

'Let him go, Jerry!' Mr Bickle growled, for the terrier had begun to dig. Then the rain came down. Dogs and hunter hurried to the Landrover, where a flask had been waiting. I dived into a nearby shepherd's hut on rusty wheels, like a bathing hut from old Brighton, and sat it out in there. In the great days of Sussex shepherds, these huts had been towed up to the flocks at lambing time, and the men had sat up all night, ready to attend to any ewe in trouble. Since the war, barbed wire and wheat fields had claimed these hills, and the huts acted as play-houses for cottage children. This one, I noticed, had been scribbled on with innocent graffiti by the Bickle brood. Pictures hung on the walls, cheap ornaments stood on the shelves, and there was a tattered rug on the floor.

'This is our Private Hut,' I read, in Julie Bickle's chalk handwriting on the wall. 'Please Move On and Leave Your Rent.'

When the rain had slackened off, I moved on and placed a penny by the notice. Returning many weeks later, I found that the money, as well as the ornaments, had gone. House martins had made their clay nests along the shelves, and when I poked my finger into one, a tiny head came out. When it saw I was not its mother and had brought no food, the little bird disappeared inside again. Reverently, I left the old shepherd's hut in peace.

21

Field sports, at their height in February and March, are events that I know very little about.

A beagling friend urged me to go to Oxfordshire, and see the Christ Church and Farley Hill Beagles, who go after hares. I found their Meet at a lonely farm at the end of a long driveway. Major Blank, a keen-faced, cloth-capped man, was greeting various arrivals and inviting them to sherry on the lawn. He looked at me with suspicion. Now I come from a long line of Communists on both sides of the family, and my boyhood allegiance was to Russia. Although I have been a loyal subject of the Crown for many years now, breeding always shows, and I bear a strong resemblance to a Party Line Commie, and an Anti Blood Sports man.

'Get off my land!' the Major shouted, his eyes popping from his head. 'Take one step further, and I'll have you for trespassing!'

Startled, I mumbled something about being a writer.

'Ha! You don't look very eminent to me. You can wait here for the Master if you like, but if you ask me, it's time to make your escape.'

Make my escape? I didn't like this. In my mind's eye, I saw my head mounted on the Major's wall.

All this while, healthy pink-faced undergraduates, presumably from Christ Church, Oxford, were parking their cars beneath the trees or standing around talking. A polite young man in a green jacket, a whip under his arm and a horn poking from his lapel, introduced himself to me as the Master. He said, in pleasant apologetic tones, that I had better do as the Major said, as the latter had been dreadfully troubled by 'Antis'.

'Don't worry, I won't let him on your land', a big red-faced countryman assured the Major, nodding towards me and clutching an ash stave in a burly hand.

I walked back along the driveway, climbed a gate a little further down the lane and doubled back on my tracks towards the farm. A big hare sprang across my path, ran long leggedly across a field, sat bolt upright for a moment and then vanished. Shortly afterwards another hare bounded past. A sound reached my ears that for a moment I mistook for a pheasant cackling. No, it was the hounds talking! My hunting friend had assured me that beagles never bark, yap or bay, but always talk.

I hurriedly changed course and felt my heart leap with excitement as I beheld the little white and red hounds running in a circle, noses to the ground. Huntsmen in green jackets and white breeches danced round them, and three hares ran by in parallel lines. Yet another hare burst through the hedge near where I was standing and scudded rapidly away.

The beagles seemed to take a remarkably long time to spring into action, hunting by scent rather than sight.

A cheerful woman in boots and a headscarf paused to wish me good day. I told her that it was my first time out with beagles.

'Ninety nine times out of a hundred, the hare gets away', she told me. 'The scents cross one another, and the hounds tend to leave one hare and go after another. When the hare sees them coming, it sometime claps.'

Claps? What with the hounds talking, and then the hares clapping, it sounded more like an animal conference than a day in the country. However, it turned out that when hares 'clap' they make no sound, not even that of one paw clapping, but lie low with folded ears and say nothing. Suddenly the beagles poured across the ploughed field I was standing in and fanned out seeking the hare. Then they were off, following first one hare and then another, as the lady had predicted. Major Blank approached me, his face quite altered. His eyes were back in place and there was a half-forgiving expression in them.

'Well, I must say, you've got resilience!' he complimented me. 'I seem to have run out of invective just now. I daresay I'll let you have some more later.'

''Allo!' a voice came at my elbow. It was the big countryman with the stick. In a broad, genial local accent, he began to talk to me about hares, almost as though we had always been friends.

'Far too many hares around here,' he said. 'Not long ago I saw fifty hares holding a meeting in that very field, and that's true! But up on that estate there, they had a drive an' shot three hundred hares in a day. One feller I know shot thirty four of 'em that day, and still there's more. Do a lot of damage, they do. Lot of foxes we have round here. Terrible for getting at the chickens, ducks and bantams. One day I was standing 'ere, no idea in my head that there was hunting goin' on, an' I sees a big old fox prowling up along the hedge. He ran into the farm gate there, doubled back on his own tracks and began to perform all variety of tricks. He ran up on a fence, jumped down, ran to and fro, leaped sideways, took two great leaps just where you're standin' an' then ran up that tree. There 'e sat in the crotch of the tree, curled up nice and neat. Huntsman came by.

'"Seen a fox?" he cry.

'"Through that gate", I answers, an' off they went. Old fox, he just sat an' watched 'em go by, following all his cunning tricks. When they'd gone, the keeper comes by with 'is gun.

'"Seen a fox?" he asks.

'"Up in that tree," I said, so he upped and shot 'im on the spot and that put an end to *his* gallop! Well, that fox had long been after my chickens.'

My face fell when I learned of Reynard's ignominious end, and the shrewd countryman observed this. For a moment a look of doubt showed that he felt I might after all be an Anti. Harking back to the hares, as the hounds and huntsmen were doing, I have been told of the enormous damage they can do to a field of cabbages. While a rabbit settles at one plant for a leisurely meal, a hare runs along a row taking strong bites at the heart of vegetable after vegetable. Were it not for the countryman's delight in foxhounds and beagles, he would, in his trigger-happy way, long ago have put paid to all hares, foxes and other interesting creatures. I had never seen so many hares before, outside the Scottish borders, until I set a muddy foot in beagle country. America and Africa have National Parks and we have hunting.

A horn blew, hounds gave tongue and the hare chase was on once more. Very wary of upsetting the choleric British Farmer, I had long been used to walking along muddy paths by prickly hedges, fearful of stepping on a single furrow. One of the glories of beagling, I discovered, was that anyone could run anywhere so long as a hare or a hound were nearby. Khaki-clad undergraduates sprinted in little groups across the middle of fields asprout with shoots of wheat. So did everyone else, and so did I. For a day I had the freedom of the fields, and hedges and ditches were there to be scrambled through or jumped over. Clouds scudded across the sky, and I scudded far below, in countryside that seemed as endless and boundless as in days before roads and villages were invented. In the distance, the beagles were musical specks of white, and a hare occasionally pelted across the skyline.

Most of us were left far behind, and there was a pause as some of the undergraduate followers drunk champagne from the bottle, or whisky from the flask, and gossiped about who was going out with whom. One young man sat writing a poem on the back of an envelope. Earlier, in Oxford itself, I had noted that the pseudo-working class blue-denimed undergrad had been completely replaced by a loud-voiced, well-dressed, super-confident upper-class variety. On the whole, it seemed a slight improvement so long as the young ladies and gents didn't go too far the other way and sneer at 'plebs' and 'proles'.

A kindly middle-aged couple, another Major and his wife, had by now befriended me, and we ran along together. The weather turned rough, and blasts of snow and sleet made us all the more determined to go on. We found the beagles massed together, a rose window of hounds, heads down and tails twirling. The Master blew his horn and seemed to be urging them to go after a hare that ran nearby. From the edge of a thorny wood, another horn sounded a discordant tinny note. It was blown by a short, stocky young man with long dark hair. One or two other young men were with him, clad in lumberjackets.

'That's the Antis!' the Major cried. 'They try and mislead the hounds by blowing their own horns. Luckily, it doesn't work with this pack, they're too well-trained. They know the sound of their own Master!'

I was surprised how young and non-intellectual the Antis looked. I had been expecting 'Guardian' readers in their thirties, not boys who looked like small but rowdy football fans. None of the Hunt took any notice of them. Soon they were left behind, as, snow in our faces and not caring a bit, we ran across a field and beheld a marvellous sight. There was the hare closely pursued by a long line of white beagles, one behind the other, sweeping by in a wide circle that seemed the perimeter of the world. The hare escaped among some earthworks and the hounds sang in excitement. My new friends turned back, but I ran hare-like to and fro for a while, before concluding that the day's sport was over, with no loss of animal life. Following the others, I walked back across unfamiliar fields.

'Owen was clobbered by an Anti in the hedge', I heard someone say.

Just then I noticed, in the near distance, two young men fighting. They were separated by a huntsman, who made them shake hands. Anti trouble!

'Did you see that?' I asked two young men who were walking side by side talking animatedly. They had, but seemed too absorbed in their conversation to take much notice. To my surprise, for I tagged along with them, I found that one was an undergraduate, the other 'a Hunt Saboteur', as he proudly proclaimed himself. This was the man I had seen earlier blowing a tinny horn, which now had been pinched off him by one of the university crowd. Both young men seemed congenial companions, but the hunter was getting the better of the argument.

'I was brought up in the country, in a way of life where hunting seems natural', he said. 'Man has been a hunter from the earliest times, long before he was a farmer, so it seems reasonable to suppose that it's part of our nature.'

'One doesn't have to give in to one's nature', the Anti could have replied, but instead he kept insisting that early man didn't hunt with dogs. a debatable point. I asked the Anti if he had been brought up in a way of life where Antis seemed natural.

'No, my parents don't approve of hunting, but they don't approve of Saboteurs either.'

This seemed very sensible of his parents. There are many pastimes I disapprove of, but I don't spend my days obsessively persecuting those who take part in them. The undergrad slipped away to join his friends at Major Blank's house, and I found myself walking along with the Anti and another young Sab, a small pinch-faced youth with staring eyes. Both told me that they were vegetarians and didn't believe human beings should ever kill any animal in any circumstance.

A farm worker shouted at us to shut a gate, with real hatred in his voice. Near the spot where I had first met Major Blank, two youths from the Hunt stood watching us.

'That one in white gloves is sure to pick on us', one of the Antis muttered. 'No, I don't think I'm an Anti out of class-envy, as I'm a student myself.'

'A student are you, old boy?' White Gloves taunted in an exaggerated upper-class accent. 'Then why won't you come to our *cocktail party?* I don't believe you *are* a student, old boy! Where at, a Polytechnic?'

That hit went home, as they say. The poor Poly-Anti walked away, followed by White Gloves, who seemed to be provoking him into striking first. 'Never hit an Anti first, as the Press might be watching' appeared to be an old hunting proverb. Just then, a white van drew up, and seven enormous Antis tumbled out and walked ominously towards White Gloves and his friend. With them was a photographer from a South London paper and a jolly-looking girl-Anti. Although White Gloves had been rude, his friend had not, and it seemed a pity if the day's sport should end in bloodshed after all.

Two of the Antis looked particularly alarming. One resembled an escaped convict, with cropped hair and a nose as flattened as if he had a nylon stocking over his head. The other had dyed blond hair standing up on end. Some of the Antis had an unhealthy look about them, perhaps because they did not eat meat. Clearly they were in the grip of an obsession that brought meaning and adventure to their lives.

'Give me back my hunting horn!' the boy White Gloves had been bullying now demanded, in a squeaky voice. Honestly! It took me back to the old days of Mods and Rockers.

'What is this, nine men against two!' I spoke up, sternly, pointing at the army of Antis and the two huntsmen. 'Do you call that fair? Why don't you all go home?'

'We won't hurt them if we can have our horn back', the first Anti said. However, the huntsmen didn't have the horn.

Someone pushed White Gloves over, in a perfunctory way. He rose up unharmed, and walked off with an Anti as if to settle it man-to-man. However, in an instant, they walked back again, shaking hands. No one wanted to fight, and the Antis suddenly decided to leave, lumbering away to their van and roaring away, the photographer with them.

'God, I hate Antis, they're the lowest form of scum', White Gloves exclaimed in disgust.

MARCH

The Hornblower of Ripon, and Magic at Pentre Ifan

The Black Bull, Ripon, is an ancient timbered inn standing a little way back from the cobbled market square, as if too modest to be seen in the company of the smart hotels mentioned in the Yorkshire guidebooks. One of these small hotels is not only disagreeably antiseptic-looking, but is also infested with mice. These rodents would stand small chance at the Black Bull, a hostelry that seems to yield new cats at every turn of the stairs. It is as if they creep from the ancient woodwork. In fact, while in the toilet admiring a picture on the wall, I heard a noise in the cupboard there, opened it and found a cat in a basket full of mewing kittens. Quaint old woodcuts, caricatures, watercolours, portraits and ornaments of every kind hang on the inn's mysterious landings. Some of these must have been handed down, almost unregarded, from landlord to landlord for hundreds of years. Others bring back memories of village hall jumble sales.

One day in March, I stood in my room looking out towards the enormous town square (market day Thursday). Outside my window hung the quaint old lantern that advertised the inn. Nearby was a book case that showed my room had once been that of the young lady of the inn, Penny Riley, whose husband served behind the bar downstairs. So for a few nights I revelled in the literature of my childhood – the Enid Blytons, the Empire Annuals, even the Beacon Readers! An atmosphere of safe cosiness, of a loving home and kind teachers at school seemed to rise from the pages as I opened them. Joy of joys, I even found the poetry book that helped me to learn to read, back in my first year at Perrin Road Church of England Primary School, and rediscovered my favourite poem of the day – 'New Shoes', by Ffrida Wolfe. A poignant reference in this verse to 'pretty pointy toe shoes' may explain my addiction to winkle-pickers in later life.

Mornings in the quiet, mellow saloon bar, where sunlight glanced through the curtained windows and on to the carpet and chairs, were enlivened by the succession of Dickensian characters who came in for glasses of sherry or stout. Most of them would probably have felt quite at home in the less dramatic chapters of *David Copperfield*. In the evening, burly, good-humoured workmen would stand in the hallway, drinking and jawing and ordering more from an opening in the wall that both revealed the public bar and acted as a reception desk. Some sat on old black Tudor benches. I was told that the inn was five hundred years old, and its dark beams, ancient stairways and spacious kitchen had not changed greatly through the years. Yawning, sleepy-eyed girls fried great quantities of eggs and bacon for breakfast. Later, carrying big black iron keys, they went up to make the beds.

On my visit, an IRA bomb blew up the local Naafi. 'The Irish make a nice change from marauding Scots,' I was told in this land of long memories, where the Border raids are still spoken of as a vivid part of local history.

Long ago, the good people of Ripon devised a warning system against Dane, Scot or any other enemy. Ever since Saxon days, the Hornblower of Ripon has sounded his instrument at the market cross, to let the townsfolk know that the Wakeman (or watchman) is on his patrols. Instead of the office of Wakeman being abolished along with the job itself, it became one of the titles of the Mayor of Ripon. Today the custom is kept up out of sheer conservatism.

Every evening at nine, without fail, the Hornblower arrives, dressed as a beadle in a cocked hat. Solemnly he blows a great bull's horn four times, once at each corner of the tall market cross. Alfred the Great ordained it thus when he granted Ripon its charter in the year AD 886, and who are we to dispute with the great Alfred? The modern Ripon townsfolk I spoke to had complete faith that the horn would continue to sound every night until Judgment Day, when I presume that Gabriel will take over.

Sad to say, the Hornblower himself, a genial man who looked like George Formby, told another story. Although the pay was a pound a night, he was unable to find a deputy. He told me that he was devoted to the custom, but nevertheless needed a holiday. As the only Hornblower, he could never leave Ripon. If no replacement could be found, he might eventually have to resign and the custom would be ended.

'There's the wife and kids at the seaside, where everything is horizontal, all beach and sea and that', he said. 'And here's me back at Ripon, all I can think of is the perpendicular – this tall old cross here, night after night. Mind you, the Mayor – he's the Wakeman, you know, a JP, Labour supporter and everything – he says he'll step in if it's a matter of real emergency. You ought to see the first Saxon horn, finished in silver and kept snug in black velvet in a secret place in the Town Hall. That's the Town Hall, yonder. It used to be the town house of a marquess till he presented it to Ripon.'

I looked at the noble building, with its steps, columns and accurate clock. It occupied almost the whole of one side of the great square. Painted high upon its gracious façade were these words, in large letters of red and gold.

Except Ye Lord Keep Ye Cittie, Ye Wakeman Waketh In Vain.

This is a Riponian paraphrase of Psalm 127, as all you Bible scholars will know. Will the Wakeman wake in vain? The Hornblower may seem absurd to some, but if the custom dies it will join Ripon's independence in limbo. The Royal Charter has been revoked, and as I write these words, the Town Hall is a Town Hall no more. Even the North Riding has disappeared, victim of local government reform. Everything in the former Town Hall has been removed to Harrogate, the town now set in administration over Ripon. The Mayor of Harrogate, willy-nilly a Wakeman, will never understand Ripon. Both towns are honourable in their own way, but each has a very different soul.

Can Yorkshire, legendary home of puddings, be standardised according to bureaucratic decree? Will the South East envelope the nation, making travel superfluous? Will Ye Lord keep Ye Cittie when everyone is too progressive to believe in Him? As I left for Wales once more, those questions remained unanswered. But if anyone wants to be the new Ripon Hornblower, they have only to let me know. I warn you, it takes quite a bit of puff.

My visit to the Price family got off to a bad start, as the bus took me only as far as Cardigan. Dragging my heavy suitcase, I staggered into a pub near the bridge to 'phone for help. I must have looked fairly wild-eyed, as the tough customers inside started back in surprise.

'Cardigan! My God, man, that's more than twenty miles away!' Mr Price roared down the 'phone, making me feel even more uncomfortable. However, he agreed to pick me up, so I stood on the bridge and watched, in the growing dusk, the steady stream of cars into town. Crumbling boathouses and crazily leaning peoplehouses receded from the mudflats of the Rivy Tivy, now renamed the Teifi. Either name recalls the River Tavy of Devon, also named by the Celts. In Daniel Defoe's time there were beavers in the Teifi, killed by the local inhabitants, who mistakenly believed that they ate fish. Gazing at the mournful river in twilight, as it flowed below the castle walls, I tried to imagine the 'broad tails' swimming, diving and slapping their tails on the mud banks as a futile warning to each other.

A small, ugly white footbridge had been built alongside the noble stone road bridge, so I crossed over and stood on it. Suddenly I saw Mr Price and his son in their brown car. To my surprise they stared at me aghast, as if I'd shot an albatross. Then they were gone, to reappear some time later heading back the way they had come. This time they slowed down and I hopped in.

'My God, man, you were standing on the *bridge*!' Mr. Price cried, his hair and beard flaring out like an effigy of the sun god, his eyes rolling to Heaven and back. 'We had to go all round town before we could pick you up! What did you stand *there* for?' Not being very well versed in the ways of motor cars and roads, I still don't know what I did wrong, but looked suitably humbled.

At the end of the narrrow lane leading to the farm I jumped out, eager to be useful, and lifted the great iron gate off the concrete blocks on which it was balanced. As the gate swung open, there was a roaring sound and Non the dog flew at me fiery-eyed and snarling. Poor Non was a golden Labrador bitch, the runt of a litter, with a twisted, leering mouth on her short muzzle, making her look rather like a demented pug. Although she had a heart of gold to match her fur, and was quite a sloppy old thing once she recognised you, I was always afraid that she might have a bite that was worse than her bark. Unhappily for Non but happily for me, she had hurt her back paw on this occasion and to prevent her from worrying the wound she wore an orange bucket for a collar, her head jammed through the hole where the bucket-bottom used to be, as if she had put on an outsize Kate Greenaway bonnet. So when she flew at my legs, the rim of the bucket stayed jammed against my knees, while her bulldog jaws snapped in mid-air, spittle flying, a safe three inches from my flesh.

'Non! Come away there, you naughty dog!' Mrs Price exclaimed. 'No one would think you were called after St David's mother, carrying on like that!'

31

Making light of my misdeed, which was now recounted to Tim with many embellishments, good Mrs P. sat me down by the fire and plied me with tea, milk-biscuits and Welsh cakes. Sycamore logs burned brightly on a bed of coal.

Next morning at breakfast a very different Non fawned on me for toast crusts, which I dropped into her mouth down the bucket shaft as if tossing coins into a well. No wonder her bark had sounded like a roar, as she wore a megaphone about her ears. Ted, Yvonne, Sharon, together with Rosie, had moved into their renovated house nearby, and only the Prices, myself, Tim and the postman sat round the breakfast table. Tom John, the postman, a cheery, round-faced man with sleek, receding black hair, always stayed for breakfast whenever he called, by standing invitation. Being a Pembrokeshire postman is no joke where houses are five miles apart, high on hillsides at the end of winding lanes.

Mr John told me, in his Dorset accent, of an otter he had seen 'over yurr' trotting up and down the pebbly river bank in the woods. The talk led to mink, which had escaped from a fur farm and made their way down the river. One had recently taken a hen from the Prices' coop. Many of the country families in the district had West Country accents of various kinds, handed from father to son over many years. An English settlement had been formed here in Elizabethan times, and one before that in the twelfth century. A certain spot on the roadside was well known as the place where the English had met the Welsh for barter in the old days. But postman Tom would have been very upset if you had told him that he wasn't Welsh. He had been rather anxious, he once told me, as to what kind of people would be buying the Home Farm. All was well, however, as 'they came from good old Wales!'

'This is the best part of Wales for me, they call it "the little England beyond Wales"', he proudly exclaimed, finishing his tea and making ready to drive off once more.

In an effort to Keep Wales Welsh, the council were buying farms and renting them to local couples on a points system (though when a council farmer retired, he had to move somewhere else). Nevertheless, there were many English settlers around St David's and the Prescellies — mostly middle-class eccentrics, very well liked by one and nearly all.

One such family were the Lawrences. Once, on a long-ago visit to Pembrokeshire, I was walking along a country road, when I saw a farmhouse in the valley below. Several unusual pens and aviaries were scattered about the adjoining fields, and in one of them I could see two brown animals running up and down. A tall man was walking towards the farm along the railway line, which seemed a foolhardy thing to do, even though Welsh trains are few and far between. As he approached his house, the animals went into a frenzy of recognition, leaping over one another and climbing up the wire. 'That was Mr Lawrence,' the postmistress had told me later, 'and the animals are otters.'

Now I found that the Lawrences' old farm had changed hands, and the cages had been pulled down

'I'll take you to meet the Lawrences,' Mrs Price told me, not long after my arrival. 'They bought a bigger place, up in the Prescellies. I often see Mr Lawrence as he drives past yere when he goes to work. He's a teacher in the new comprehensive school. Some people say he's so keen on animals that he neglects his own children, who run around barefoot. I don't know if there's any truth in it, mind.'

Mrs Price seemed to enjoy the occasional excursion. On our motorised ascent of the Prescellies, steep-sided primrose lanes formed a maze between the sea and the top of the mountain range. 'Those little white flowers grow mostly on the cliffs, we call them 'Eyebright', she was saying. 'Ah here we are, it's down this lane. It's an old water-mill they've got now, by a stream'.

A stag's skull with antlers looked down on us as we rang the ship's bell by the door of the mill, a rather grand, white building. Very friendly in their amiably dotty, homespun upper-class style, the Lawrences welcomed us effusively. Children's drawings were pinned to the walls, and sitting in easy chairs around the room were kids of both varieties, human and goat. It was a joy to see the little black and white baby goats jumping from chair to chair, while a grey parrot in a cage squawked enthusiastically. Mr Lawrence reverently showed me an eight-foot python in a heated tank and a moss-filled vivarium where black and gold salamanders squirmed.

Outside, the two otters climbed the wire on their pen, fixed their tiny eyes on us and whistled keenly. They were of the small Malayan short-clawed variety, and now had a section of stream to bath in. Imported kites and buzzards from Africa flapped around in the aviaries, and owls hid in the shadows beyond. In the whitewashed room which enclosed the great, gnarled mill-wheel, now at a standstill, Mrs Lawrence's beloved spinning-wheel had been installed. I had already met the small flock of Lincoln ewes, and their lambs with shining white legs and faces emerging from off-white wool, and I noticed that all the Lawrences wore chunky cardigans.

'I really must get a pair of Alpacas from Peru,' Mrs. Lawrence told us over tea. 'They're a kind of woolly camel, very good for spinning from. I'll have a look in the *Cage Birds* paper; they advertised an elephant last week, so you never know.' 'Buy us an elephant!' the children chorused, but Mr Lawrence just laughed.

We were soon on our way, as Mrs Price wanted to show me Pentre Ifan, the great cromlech, a Bronze Age chief's grave on the other side of the hills. Silent for a while, Mrs. P. seemed to be musing on the bohemian household we had left. Perhaps she was slightly scandalised. Her friend, Ted, who was now a small farmer himself, scoffed at the English back-to-the-land movement. It's all right for the Celts! An Irishman can drink in the same pub in Camden Town for years. Then one night he learns that his father in County Mayo has died, and off he goes to take over the farm and to run it as easily as if he'd never left his native soil. Ted, Yvonne and the Prices had lived among coal-mines and ribbons of mountainside terraced houses most of their lives, and no one would now suspect they had not all been born in Pembrokeshire farmhouses. Saxons, however, cannot take easily to farming in middle age. Real farmers come to watch them over their tumbledown walls, as a form of sardonic entertainment. (I didn't think the Lawrences were doing too badly, all things considered. What's wrong with alpacas?)

English back-to-the-landers in particular had annoyed Ted, as these men continually appeared on television leading shire horses or holding organically-grown turnips. Apparently when the cameras had gone, they would secretly drive a tractor and use chemical fertilisers in between preaching on self-sufficiency. Why anyone should want to live in a populous land as if he were Robinson Crusoe I find hard to understand. Even the Ancient Britons are supposed to have bartered with the Phoenicians.

After a long, slow climb, the hedges vanished and we entered a wild, open moonscape of moors, a vast, eerie brown plateau on the Prescelly heights. Sheep and cattle wandered freely, and eyed us suspiciously. A mountain mist came down, and when the sun shone through again, we found ourselves among primrose banks once more. A gate in the hedge led into the field of the great grave, Pentre Ifan.

Pentre Ifan, one of the sights of Wales, consists of a huge boulder raised from the ground and balanced on two others, as if a giant had begun to make a card house out of pebbles. A strange, almost menacing atmosphere could be felt, for we were walking round and into a desecrated Bronze Age grave. Wind and rain over the centuries had swept away the earth and turf covering, leaving just the skeleton of a grave, or cave. For the Bronze Age men, for reasons best known to themselves, built their graves upwards, not downwards, somewhat on the lines of family vaults in Victorian cemeteries. I ran down the hill to survey the ancient grave from a distance, then up again in time to meet another party of visitors. Did the old chief suspect his tomb would be visited thousands of years after his death? Very probably.

The newcomers were cold-eyed, well dressed hippies. 'There is a force field here, can't you feel it?' one said. 'We believe this spot has a universal significance. It links up to a ley line, and there are marker stones stretching almost from here to the sea.' This was true, as every fifth field seemed to have a standing stone in its centre. Buzzards perched on them, and cows liked to scratch against them. Farmers were said to leave them alone for that reason, and some kind-hearted farmers, sorry for itching cows, may have raised standing stones of their own.

There is no doubt that the Prescellies are a magic place. Stonehenge was made partly from Prescelly boulders, and a reader of *Elvis Monthly* once wrote in to suggest that 'Presley' was a corruption of 'Prescelly'.

'Do you think the Bronze Age religion still has power after all these years?' I asked.

'Religion!' one of the intelligentsia scoffed. 'It's science, an electro-magnetic force field. If a hare gets on to a ley line it has to run straight on it as if fixed to the track.' He made it sound just like the dog races. Mrs P. was already in her car, so I galloped off and we had to leave it at that. Ley lines appear to have been made by the first prehistoric surveyors of our island. Roman roads were sometimes built along these straight and narrow paths, and my mad uphill dash to school as a boy in Brighton, which took me through St Anne's Well Park, followed the course of a ley line.

The fascination of Bronze Age magic stones has come full circle, and there are many shaggy young people of university background who venerate the stones as much as any spear-throwing herder or warrior could have done. In the Bronze Age, however, stone-worshippers presumably had a common idea of the significance of the boulders, as of other parts of the natural world that they saw around them. Our modern stone-worshippers more closely resemble 'the heathen in his blindness' of the popular hymn. They venerate they know not what, whether science, unknown gods or the ecology of the environment. Brooding on sacred sites, they produce rival typed-out magazines, and walk around sunk in a private world, ley lines on their foreheads and Bronze Age circles under their eyes. It always seems odd to me how intellectual movements operate almost in a secret world – the postman, the milkman and passers-by having no inkling of the turmoil in the minds of those absorbed by abstract ideas. Clearly the ley-liners are feeling for a religious significance to life, even if they name it 'science' and have gone back several thousand years too far. Pentre Ifan is not the only empty tomb in history, nor the only church founded on a rock. Most ley liners, when scanning maps for 'sacred sites', accept churches as sacred if they are on the sites of pagan temples. I've never heard of them turning up at services on that account, though.

We stopped at the beautiful old church of Nevern on our way back to the farm. A crumbling mounting-block stood outside the gate. Inside we walked along a short, dark avenue of ancient, twisted yews. One of these was the famous Bleeding Yew of Nevern. Dark-red 'blood' oozed from under its withered limbs, presumably sap of some kind. Nevern churchyard is unique, as it has been a Christian burial-ground since Romano-British times. The star attraction here is a tall Celtic cross from those days, with Ogham writing on it and curly patterns beloved of the Celts. Smaller Celtic crosses stand nearby, with similar patterns perhaps deriving from earlier ideas of eternity as a serpent eating its tail. Some graveyard crosses have been taken inside and made into window ledges in the church. Here the old religion merges into the new. Stone crosses and gravestones appeared as a continuation of the standing stone tradition, and the yews formed a sacred grove, complete with blood sacrifice, that would have delighted many a Druid.

Hurrying back in time to cook for the others, Mrs Price followed a school bus along the narrow lanes. At lonely farm gates the bus would stop, and children could be seen walking along hillside paths to invisible farmhouses or cottages. We stopped to pick up Davey and Tim, who were wandering along the edge of the wood.

'Did you have a good day, Porridge?' Mr Price asked with amusement. (That was his pet name for me.) Later that night I watched as he had a haircut. A gentle patriarch, he resembled a mellow Abraham, as he sat with head back and eyes closed, a bib tucked under his tangle-bearded chin. Mrs Price snipped away carefully at the grey locks hanging over the back of the chair, sometimes asking him to move this way or that. Above them on the wall hung the row of love-spoons carved by Mr Price for each stage of their life together. One spoon had a ring carved on it, another a church window in Gothic style. A third formed a cradle, and I looked from the wall and down to the practical young man in a corner chair reading a farm catalogue. My favourite spoon, however, must have been a private joke or else inspired by a nightmare. From the handle of the spoon grew a demonic toad with bat's wings and shining yellow glass eyes. Mrs Price took away the bib, gave her husband a mirror, and wandered off into the kitchen singing a song about a little saucepan.

Afterwards, lighting his pipe once more and stirring up the fire, Mr Price told us of a hell-ship he had served on, sailing beneath a blazing sun to Cairo with a contraband supply of whisky locked firmly below one of the hatches. The 'Old Man' had made a private deal with an RAF officers' mess ashore. Water was rationed, there was no other alcohol on board, and no ports were called at on the way, for the war was on and the seas were dangerous. The crew grew maddened with thirst, and mutinous. One day they could stand it no longer, and shouted at Mr Price to bring out all his tools so they could force the hatch open. He did not dare to refuse, and in fact was very glad to agree.

'The Old Man could see what was going on, but as our leader was a great wild-eyed mountain of a fellow holding a crowbar, nothing was done to stop us. So with loud cries, the men forced the hatch open, tearing at it with their bare hands. When we opened it, what do you think we found? Soap powder, boxes and boxes of it! Swearing and cursing, with roars of rage, we hurled it all in the sea. The ocean was like a bubble bath after that, and we steamed along with a wake of soap suds behind us. So we ran to the next hatch, and began hacking and tearing again. This time we picked the right one, and fell on the whisky like madmen, drinking from the bottle. Everyone stayed drunk for ages after that. We were singing "Whisky is the life of man, whisky for my Johnny!"'

I remembered that the Irish accordion-player had sung a similar song the night we had the dance:

> I'll eat when I'm hungry, I'll drink when I'm dry,
> If the whisky don't kill me, I'll live till I die.

Mr Price had set up a small smithy in one of the outbuildings, where he could repair farm machinery. One of his proudest nautical possessions was an anvil on a wooden base made from the keel of the *Havana*, one of the ships that accompanied the *Bellerophon* when she took Napoleon to exile on St Helena. For some reason this historic piece of wood had been presented to a South Welsh workhouse. When the workhouse became a 'spike' or hostel for tramps, the *Havana* was the chopping-block on which they cut wood for the furnace to earn their keep. It was later that it became an anvil, and here it was, after many vicissitudes, in the middle of Pembrokeshire.

'There's supposed to be some stones a bit like Pentre Ifan about a mile up the lane, there, in a field,' Mrs Price told me. 'A cromlech, they call it. Perhaps you'd like to go and look at it tomorrow?'

It was dusk the next day before I set out. The lane wound up a hillside, and I stepped gingerly over cow-pats or flattened against the bank when a tractor passed. Looking back, I admired the white mansion house among the trees, the lights in one or two windows giving the impression that the landed gentry had survived. In fact, problem families were now being sent there by the DHSS as the place had become a bed-and-breakfast house. Some of them had taken to poaching trout or salmon in the river, hitherto the privilege of Ted, Yvonne's husband, and his gypsyish friends and relations. Ted had caught a man fishing one day and had asked for his permit, pretending to be a water bailiff. With many threats and warnings, he let the wretch go. From the wood I could hear a low 'boom boom', the electric pump on the river, installed to bring water to the Big House before the war and still in use.

A church lay half-hidden in the ivied woods by my path and I saw a large tawny owl glide over the tombstones. Eager to see the bird at closer quarters, I began to walk round the church. Suddenly I looked round and saw a dark figure staring at me from among the trees. 'Hello!' I shouted enquiringly, whereupon the man jumped behind a tree and hid. As I hurried back to the lane I could see him following me, bounding from tree to tree. When he realised I could see him, he stood staring with his hands on his hips. Then he disappeared into the wood.

'A robber!' I thought, and walked on in dread, expecting him to jump out on me from the hedge. At the top of the hill I noticed, through a gateway, a tractor standing with its engine running. Obviously the mysterious stranger was the driver and consequently a great deal less mysterious. A stile marked the site of the cromlech, an eerie spot, made more so by a rusting bulldozer with scoop erected like a dinosaur's head peering over the bank on the opposite side of the lane.

Crossing the stile in semi-darkness, I picked out a rocky outcrop at the top of the field, the kind of place that might once have been a wolves' lookout, their caves dug beneath scattered boulders among the thorn bushes. Wonderingly I stepped among the stones, and found what seemed to be a cave-like grave, a smaller version of Pentre Ifan, half-emerging from the earth. Ahead of me the overhanging rocks loomed, pale and silvered by the full moon. My mind was acutely clear, my nerves tingling slightly from the encounter with the 'robber'. Looking round, I was surprised to see a long ribbon of yellow light passing across the field towards me, rippling over the stones and illuminating the grass. It passed over me and was gone. Inspired by the magic of the stones, I climbed the rocks, fitting my feet into step-like crevices. As I descended, a similar line of light crossed the field once

more, reminding me of a gentle breaker sweeping over a beach. Leaving
the field for the lane, I wondered what I would have seen in that light if I
had had 'the gift'. A neolithic burial party, possibly, or something
equally mournful.

Safely at the Prices' hearthside once more, I told them about the man in
the wood.

'That would be Henery Morris, the farmer who lives near us,' Mrs
Price told me with a laugh. 'He's always suspicious of strangers, and he
must have thought *you* were the robber, about to break into the
church. He was christened a Henery, mind, not a Henry. They have
some funny names yere. There's a man we know who was christened
Sunaway, what do you make of that? Do you remember him?' she asked
her husband. 'He's married to the woman who comes to the WI and
whistles.'

'I know who you mean,' he replied. 'His wife might whistle, but she
makes a damn good tractor driver.'

In a village near Lydford on Dartmoor live Mr and Mrs Davey. They
used to own their own farm but lost money, and now hope to convert
their cottage into a tea shop. When I met them they were both busy
gardening, and a request for directions to Lydford gorge and castle on
my part led to a whole saga about Dartmoor on theirs, the husband and
wife taking turns almost breathlessly.

Mr Davey is large and jovial and when I saw him he was wearing a
white open-necked shirt under big black braces, with enormous boots
and an old hat. Mrs Davey is short and plump and very earnest.

'It's a brave old walk to Lydford, but if you step on it, you should get
to 'ee in bad time,' Mr Davey said, meaning 'in good time', as it
happened.

He went on to tell me that some time before, a young soldier from
one of the training camps had taken a short cut across the moors at
night, to get from one pub to another. The night was dark, and the
soldier had missed his way and crashed through the bracken down into
the Devil's Cauldron at the head of the gorge. There his body was found
in the morning, spinning round and round, face downwards in the
swirling waters.

'It's his family I'm sorry for,' Mrs Davey told me. 'Now as for
Lydford, you see Gibbet Hill over there?'

'Gibbet Hill? Is that anything to do with Judge Jeffreys?.

'No!' Mr Davey butted in. 'In Judge Jeffrey's time they took 'em to
Lydford to be hung. Time was, they say that hill was black with

gibbets, but that was before the judge's time. The old judge went all over Devon, looking for people to be hung. Once, in old Napoleon's day, the folk not far from 'ere hung an ape they found, escaped from a show. Thought it was a Frenchman! Since then, many people told me, they seen the ape's hairy hand, rapping on their car windows. Before the cars it was coaches, same as the White Lady.'

'What White Lady was that?' I asked.

'Oh, she was a very bad lady lived hereabouts – poisoned 'er 'usband, they say. They put 'er to death, like, but now 'er ghost rises up real quick, at night in front of cars. Many drivers go off the road that way, swerving in fright, and has accidents. One time it was horses that went wild, turned the coaches over, going to Okehampton. I've met many farmers seen the White Lady – they all swear it's true. But I don't know.

'One night I was driving back, when whoosh! up from the moor right into my headlights, there was the White Lady! Well, I went off the road all right, but I just missed the marker stone, and swung right on again.

'Since then, I've often wondered about that. I think that somehow it's a flash o' white light from off a pool down there, just in the *shape* of a White Lady. There's a ghostly coach an' horses on the old Okehampton road to this day, but I never seen that.'

They showed me the path to Lydford, and also the distant ruins of a silver-lead mine whose 'cap'n', or head overseer, had once lived in their cottage.

'The cottage is haunted, too,' Mr Davey added.

'Really? What by?'

'Well it's a poltergeist,' the haunted man told me, thoughtfully. 'We all seen cups an' jugs lifting themselves up and flying around, like. [Mrs Davey nodded.] Now a gypsy told me a poltergeist is a child's ghost. And that's a true thing, 'cos we all heard a little girl crying many times out in the garden. Twice, on different nights, we 'eard 'er cry "Daddy!" in such a voice of despair it'd make you sorry. Then, after snow, we found a little girl's footprints all over the garden, in early morning. Prints of a little girl's shoes, they was.'

'Poor little mite!' I exclaimed. 'Have either of you ever seen her?'

'No, we never have. Our girl Mary has. Mary!'

A girl in her twenties emerged from the kitchen door. She had long brown hair and a round sleepy face with small eyes. Eagerly, she launched into her story.

'I work on my uncle's farm, you know, and they all there starts almost when it's light, and goes to bed every night at nine. You know how it is when you wake up and lie there, not sure what's going on yet.

One morning early I'm lying in bed and I hear a quiet crying all going on right near me. Very sad, it sounds. I opened my eyes and there, on a chair by my bed, is a dear little girl of seven, in old-fashioned clothes. She was sort of whimpering and rubbing her little hands into her eyes. I starts to drop off again, and suddenly I thinks, "Who's that?" But when I look again she's not there!'

'How strange!' I said, 'Well, I really must go, if I'm to see Lydford. If I have time, I'll try and get to Wistman's Wood as well and see the stunted oak trees.'

Surfeited with legends, my mind reeling, I said goodbye and started wandering down the road.

'Don't go into Wistman's Wood, it's full of poisonous snakes and deadly bogs!' Mary called after me urgently.

The Britannia Coconut Dancers, and a Modern Cult Revived

On Good Friday, as Easter bells rang out, I took a bus from Rochdale in Lancashire to Bacup, in the Rossendale Valley. Rossendale resembled a more spacious and less grim Rhondda Valley, with worked-out granite quarries instead of coal-mines. Chimneys of demolished cotton mills stood like obelisks. Green Pennine ridges swept down to the strips of cottages below.

Next morning, on Easter Saturday, I stood with a small crowd a mile out of town outside the Travellers' Rest, waiting for the Britannia Coconut Dancers. This part of Rossendale is called Britannia, perhaps after the Royal Brittania Mill (now a garage) where some of the dancers' ancestors had worked. Half the crowd were parents with children, the other half earnest folklorists with tape-recorders. Policemen prepared to direct traffic around the dancers.

Before long, the 'Nutters' as they are called, emerged from the pub in all their finery. They were middle-aged men, all locals, and their eyes blinked with pink lids in heavily blackened faces. Even the backs of their necks and ears were black, though not their hands, on which they wore inverted knuckle dusters of maple discs, known as 'coconuts.' Perhaps real coconut shells had been used in the past, and these discs, also fastened on the knees and about the waist, produced the same clippety-cloppping effect. The eleven dancers wore patriotic colours, including red and white turbans with blue feathers in.

'The Gregories, the Flynns and the Shufflebottoms are all dancers here,' a sage in a working men's club had told me. 'They say the dance came up from Cornwall when the old tin-miners came up here to mine granite. In fact my father's father was Cornish.' But now eight young men from the Stacksteads Band, Bacup, lined up holding their brightly polished instruments. We were off!

Every year the Nutters spend the whole day dancing from pub to pub in their bells and gaiters, knee-breeches and clogs, followed by enthusiastic local supporters and twenty or thirty folklorists who try hard not to influence events. Well aware of the lethal power of folklore-collecting on a custom, they scarcely dare to speak to a Nutter in case he should cease to be 'unspoiled'. But it would take a lot to spoil these cheerful giants of Rossendale, whose good humour seems as boundless as their thirst. Once upon a time, however, the brass band's manager told me, hordes of hippie-like folk hooligans would arrive in coaches from Manchester and Liverpool Universities, bringing an atmosphere of protest and rowdiness to the town. These were banished at a dreadful cost – the pubs were no longer allowed to stay open all day.

'Nice variation, lads!' the band leader commented, as a brisk dance tune started the day, and the Nutters began their rounds. Each dancer held a 'garland', an arc of bamboo swathed in red, white and blue tissues and grasped in each hand. Round and round the Nutters waltzed, twirling each other and holding the garlands aloft, sometimes joining to make a crown of them, sometimes bounding apart in pairs. The eleventh man was a ringmaster with a whip-like baton and a collecting-box.

Sometimes he blew a whistle to announce a change of dance. After a few minutes, the men threw their garlands to a mournful young girl who hung them about her shoulders. Now began their intricate coconut routine, as they beat up a brisk castanet rhythm by clapping the discs on their palms on to the discs on their waists and knees. This they did with extraordinary agility, bending their knees in and out as in a 'twenties dance, crouching, springing up again, hopping backwards and forwards in perfect line formation on one spot, and rolling their eyes at all and sundry. Clackety-clack, clackety-clack and oompah from the band!

Springing to his feet, each man then played pat-a-cake with his partner, pointing a finger between each pat and withdrawing it before it could be crushed. Forming into two lines, they danced straight at one another, kicking in between each other's legs but cleverly avoiding mayhem. The most amusing dancer was a gnome-like man, one Brian Daley, with a smile too big for his blackened face and greying hair hanging strangely forward.

Now the band formed a line and marched into Bacup, blowing a sprightly hornpipe called 'Claybank'. Forming two lines on each side of the road, the Nutters skipped along, nimbly throwing their belled legs up in the air. Men who were big and blundering in repose skipped like the high hills beloved of the Psalmist. As they hopped, they jangled and clacked, and the ringmaster greeted the families gathered in cottage doorways along the road.

Outside Bacup, the men danced down a farm track, avoiding a large family in a painted, pony-drawn gypsy cart, and then performed all their dances again on the paved front garden of a bungalow where one of them lived, as a treat for his family. Then on they went, the band following, until they reached a big house with a drive, set among rhododendrons – the old folks' home. This was rather a poignant occasion, for Frank Ashworth, once a leading dancer, was now a resident there. Clearly moved, he stood in the doorway among elderly ladies propped up by nurses, and watched his old comrades perform. He watched them out of sight as they waved goodbye with their clackety hands, and danced on down towards the mill.

Ross Mill, an enormous red brick cotton mill with a fine chimney dominates Bacup, and it seemed in such good condition that I was surprised to find it closed and up for sale.

'Aye, they began laying men off in hundreds these past few years,' a local dance follower told me. 'Then, a couple of months ago, to everyone's surprise, the whole place closed. There's still four or five cotton mills in Rossendale, but most o' the other mills are put to different purposes, like.' I had noticed an engineering works and a shoe factory in what seemed to be former mills, and one mill now specialised in 'pigeon accessories'. Lorries of cooing crates, marked 'pigeon transport', passed the dancers every now and then, for pigeons are evidently big business in Rossendale.

Next stop was the fire-station, on a hill slope by a large council estate. Here an enormous crowd gathered, and waited outside patiently while the Nutters drank tea with the firemen. Downhill through the council estate went the procession, children running from every doorway, leaving their parents behind. Then on through terraced streets with washing strung across back alleys, and cobbles ringing once again to the sound of clogs as in a Lancashire of long ago. Down Gladstone Street, past Inkerman and Alma Streets, and so to the Joiners' Arms. Children poured into the pub behind the dancers, for Bacup's pubs were to resemble school playgrounds for the rest of the chaotic day.

All Bacup filled the town centre, stopping traffic as the Nutters danced in the road and the band played a melody that sounded like 'Bibbety Bobbety Boo' from Walt Disney's *Cinderella*. Young people perched on the disused fountain for a better view.

After lunch upstairs at the George, the Nutters and the band split into two halves, the better to cover every pub in town before the afternoon closing. The half I followed serenaded some old people in their flats, then skipped along by the banks of the Irwell, Manchester's pride but here only a muddy stream. Terraced streets, the tiled roofs curving up the steep slopes, led to council estates where Bacup's Irish population had been rehoused. This was supposed to be rather a rough area. The night before I had narrowly avoided flying bottles that shattered on the cobbles as children played. In a pub here, the irrepressible Mr Daley let one boy try on a turban, and loaned another a pair of 'nuts' to strap on to the palms of his hands. This entranced the boy, who shot looks of hero-worship at the Nutter. The nine-year-old skinhead was to dance behind the Nutters for the rest of the day.

For two hours or more the Coconut Dancers led me a confused, sweaty dance in and out of more pubs than I care to remember, through a market crowded with shoppers, and to the local Irish Club. Here a notice warned against 'abusive behaviour or violence'. Wrong-doers, it seemed, would be hauled before the committee. Irish and Lancashire-Irish alike acclaimed the dancers, and then returned to loud discussions about race horses and politicians: 'Labour or Conservative, they're all pigs of one sow.'

Finally, dancers and band reunited in the town centre near three crosses placed by the Church to commemorate another aspect of Easter. (At nearby Waterfoot, a cross is placed each year on a hilltop above the village.) Then they set off to dance right down the valley, through Stacksteads and Tunstead Mill to the Glen, where the mountains begin – a journey of several miles. As agile as when they had begun, five hours before, they entertained with more garland-dancing outside the Victoria Working Men's Club on the corner of Foundry Street. Along Newchurch Road, among scenery that resembled every southerner's idea of the north, I saw alleys, chip shops and ruined mills, with quaint bridges over the Irwell and curious steps and balconies jutting from the end-of-terrrace houses. Great slabs of granite stood upright like teeth in an aged jaw, forming a low wall. Small skinheads in baggy half-length jeans and big boots completed the nineteenth-century illusion. I heard a young mother, taking the washing down from the line across an alley, shout 'Willy! Can thou 'ear me?'

But it was no use. Willy was off, dancing in a conga-line behind the pied-piper Nutters, one of the many children who followed on, imitating the dancers as they went. The young adults here seemed unaffected by teenage fashions, although in the Rossendale Working

Men's Club, a later stop, a hippie-like group attempted to bring folk music to the people, ignored by all and soon drowned out by the Nutters. Everyone surged into this club, to the annoyance of the committee, who tried to levy a fee and sign the strangers in. I went outside and admired the figure of the Virgin, daffodils at her feet, in the grotto outside the Catholic church.

The dance continued with sad pauses of respect outside the closed pubs. At the Glen it all ended in a grand finale – coconuts clashing, brass blaring and bells jangling in the forecourt of the Glen Service Station, among the petrol pumps. By now the garlands were losing their paper petals, and the hilltops glowed in the evening sun. Townsfolk and children started for their homes; and the Nutters, the band, and a few diehard folklorists, their tapes still running, adjourned to the Dog and Partridges, which had just opened. With scarcely a break, the men had danced and played from nine in the morning until six at night, covering about ten miles.

Now, as they sat exhausted, they had to put up with my peppering of questions, and I learned that the brass band had been formed about a hundred and ten years before, but that Nutters had been dancing since the seventeenth century. A bandsman showed me a stone shaped like a fox's head, with cartoon eyes painted on, that he said was his mascot.

'There used to be lots of dance teams, competing against one another,' Brian Daley told me. 'We're the last one. No one knows how the dance began, that's part of the mystery.'

'Soot! We 'aven't used soot for fifty years!' exclaimed the whipper-in or ringmaster, quite shocked at my enquiry about his make-up. 'We use Max Factor pancake!' And both set about demolishing the row of foaming pints in front of them

That night, after bingo in the Victoria Working Men's Club, a noisy electric pop group came on stage, and the younger members began to dance. Two of them clutched babies as they swayed. In their leaping dance, with hands thrown behind the head and then clapped in front, I could see more than a trace of the Britannia Coconut Dancers. Perhaps the Coconut Dancers will flourish when rock-and-roll has become a thing of the past. Old customs, long thought forgotten, have a way of rising from the tomb, a suitable reflection at Easter Time.

On Easter Sunday I booked an afternoon coach tour to the seaside, and spent the morning wandering in the hills above Bacup. Open moorland alternated with disused granite quarries ringed by rusty barbed wire. I climbed up the stone ledges jutting out of a farm wall and saw a goat and kids frisking around a tumbledown farmhouse. A sheepdog barked furiously, but nobody seemed to be at home. A notice painted in wobbly white capitals on a large boulder read 'All Rabbiters and Foxers Keep Off'.

Later, in a coach full of garrulous old ladies, I crossed Lancashire and went AWOL at Morecambe, the county's number two resort. Swinging my possessions in a plastic bag, I signed in at the Elfordleigh Hotel, a jolly place on the seafront with such gems in the visitors' book as 'Very friendly people, but look out for John alias "The Stud".'

To my amazement, the town was full of Mods in khaki anoraks, who sat in rows on the wall in front of the hotel's locked doors, gazing towards the sea. The National Scooter Club was holding its Easter rally, and the scooter fans numbered between six and ten thousand. 'Every year they go on the rampage and smash the town up,' I was told. 'Mind you, they bring money into the town, all spent on drink.'

Mods drove up and down the seafront in convoys of twenty or so. Others larked about, throwing one another into the sea, walking on parapets, playing leapfrog and generally showing high spirits. Holidaymakers watched them with scandalised pleasure. Of course, these were neo-Mods, consciously aping the fashions of the 1960s. I quite liked the look of them, for they seemed to be decent lads merely over-excited by their enormous numbers. They reminded me of young soldiers, though if eight thousand soldiers all had leave on the same night, who could suppose they would do as little damage as the Mods? Thirty arrests were made over the holiday, and a special court was set up to deal with the fines. Youngsters from every town in Britain, it seemed, were showing off their Vespas and Lambrettas. No events had been organised by the Scooter Club – just being there was enough. All-night discos were held on the pier. I peeped through the door of a pink perspex dome and saw a 'roller disco' for the first time. It differed from the skating rinks of my youth only in the volume of the piped music.

National Service, which often proved a horrifying ordeal for bookish youths, seems to have suited the less academic masses down to the ground. Ever since it was abolished, teenage stylists have sought to recreate it, rejoicing in the attendant sense of camaraderie. Many of the Mods wore combat jackets, and one scooter driver had camouflage branches on his tin helmet. Congregating in the King's Arms, they proceeded to drink the bar dry and then to dance on the tables, watched through the door by austere mounted policemen. The police did a very good job of keeping order, and some joked affably with the Mods.

Approaching a group of boys and girls aged between sixteen and twenty, I asked them where they were from and what their views on life might be.

'We're from Clitheroe!' they chorused, gathering around me, eyes shining with pleasure. 'Are you really a *real* book-writer?'

'Certainly,' I replied, feeling benevolent, like a store Father Christmas. 'Now, one at a time please.'

'I'm the Face from Clitheroe,' announced the tallest youth, Chris Biddulph. In Mod parlance, a face is a leader, someone who stands out from a crowd. 'We believe in following the fashions of the original Mods of twenty years ago.'

'Put my name, put my name!' urged Debbie Coward.

'Were your parents Mods as well?'

'No, they were rockers!'

'So were mine!' 'And mine!'

'So in becoming Mods you are rebelling against your parents?' I suggested, and most of them agreed.

'As there are no Rockers around, who are your enemies now?'

This was a poser, but eventually Neil Jones suggested 'trendies'. At once I tried to look as untrendy as possible, a feat easily accomplished.

'I'm serving my country, as I'm in the Army,' he continued. 'This Union Jack badge isn't satirical, it's real.'

After naming their favourite pop groups and scooter magazines, the Clitheroe Mods departed, along with Patrina Aspin of Blackburn, who said I had to put her name in as she was a girl. I didn't have the heart to tell them that they weren't a bit like the original Mods. Immortalised by the novelist Jane Gaskell in *The Shiny Narrow Grin*, the 'sixties Mods, as I remember them, were sharp, sarcastic and weasel-faced, with very expensive hairstyles. Their distaste for Rockers was partly snobbish, as Mods tended to pass their 'O' levels. They wore rabbit-fur lining in their anorak hoods, and had enormous radio antennae on their pale-blue scooters. A rabbit scuttled across the Morecambe seafront, from one flowerbed to another, safe in the knowledge that neo-Mods wore no fur. These youngsters, who spoke reverently of a past Golden Age, made me feel I might be speaking to members of Disraeli's Young England movement, who idealised the Middle Ages. I am a great one for Golden Ages myself, favouring the eras between the reign of Alfred the Great and 1956.

On Easter Monday the Kings' Arms and the railway station remained closed, as did most of the town's pubs. Regulars gave secret knocks and were admitted. Thirsty Mods, red-eyed from sleeping on the beach in their baggy parkas, roamed the streets in an ugly mood, looking for off-licences. I saw one of them tip over a postcard stand, though as the cards were vulgar this may have been part of a drive for moral purity.

'There's been a riot at the King's Arms, the whole place got smashed up and the police rode into the bar on horseback!' a taxi driver informed me. Next day as the Mods were leaving, the King's Arms opened as usual, a smart pub full of middle-aged holidaymakers. Some glasses and light-bulbs had been smashed, but the 'riot' was a myth, a barman assured me. No cowboy film scenes had occurred, for the police had simply asked the landlord not to open. I felt rather disappointed.

In the past, old men would boast to the young of the hardships they had endured walking to work over the moors on freezing winter mornings, breaking their backs in mills, mines and factories. Soon the modern grandfather will be scoffing at youngsters too 'soft' to endure hitch-hiking to pop concerts along ice-bound roads at dawn, sleeping in railway stations or under seaside piers, and dancing non-stop for twenty-four hours or more at 'weekender' discos. People, it seems, love to make difficulties for themselves. Why, when I was your age, I was writing novels eighty thousand words long!

Pentecostals, Chapel,
and May Day Celebrations

Minehead, a seaside town in Somerset, is known for its May Day Hobby Horse. Another annual custom of a more modern kind takes place there between 3 and 10 May the General Conference of the Assemblies of God, held at Butlin's Holiday Camp.

'Assemblies of God' is the collective name for Britain's many Pentecostal churches, whose members speak in tongues. At 'Meadowvale Dell' rehabilitation centre, I had met a young Greek girl, Lula, who walked with a slight limp. She had been 'saved' and she taught in a Pentecostal Sunday School. When we had both been rehabilitated, or at least released, I called at her house to find out about the conference. Lula's front room, glittering with ornaments, was filled with brothers, aunts and cousins. It was surprising to hear the gruff English accents of her Mediterranean-looking brothers, who probably expressed themselves more fluently in Greek than in Comprehensive Cockney.

When my visitor's pass arrived, which would allow me past the formidable security guards at Butlin's, I took a coach at once to Minehead. Arriving at night, I was bewildered by the neon lights and the crowds. It was a week before the tourist season, and 7,136 Pentecostalists were staying in the camp. A thousand more, including myself, were coming in as day visitors. Religious music blared from the loudspeakers, and I fled to my guest-house, where all the other guests were Pentecostalists.

Next morning, in calmer mood, I was better able to take my bearings. The funfair was free, and I rode above the camp on the monorail, noting the ballrooms, pubs and theatres all put to Pentecostal use. One bar had been taken over by the Junior Christ's Ambassadors, very noisy children who played tambourines. According to my timetable there was a 'business session' in the Pig and Whistle. The sessioneers, glimpsed through a window, seemed a grim lot – stocky men in grey or brown suits. Later they held a court of appeal, Plenary Session, for court members only.

Every day I found the camp turned into a rantorama, with three packed-out religious services being held simultaneously. Congregations were of all ages, the girls in Princess Anne hats, as they had been ordered to cover their heads. All seemed mild, gentle souls. Ferocity and imagination were qualities to be found in the pastors who addressed the meetings. Such wild pastors they were, too, bawling and shaking their fists in the air like minor characters in a Dostoevsky scandal scene. With faces contorted in fury they jumped up and down, bellowing about the devil, materialism, Divine Compulsion, and the end of the world and from one, in an inspired moment: 'Oh my friends, the fortune, fun and filth-seeking people are passing away!'

The response to this frenzy in the gaudy Regency Ballroom was mild in the extreme, and the mood was one of quiet satisfaction, as if this was what the crowd wanted to hear. Most of the preachings were in a sub-American accent, and a husky, 'sincere' tone alternated with a high-pitched screech or roar, with now and then a give-away 'yere' to show the pastor was a Welshman. One young minister who had spent years in South Africa kept breaking into a comic African accent. Young people in the congregation raised their arms in the air in a kind of stolid ecstasy. Songs were accompanied by fast hand-clapping.

I had never been in a Butlin's before, and I was startled when a figure glided past the blue windows of the coffee bar. Then I realised that the windows, with their peeling stickers of fish and other underwater creatures, looked out on the swmming-pool from below. Young men were lounging about, identifying their apparently headless girlfriends through the glass. Some teenage Liverpudlian boys were discussing girls in a familiar fashion, and among the crowds, northern and Welsh accents predominated. West Indian women sat in little clumps looking, and no doubt feeling, rather out of place.

Strolling round the camp, looking at all the kindly people there, I wondered what life in Britain might be like if *everyone* was Pentecostal. There would be no strikes, promiscuity, divorce or drunkenness. If everyone in Britain was 'saved', we would be a docile, harmless folk, hardworking but producing no art or exceptional talent other than singing. It might conceivably be a pleasant fate, but we would be ruled by furious totalitarian ministers, which would detract somewhat from the fortune and fun. Many young people, I believe, get 'saved' in order to escape the horrors of the teenage world, with its emphasis on drink and discos.

This was, of course, a teetotalitarian occasion, though one bar served drinks to off-duty staff members. A cheerful little waitress told me that she felt no differently about the Pentecostals than about ordinary tourists. 'It's all the same to me, as long as they let us do our job in peace,' she said. A veteran on the staff told me that in holiday times they had 'a lot of trouble from delinquents'.

I was sorry to find the enormous South Sea Bar closed, as it was decorated as a series of pagan groves set in plastic tropical scenery. What kind of sermon could have been preached among grimacing heathen idols? On the other side of a lawn, among avenues of young trees, the chalets stood in brightly painted rows, like an ideal South African township.

Meetings ended at midday and started again in the evening, so I took a walk along the seafront into the town. North Hill, wooded and dotted with villas, rose steeply from the harbour. Near the top, with its old steps and cottages, stood a tall-towered church – dedicated to St Michael, as on most such high places. Perhaps a real pagan grove had preceded it, and St Michael was needed to battle with the devil. The higgledy-piggledy lanes bore such names as Hemp Garden, Watery Lane and The Bell. Thatch on the cottages rose to a widow's peak at each roof end, a style characteristic of this part of Somerset.

Talking of hemp gardens, no trace of hippies or Oriental–mystic types could be found at the conference, and very few young people there seemed the sort to have led wild lives before being 'saved'. The Pentecostal Church is worlds away from the sinister new cults that began by recruiting drug addicts. It is closest in tone to the Elim Church. Older Pentecostals seemed, from their sniffy comments, to regard the Elims as rivals, but Lula and her friends just called themselves 'Christians' and accepted all 'saved' evangelicals as equals. When I finally met Lula among the crowds, she introduced me to a childish old Yorkshireman who frolicked about, singing the theme song of the conference, 'I will put on my Garments of Praise.' At once he buttonholed me and began a long, involved story about his car breaking down on the Yorkshire moors, which led to a chance meeting with a long-lost relative, his wife's cousin's brother-in-law. 'It was the Lord made me break down like that,' he assured me. This *did* remind me of a hippie I once knew who would say things like 'I was only *talking* about this guy, you know, and there he was! It must be cosmic!'

'I couldn't go to the ordinary Butlin's,' said the old Yorkshireman. 'There's drinking and swearing, even in front of ladies.' I put his happiness down to simple faith, but one unkind soul told me it was because his wife had just left him.

Lula was with her Youth Fellowship, an engaged couple, another girl and three spirited boys, all aged about twenty. The boys were not interested in girls, only in judo and karate, which they practised on one another. However, the girls were very interested in *them*, and trailed after them forlornly. Lula's situation was rather unfortunate, as her parents believed in arranged marriages and wouldn't let her go out with a boy until they were engaged. The conference should have been her opportunity, but instead the boys spent hours at a time in the crowded billiards hall.

Few of the young people ventured outside the camp, and when they did it was to the amusement arcades. On this occasion we went to the coffee bar with the swimming-pool windows, where the Youth Fellowship queued up for knickerbocker glories. A folk group played at one of the tables, and young people around it danced and clapped, while one wheeled round and round with his arms outspread, as if playing at aeroplanes.

'You should have been here yesterday,' a lady in the queue told me. 'They were dancing out on the floor there, with guitars and tambourines. Lots of the old people were joining in, and our pastor's wife danced very cleverly with a young man. I've never seen anything like it before, and I've been coming ever since I was saved'

As in most evangelical gatherings, the very old and the very young predominated, though most of the pastors were middle-aged. The engaged couple attended Bible College. You have to pay to go to such colleges, but when you leave, a place is nearly always found for you in some evangelical organisation.

We all crowded into Lula's gloomy little chalet for tea and biscuits, in a seedy corner of the camp reserved for self-catering customers. Lula shared these cramped council-flat conditions with the two other girls. 'It's like a prison here,' said Lula, 'I'm ever so sleepy, 'cos we got up for the morning meeting at six-thirty, and we have to sleep three in a bed. The other bed there is full of dead fleas.'

'You should complain and they'll move you,' said the blowzy pastor's widow who had just dropped in. 'My complaint is the meter men. They just barge in to empty the meter without knocking.'

'Our meter's broken, and we've got no electricity at all,' said one of the boys. 'What's more, the lavatory don't flush, and we have to empty buckets down. The lady next dooor's got a mouse – she makes enough fuss about it, you'd think it was a rat. Her roof's leaking, she says. Or is it the tap?'

The vivacious Bible College girl, began describing a lovely cathedral she'd seen, but the widow cut her short. 'You don't need any of that stained glass and stuff to see the Lord,' she admonished. 'I was saved in a tin hut. Yes, a tin hut! No, I tell a lie, it was a stable.'

Lula pulled a book out of my pocket curiously, but returned it disapprovingly when she saw it was not evangelical. She gave me a pamphlet to read instead, which told a warning story about a young man who, though 'saved', wasted his time by tinkering with wirelesses instead of serving the Lord. 'Oh, beware even of legitimate hobbies lest they steal God's time,' the tract ran, going on to inveigh against 'unwholesome reading'.

Once they are 'saved', evangelicals do not always consider that they have to help others outside their Church and tend the sick and unfortunate, but instead are urged by their pastors simply to evangelise until as many more as possible are 'saved'. To be fair to the Pentecostals, they run organised charities and orphanages, but on the whole they make the saved feel more important than anyone else. Reading of an orphanage where every boy but one was 'saved', my heart went out to that child. Older churches and cathedrals baffle most evangelicals, whose minds usually jump straight from the New Testament to the *Pilgrim's Progress* or the nineteenth century, and can make no sense of the years in between.

'Do you think a Catholic or an Anglican is a Christian?' I have often asked them.

'He *can* be, if he's saved as well,' is the usual dubious reply.

If I tell someone under forty-five, someone of the pop generation, that I am a Christian, they automatically think I am a 'saved' evangelical, as this is what the word 'Christian' has come to mean. These days, 'Christian behaviour' is often interpreted as going around asking everyone if they are 'saved'.

'That pastor last night wasn't half using long words,' complained the widow. ''E never used to, it must be 'cos 'e went to Australia.'

'Yes, it was really intellectual – I went to sleep,' Lula agreed seriously.

'I missed that, as I went to the Pastor's Meeting,' said the Bible College boy. 'They have meetings about meetings nowadays, but yesterday they finally passed the Evolution Bill. Now we're going to make a petition to the House of Commons, asking for school curriculums to be changed, so that children aren't brainwashed into thinking the evolution theory is fact. As it is, they teach it as if it is proved, and never mention God at all.'

Evening meetings began, and we hurried off to the ballroom.

A benevolent elderly pastor was speaking, and the place was so full that we ended up perched on tables. Sometimes arms waved and groans of rapture rent the air, but on the whole the occasion was a placid one. Two young girls sat drawing cartoons as the pastor spoke, but clapped as wildly as anyone else during songs. It occurred to me that the conference and the meetings demonstrated not religious fervour, but togetherness. Our Lord's name was repeated so often, without any sign that His message or character were understood, that it became merely a means of whipping up excitement. For Lula's friends, enjoyment and religion could both be conjured up by an emotional pastor, responded to in a traditional way, and then be switched off until the next meeting.

'The ways of the Lord are surprising,' intoned the pastor. 'We have always thought that God would only go in the Pentecostal churches, but now God is in the historic churches too, where people are being baptised and saved!' At this point a man appeared by the platform, silently holding up a box with a lit-up message on it: 'Baby crying in Green Chalet Number Two.' Many such electronic baby warnings were scattered about the camp.

Then a girl and a young man each sang a song, he in country and western, and she in soul style, to great applause and admiration. A bowl was passed from hand to hand, and one of the boys remarked that the collection would come to two thousand pounds, as there were two thousand people in the ballroom, and most seemed extremely generous. I dropped my coin on a salad of pound notes.

'Last week,' continued the pastor, 'I prayed for gifts from the Lord, I went to bed and later woke the whole house singing psalms in tongues! Someone told me I was saying "Oh Lord, when will our church revive?" in modern Greek. Now Lord, we ask for miracles! We ask to speak in tongues!'

At once everyone did so, in a steady mumble, sometimes breaking out into the contrived voice with which they shouted, 'Yes, Lord' or 'Help me, Jesus!' I think the babble was meant to sound biblical, but the only words clear enough to spell were 'alleganempty allagaseah'. In a West Indian church I have heard tongues spoken in a hysterical frightened manner, which suggested that the words came from the unconscious mind. Pentecostals try hard to be like Negroes, but have to act emotions that are not natural to them, and force themselves to get up and perform 'spontaneous' clodhopping dances. Once I took a girl from such a meeting to a West Indian church, and she was terrified by the screams of genuine hysteria.

As the meeting ended, the hum of tongues from the congregation continued, and one coloured girl was jumping up and down. I thought of throwing in a ramalamadingdong, but decided it might lack sincerity. Someone shouted several phrases in what sounded like Russian. When the meeting ended, three young men stood hugging each other in the emptying hall and beseeching the Lord, with closed eyes, to give them tongues and larger congregations.

Next, we all hurried across to the camp theatre for a film-show. The young pastor with the South African ministry had made a very professional film, the highlight of which showed a large tent full of stocky African women in headshawls, who had suddenly decided *en masse* to get 'saved'. They surged forward to the platform in thousands, toppling chairs and one another, rolling on the ground and sobbing – either from ecstasy or from anguish, as some must have been trampled on. Such a heaving heap of humanity seemed to me a degrading spectacle and a warning against playing with mass emotion, but all the other film-goers were entranced, especially Lula.

'It was wonderful – the Lord meant us to see it!' she said. 'Why can't *we* be like that?' All the young people seemed elated, and burst out of the cinema talking loudly to one another.

I went back to the coffee bar. There a real-life drama was taking place, for a three-year-old West Indian girl had been found sitting there, and no one knew whom she belonged to. It was now nearly midnight, and the solemn-eyed child hugged one of the conference organisers, only taking her thumb out of her mouth to say that her name was Sheryll.

The dilemma had united Butlin's staff and Pentecostals, and they gathered round poor Sheryll suggesting names of pastors and of towns to her but in vain. With sleepy gravity she shook her head every time, without disturbing her thumb. 'Surely someone will be looking for her by now,' said the organiser. 'Where do you suppose she's from?'

'Tooting!' Sheryll said suddenly, and recorked herself amid cries of relief.

I never found out what happened to Sheryll, because at that moment a tall Assemblies of God bouncer told me, very fiercely, to finish my coffee and leave, as the place was closing. He was one of the dreaded 'God Squad', as the boys called them, who made sure that there was no hanky-panky round the chalets.

The next afternoon I stood watching the children in the funfair, when a bull-necked, thick-set young man in a suit too big for him, ran past sobbing wildly. 'Oh my God, oh my God, where's the chapel?' he cried – then tried some doors and ran up the stairs into an empty meeting hall. No one else seemed to notice him, except a young American girl that he brushed past. 'What ought I to do?' I asked her. 'Go up after him.' she said; so I did, and she followed.

When we had at last found him by his loud moaning, we sat him down, as the American girl was afraid he would jump out of the window and I was afraid he would attack me. He ignored my queries, but the girl cooed at him winningly.

'What's your name?'

'Steve.'

'What's the matter, Steve?'

'You won't believe this – you won't believe this – but I went to God! I was happy, fit and strong as anything, and then I went to God! Amnesia, I've had amnesia, and I can't remember things. I died and went to Heaven, and yet here I am! Visions, I saw visions, it was wonderful, and then it was awful.'

'Look after him while I find his pastor,' the strong-minded girl commanded, and vanished. After an age, during which Steve sobbed uninterruptedly, she returned with the pastor and then left him to it. He was a tall, hook-nosed young man with a sleek Beatle haircut and a grey suit. Expecting compasion I was in for a nasty jolt.

'Now, Steve, what's all this?' he snapped. 'You've caused a lot of people a lot of trouble. To be frank, I thought you shouldn't have come. You're an embarrassment to others and to yourself, and an embarrassment to *me*. Why don't you go home if you can't pull yourself together?'

'Oh Pastor, when you exorcised the devil out of me, I felt great, but now he's come back!'

'Who are *you*?' the pastor asked suddenly, giving me a nasty look. So I left too.

It's a tricky business, this exorcism. I was once at a delightful Pentecostal 'house fellowship' in a middle-class home in Surrey. The star turn was a visiting healer and exorcist from the Channel Islands, a rascally looking fellow but very much revered by my hosts. Craning his head, he had looked us over, sniffing for devils, and settled on a rather unstable thirteen-year-old girl in pigtails, who lived with her grand-mother.

'Satan, come out of this child! I command you in the name of Jesus!' he roared.

'No, no,' faltered the terrified girl.

'Yes, Satan, yes!' the man insisted, taking her voice for Satan's. 'Out, I command you!'

'No, stop, stop!'

'I won't stop, Satan! Out, I command you! Satan, get out of this child! Satan, I rebuke you!'

At this the girl fainted, and lay breathing heavily in her armchair.

'The demons are leaving her now,' the man said with satisfaction.

(Later I heard that the girl never quite recovered her senses, and was put in a council home.) Then the roving evangelist turned to me, and with a shrewd glance diagnosed seven devils all raising hell. 'Come forth, demons! Come forth in the name of Jesus!' he roared.

Tit for tat, I decided to roar right back at him, and rose from my seat emitting a hoarse growling rather like a bear. Very pleased, he exorcised and I growled, until I got fed up and stopped.

'The demons are gone now,' he announced, his prestige increased enormously.

'Thank you very much, I feel better now,' I said relieved.

With a cry of horror he began exorcising all over again, and I realised that a truly exorcised person would not know what had been done to him. 'I rebuke you, Satan! I rebuke you!' several people cried. It seemed expedient to faint, so I made for a comfortable armchair and did so.

'The devils are passing away through the top of his head,' said the exorcist.

His next trick was to 'heal' a young man with a bad back, who, when it was over, jumped up and down with joy, crying, 'I'm cured! I'm cured! (But shortly afterwards he had to go into hospital more ill than ever, for the 'cure' – a mixture of massage and loud prayer – had served to conceal the pain only for a time.)

I 'came round' after that, and the witch doctor looked at me with a great deal of interest and amusement. He knew I had been acting, I'm sure, and was wondering how to ask me to become his assistant. As he left the house a wealthy man, my joke misfired, and I have never cared for exorcism since.

Back at Butlin's, I went with Lula and her friends to hear the South African evangelist in person at the Gaiety Theatre. A chubby-faced man with bushy sidewhiskers, his sermon was chiefly a plea for money. Remembering the film of the women in the tent, everyone looked at him expectantly, and his voice grew louder and louder as the collecting bowl went round. The climax of his story was that a rich South African woman had offered him £25,000,000 for his missionary work, but he turned it down because of a dream in which he was frightened by a hippo. This made a tremendous impression..

Encouraged, he shouted still louder, breaking into tongues and back into English, urging those who wanted to serve the Lord to come up to the front. Instantly an emotional bomb seemed to go off: everyone in the packed theatre rose, many of them making their way politely to the centre aisle, only to rush down it like the South African women had done. Lula and most of her friends went to the front, leaving the Bible College girl and myself. I felt nothing at all, but the girl was clearly transfixed with tears in her eyes.

A loud babbling of tongues broke out all round me – 'Shollygoblin! Shollygoblin!' With a triumphant cry of 'Crowbush salamander!' the pastor threw his arms up in the air and the girls began to scream. Everyone embraced each other tearfully, and though I thought nervously of the Bible College girl's six-foot fiancé, I needn't have worried. She fell forwards on to the person in front of her, and appeared to be on the verge of convulsions. In the midst of this confusion, an old lady tottered feebly onto the stage and said that now she could walk again.

The meeting ended abruptly, and everyone left the building talking happily, for they had got what they came for.

'You have been baptised in the Holy Spirit!' the pastor announced.

Lula, radiantly happy, compared notes with some other girls. 'There was a rushing wind going round the hall!' cried the Bible College girl. 'You could hear it!'

'This must be like Heaven.'

'Oh, when we all hugged each other! Oh, that pastor! I wouldn't mind cuddling *him*!'

'When I fell over, it was just like I was pushed!' Lula exclaimed. 'I don't know why I was screaming, but I was! And although we were all falling about, the pastor just stood there as calm as anything. He looked like an angel!'

I was reminded of descriptions I had read of Beatles concerts in the mid-'sixties. Clearly what the Pentecostalists hoped for was a Beatle-like experience. The pastor was all, and Jesus was irrelevant. Perhaps if the Beatles had sent round a collecting-bowl instead of charging admission fees, they would now be even richer than they are. In 1960 I went to my first and last pop concert, to see Adam Faith, who then wore a shiny grey suit like a pastor. Girls screamed at him, but the boys were jealous and threw screwed-up fag packets. So I was not surprised, now, to hear the boys grumbling about the charismatic pastor.

That night, I saw some rough young men being turned away at the gate by the security guards, for the main Butlin' season had started, and no seasonal workers would be admitted until the conference was over. The young men, some with bundles, sat on kerbstones on a freezing night, and wondered what to do. The police moved them on, which didn't help.

In the morning I said goodbye to everyone, and headed home in a coach full of Pentecostals singing about garments of praise. But, I prefer the older churches and I thought instead of a rhyme on the tombstone of Captain Benjamin Forest, who died in 1823, and is buried at St Michael's, Minehead.

> The Boreas' blasts and Neptune's waves
> Have tost me to and fro,
> Yet spite of all, by God's decree
> I harbour here below.
> Where now at Anchor here I lie
> With many of our fleet,
> I hope one day to sail again,
> Our Saviour Christ to meet.

Knutsford, the little Cheshire town Mrs Gaskell described as Cranford, has one of the grandest May Day pageants in Britain. This takes place on the first Saturday of the month, so there is often time to visit other May ceremonies first. On my way to my friend's house in Gaskell Avenue, I basked in the gentle atmosphere of a town whose drivers stopped at once if you so much as glanced at a zebra-crossing.

Older than the present May Day ceremony at Knutsford, which was revived by the Reverend Barnacle in 1864, is the ancient custom of 'sanding'. Sanding may be a relic of a pre-Christian fertility charm, possibly brought from the East by the Celts. Be that as it may, for centuries, brightly coloured patterns of sand have greeted newly married couples as they step from the church. This custom is still kept up, and now extended to May Day; the sanding is carried out by Mr Ray Veal, his son Colin, Mr Veal's brother-in-law Alf Gilbert and his son Jim, all salt-of-the-earth as well as sand-on-the ground types.

On the evening before the festivities, I called at Mr Veal's house, which is built into the side of the eighteenth century Session House, as part of the wall that once surrounded the local prison. Mr Veal appeared

The Haxey Hood Game   The Chief Boggin throws up the 'children's' hoods before the start of the main game. If children succeed in getting these sacking hoods to a pub, they win a small sum of money (Homer Sykes)

The Haxey Hood Game (above)   The Lord Boggin, his willow staff of office in his hand, and the Chief Boggin lead the singing and drinking in a local pub, prior to taking to the streets for the game. The fool stands between them (see p. 1) (Homer Sykes)

The Hornblower of Ripon (below)   At 9 p.m. each night the horn is sounded from each of the four corners of the obelisk in the market square. The office of Hornblower dates from 1604, but the custom is much older and probably originated in Saxon times (see p. 29) (Homer Sykes)

Nutters (above)   On Easter Saturdays the Britannia Coconut Dancers perform all day in the streets of Bacup, Lancashire (Homer Sykes)

Inside the 'Big Top' at Minehead (below)   Early each May a week-long convention of members of Britain's pentecostal churches, The General Conference of the Assemblies of God, is held at Butlin's holiday camp, Minehead (see p. 50) (Butlin's)

May Day, Oxford   At 6 a.m. on 1 May the choir of Magdalen College gather on the top of the bell tower and sing a hymn and a madrigal (above). The large crowd of revellers that gathers for the event is assisted by nearby pubs being open. Three women in the crowd buy fertility cake from a street trader (below) (Oxford and County Newspapers)

May Day, Oxford A local vicar in fancy dress makes his own unusual contribution to the early-morning celebrations (Oxford and County Newspapers)

Morris Men, Oxfordshire Morris dancing, long associated with May rituals and fertility, has been rescued from extinction by the enthusiasm of local groups. Most towns and villages of any size in England now boast a team of Morris dancers (Peter Smith)

Well Dressing   This elaborate panel from Youlgreave in Derbyshire, composed entirely of flowers, is an example of the kind of decoration applied to wells and springs at Ascensiontide. The custom is particularly prevalent in Derbyshire (Janet and Colin Bord)

Reschtach   Couples about to be married in Mallaig, Scotland, are drawn through the streets in a bathtub and pelted with flour and eggs (Homer Sykes)

Durham Miners' Gala   Originally a grand procession and picnic, with bands and banners, drawing miners from over fifty Durham pits, the July Gala is now in serious decline as the mining industry contracts (Homer Sykes)

in his shirt sleeves beneath a large archway, and we stood on the cobbled driveway talking. He was a good-humoured man with an alert face and a bush of grey hair.

'I came to these parts as a boy from Lincolnshire, and I learned sanding from my late father-in-law, who had been doing it for nearly thirty years. I've been sanding for twenty years now, and my son is carrying it on. You know how the custom began, don't you? We've got a little river here by the moor, and in the old days it must have been bigger, as King Canute had to ford it on his way to Scotland or somewhere. That's why we're called Knut's Ford. Anyway, the king had got over all right, when he stopped to shake the sand from his shoes. A bride and groom passed by, coming from church, and the king said "May you have as much happiness and as many children as there are grains of sand in my shoes." Well, I hope they didn't have that many children, but that's how the custom started. Weddings are still our main thing. I live here in the Session House because it's my job to help the judges on and off with their robes. I wear a grey uniform with 'Court Keeper' written across it in gold braid when I'm at work.'

Saying goodbye to the Court Keeper, I promised to meet him at six o'clock next morning to see the sanding. Judging by the state of the funfair on the heath, which stood in a sea of mud, the story about King Canute was false. There was no sand to be seen anywere in this town that slopes steeply down a hill towards a marsh known as the Town Moor. Knutsford chiefly consists of two parallel shopping streets on the hillside, known unofficially as Top Street and Bottom Street. They are connected by a great many alleys and the courtyards of former coaching inns.

May Day dawned bright and fair, the pavements wet from the night's rain, which Mr Veal had assured me was good sanding weather, as it made the grains stick and show up brightly. Hurrying along Bottom Street, I soon found the four sanders at work, accompanied by Alf Gilbert's little grandson Stefan. Mr Veal slowly drove the sand from one place to the next in his van, the back open to reveal buckets of it, dyed by the men themselves. Working briskly, the sanders each filled a funnel known as a 'tundish' with sand, and, with one finger over the spout to control the flow, poured it out in sweeping arabesques several feet long, up and down the pavements. Each curly line was accompanied, rainbow fashion, by lines in other colours — scarlet, chestnut, blue, green and natural white. Most of the large inscriptions in block capitals or handwriting read 'Long Live Our Royal May Queen', and nearly all the Bottom Street pubs had their doorways adorned with peacock-tail designs.

As they worked, with great dedication, the man chatted to one another, rolling cigarettes, or remarking "E's a rum bugger' of some absent friend. They were more like unusually keen early-morning workmen than creative artists.

We then drove out to the suburbs and council estates where members of the May Queen's court lived, all due for special treatment. Court members hung bunting outside their houses, for the while occasion was taken very seriously. What an extraordinary honour it must be for a twelve-year-old girl to be chosen as May Queen and have the whole town at her feet! No wonder the former Queens kept their crowns and talked about their day for the rest of their lives.

'Long Live Our Court Lady' and 'Long Live Maid Marion' were duly inscribed. If sand-wishes alone would help, Knutsford was well on its way to being a town of octogenarians. A Court Lady ran after us with a crisp money-filled envelope from her father; being associated with royalty has its perks. Now the sanders were searching in vain for another court member who had neglected to put out coloured streamers and bunting. 'If he don't take the trouble, why should we?' someone said, disgruntled. The offender had a sandless May Day.

Hunched up in the van, as we hurtled through streets bright with almond blossom and fresh springtime greenery, I was fearful of getting dyed sand on my suit. No such calamity occurred, and soon we reached the home of Paula Williamson, the May Queen herself, which was decorated from top to bottom, with a banner on the roof and a triumphal arch of greenery in the front garden.

Wasting no time, the sanding team drew a crown surrounded by rococo twiddles, and added a little poem for good measure:

Long May She Live, Happy May She Be,
Blessed With Contentment And From Misfortune Free.

Looking as harassed as a bride's father, Mr Williamson invited us all inside and gave us each a cup of coffee well laced with rum. Another envelope changed hands, and I felt some of the glory of being a dustman at Christmas in an unusually generous neighbourhood.

Bidding the sandmen farewell, I was a little saddened to see that a shower of rain had softened the bright colours of the sand patterns, and washed the chestnut dye away into the gutters. But the writing remained intact, in spite of being walked over by unheeding passers-by.

The weather brightened, and with thousands of others I stood expectantly at the roadside waiting for the procession to begin. As the silver band struck up, horses with ribbon-plaited manes tossed their heads coquettishly, and tall schoolboy guardsmen twirled their batons. I was reminded of the royal wedding of Charles and Di. Rows of children in peasant costumes represented the peoples of the world in good *Children's Encyclopaedia* style. The carts, drawn by shire horses and referred to as 'lorries', showed scenes from fairy-tales, nursery rhymes and idealised English history. Well hung with polished brasses, the shire horses were proudly led by local farmers. This parade, with its Victorian fire engine and penny-farthing bicycles, was a celebration of the past – a past where even the less happy features, such as marauding pirates and Vikings, seemed delightful when impersonated by small children. This was not really a grown-ups' occasion, despite the troops of bespectacled or bearded Morris dancers and the ranks of brass and silver bandsmen.

Mabel Telfer (my Knutsford friend) and I took our seats in the grandstand facing the green and the pavilion where the queen would be crowned. Her Majesty, Queen Paula I, a merry, pink-cheeked girl with long dark hair, was led to her throne, and a boy in a red tartan kilt, crown-bearer James Campbell, aged fourteen, approached her, carrying the crown on a cushion. The less privileged onlookers sat on benches in a wide circle around the green. Beyond this perimeter, the caravans of the nearby fair formed a wall, and the Big Wheel rolled round and round, its engine rather muffling the royal proceedings in the ring.

'In Lord Egerton's time that would never have been allowed,' someone remarked, for Knutsford is a town that feels the absence of its nobleman. The horse-drawn fire engine used in the parade had once belonged to the Hall.

'I crown thee Queen of May!' James Campbell cried loudly, and everyone applauded. A wooden dance floor had been laid on the turf, and as the Knutsford band struck up with 'Cock o' the North', miniature sword dancers in highland costume leaped into action.

The weather now looked threatening, and the band put on scarlet oilskins. Nevertheless the dancing teacher began to unravel the maypole ribbons, and 'Bring on the dancing girls!' seemed to be the unspoken cry. The white maypole, closely surrounded by six others, reminded me of a stone circle I had visited recently on a lonely hill in the Hebrides. There the tall, upright stones had been bleached white by the weather and were marked with natural whorls reminiscent of the sandman's art. Perhaps there the May Day ceremony in its earliest form may have taken place, to the music of a bone flute and deerskin drum.

Back in present-day England, the rain suddenly fell in torrents, beating heavily on the awning above our heads. All the same, the young dancers took their places, soaked to the skin but ready to carry on. However, as the bandsmen's instruments slowly filled with water, further celebrations were cancelled, and a car ploughed through the mud to collect the Royal Williamson family.

To cheer up the queen, who bore her disappointment bravely, the announcer passed on a message of goodwill from a party of visitors from Radcliffe, near Manchester. Considering the splendour of the occasion, it was rather touching that the approval of Radcliffe was welcomed so avidly. That night, as I looked from my window across the heath to the flashing lights of the fair, it seemed to me that if the Knutsford May Day received the national recognition it deserved, the thousands of visitors in charabancs would trample away every trace of Mr Veal's sandwriting. And that would never do.

Mabel Telfer, my Knutsford hostess, lives only a few doors away from Mrs Gaskell's former home, in a Victorian house of dark bricks and curly water pipes, with a red wooden gate in the doorway. Once a Lancashire country girl, she has grown into the Knutsford equivalent of a Hampstead thinker. We went for a walk in Tatton Park, superior to Hampstead Heath in every way. A long driveway to the Hall is flanked by meadows where highland cattle, Jacob's sheep and fallow deer graze unconcernedly. Herds of red deer graze more warily on the edge of the woods. 'In Lord Egerton's time, the fallow deer were better able to withstand the winter, as he fed them on sacks of imported locust beans,' I was told.

At the turn of the century, a wealthy evangelical named Watt bought a great deal of Knutsford, and introduced into the unassuming little town a touch of Follydom. His architectural ideas, which might have pleased Clough Williams-Ellis, had been influenced by visits to Italy, Turkey and other sunny lands far from the meres of Cheshire.

Jutting out from among the Tudor shops and cottages of Bottom Street is the King's Coffee House, which has a remarkable tower. It was built on the site of a former inn, and the king in question is Jesus. Watt intended to promote temperance, but instead provoked annoyance, and most of his creations had fallen into ruin by the 1970s. Now the steam laundry and the stone chalet-like houses have been smartened up and turned into homes for 'young professionals' from Manchester. The Coffee House, with its art nouveau windows, has been renamed 'La Belle Époque' (pronounced 'la Belly Pork'). A new block of flats has recently been built in the Watts style, a compliment indeed.

Watt's masterpiece, a building that once epitomised Knutsford for me, has recently vanished, however. Behind an overgrown garden with beehives once stood a lone green and red minaret straight from Old Baghdad. It was a most amazing sight, eminently suitable for calling the faithful to prayer. I'm surprised that no astute muezzin from Rochdale, Leeds or Bradford made a bid for it, to re-erect it among the Moslem terraced streets of a grim industrial hillside. Now it has been pulled down for the same reason that it was put up – that is, for no reason whatsoever.

One of the loveliest old dwellings of Knutsford is the farmhouse, stranded at a corner of the ugly, vandalised concrete bus station. Ash House lost its fields to the buses, which seldom come nowadays. A victim of council reorganisation, Knutsford has now been delivered into bondage to Macclesfield. If the town had been given to *me* instead, I would have provided gentle grey donkeys with panniers to carry people's shopping up the hill from the Moor to the shopless council estate. The soulless clowns of Macclesfield would never think of a thing like that.

Talking of clowns, I well remember the day the circus came to Knutsford. Mabel Telfer, who campaigns tirelessly against cruelty to animals, refused to go and see it. It was a small northern circus, run by gypsyish people of enormous optimism. Soon I saw what Mabel had been driving at.

I asked three merry little children, who were playing among the guy ropes, where I could find the circus zoo. 'The monkey's hung himself!' they cried in great excitement. 'He had a collar and rope round his neck, and when he jumped off a branch he got hung.'

'Oh dear! What about the python, can I see him? He was advertised on the poster.'

'No, he got ill, and the vet in town is looking after him. He's a lovely python – we love to see them feeding him rats! Once he got so fat we could hardly carry him. We've got lots of animals here. It's a shame how they whip them, but they only do it when they're naughty. That over there is a zebrorse, a cross beween a horse and a zebra. In that tent there's two elephants, and my dad says the big one's Indian and the small one's a baby African. And in that caravan, there's two bears.'

Inside the tent I found a young Indian elephant with a sore back and an adult African forest elephant – a prize indeed, since these are seldom seen in captivity. Some naturalists consider the smallest of this variety of small elephant to be a separate species, the pygmy elephant. Almost all the African elephants shown in the West are the enormous plains variety, as seen in national parks. Few white men have seen the elusive forest elephant of West Africa, which can melt away among the great trees without a sound. Unfortunately, the proprietors of 'The Greatest Show in the North' didn't realise the animal's value, and had almost let it fall to pieces. It's tail had rotted off, leaving a stump, one ear was inflamed, and its dead white eyes stared vacantly. The strange, dark, blind creature of the rain forest snuffled for food with its hairy trunk. The only other specimen in Britain is at Whipsnade.

The bears' cage was a small barred section at the end of a living-caravan. Both the bears were bald. These half-grown black bears from Canada, looked friendly, and weaved monotonously up and down their four-foot-square. Both wore collars, and the baldness may have begun on their chafed necks and spread. Only their heads and legs were fully clothed in fur. The rest of their bodies resembled a worn settee of dark grey leather. This circus was a contrast to most others I had seen, as a delight in performing and being useful is normally a tonic to wild animals, and brings their fur out in a gloss.

I was glad to be back in Mrs Telfer's elegant front-room, looking at her books and admiring her peaceful cat Tess, a patchwork-quilt tortoiseshell with an orange triangle on her face. My hostess walked about the house singing. She had been brought up in a small Lancashire village, but left home to be progressive.

'I remember at our May Day when I was a girl, the farmers would lead all the cart-horses through the village, with their brasses polished and shining. We never had a school holiday, so we couldn't see much of the goings-on. It was a censorious and inbred village, ours was. When the shutters were up for a funeral, *every* cottage had its shutters up, as we were all related. They used to let us children look at the corpses. I used to sing around the house then, and still do now, all the same songs. You'll have to excuse me.'

No excuse was needed, as I love the hear the old ballads sung in snatches, floating from the kitchen along with the aroma of cooking.

> Our daughter Jane is far too young,
> We cannot spare her flattering tongue. . .
> Oh, I'll clothe her in silk and wash her with milk,
> And write her name with a gold pen and ink.

'Have some more elder flower champagne', Mrs Price urged me, for once more I was staying at the old Pembrokeshire farm. 'It's a summer drink I make every year.'

'I'll have another glass, Mrs P,' the curly-headed Tim volunteered. The champagne was fizzy, non-alcoholic, and delicious, and went well with roast dinners.

Ted and Yvonne were there, full of plans for renovating their house. Several of their relations had turned up in an expensive trailer caravan parked at the bottom of their garden. Rosie, the gnome-like milkmaid, had now been adopted by this family, whose home was only a few fields away, so she could still reach the Prices' byre by milking time. I was rather alarmed by Ted's male relatives – enormous, swarthy gun-toting men in camouflage jackets. Ted himself went out almost every evening after rabbits, as did most of the neighbourhood's young men.

'Every night I go to the same place, a bank at the end of the woods,' he told me. 'There I lie down facing the field above me, and pick the rabbits off as they appear, like. If I stay too long after sunset, the badgers come out. My hiding place is bang in the middle of a badger-run and one night last week, I felt something on the back of my legs, like, and realised it was a badger! He was so short-sighted, he just walked over me. As long as the wind's right, and they can't smell you, you can go right up to a badger. Last night I poked at one with my shoe, just a nudge, and he made off fast enough. One badger I see there sometimes looks like a bear! He's black all over, not a grey hair on him. He's the biggest badger down there, I believe,'

'Will you take me to see them, Dad?' his daughter asked.

'And me!' I chimed in.

So a badger expedition was planned. We would leave at dusk – Ted, Yvonne, Sharon and myself. I'm not too fond of wild woods at the dead of night, but with so much company I could hardly expire from terror. Once part of the nearby mansion's estate, the forest was overgrown with rhododendrons. By day at this time of year they made a wonderful sight, rising above bramble, bracken and crooked oak in wall upon wall of red and pink blossoms. At night, however, a ghost was supposed to roam the rhododendrons – a young lady from the Big House who had been imprisoned in an old keeper's cottage to prevent her from running away with the groom she loved. The poor girl pined, went mad and died, and is now known as the Grey Lady. A mad ghost seemed a particularly alarming phenomenon, and I hoped I wouldn't meet her.

As the sun went down behind the Prescellies, we four conspirators set out, leaving the Prices and the two boys in the house. We crossed the meadow and climbed over the fence at the far corner, near the grove of trees where Mr Price said he would like to be buried. Through the black trees we could see the bright lights of the great crumbling mansion. To reach the badgers' haven, we had to cross the fast-flowing river across a fallen tree trunk which acted a a bridge. Ted and Yvonne managed this easily, and Sharon got over with a suppressed shriek or two. I edged myself along the trunk and around the branches very slowly, to the impatience of the others. A little further on, the river ran into a rocky gorge, but here the drop was only a few feet from the tree to the river bed itself, so I was in no real danger. At last I was over, and we skirted the brambles and made for the trees upon the hillside. Here Ted showed us the ditch, and we crouched there peering out across a misty field where a few cows still grazed. Yvonne, a slight, boyish woman, seemed to think it all a great adventure.

Something seemed to startle the cows, who jerked their heads in annoyance and moved away. Two half-grown badgers came whiffling through the grass, their silver-grey bodies effortlessly rolling along without visible legs, black and white heads close to the ground and noses twitching for slugs or snails. We held our breath, and they paused about six feet from where our heads poked out of the ditch. Neither animal saw us, as they nuzzled at one another, and snuffled round back to back in a circle. Their small tails seemed far paler than the rest of their bodies. Black paws appeared from a fringe of bristly hair, for these badgers moved low over the ground.

Ted licked his finger, held it up to the breeze, then beckoned to us. Bent double, we followed him around a bush and then strolled right up to the badgers. Unconcerned, they grubbed around almost at our feet. Impatiently Ted swung his foot near one of them, and all at once they saw us. I have never before seen two such surprised animals. One looked me full in the face, in utter amazement, with round open mouth and eyes, before rollicking off into the wood. Following Ted, we came to a grubbed-up piece of ground where the surrounding grass had been flattened.

'That's their rolling place,' Ted explained. 'The sett's over there under the roots of an oak tree.' As we neared the sett, a flash of grey rushed past on galloping black legs, and we saw it tear down the hillside for all the world like a wild pig.

'That's the old boar!' Ted said. 'Look, there goes another.' Straining my eyes in the half-light, I could see another pair of badgers some way away. Ted, with his sharper sight, could see two more among some far-off bushes.

Yvonne and Sharon, meanwhile, who had been moving nearer the farm, suddenly called to us. Ted, expecting another badger, was annoyed to see nothing more than a flowering may tree. The moon sailed overhead, sending shafts of silver light through the fringe of white blossoms and on to the mossy ground. Sweet perfume, a bower of white around silver paths and dark shadows – surely this was paradise.

'You've brought Porridge back safe and sound?' Mr Price asked, I hoped humorously, on our return. 'Pity, I thought you'd lost him in the forest.'

Davey, the Prices' son, was avidly reading a paperback novel about a cowboy called Edge. For years his parents had despaired of him as a reader, urging the classics on him in vain, until one day he had discovered Edge and never looked back. Now in his room there was a whole ledge of Edges, along with his catalogues for guns and tractors. Before Ted, Yvonne and twelve-year-old Sharon had departed, a few coy jokes were made about the girl from the Milk Marketing Board who would be coming the next day to get the cows 'de-bruced'. This capable young lady would be testing the cattle for possible brucellosis, by taking blood samples. It was vaguely hoped a romance between her and Davey might spring up. Uninterested in girls, he seldom went to Young Farmers' discotheques. When the morrow came, and with it a jolly girl in khaki and boots, the de-brucing took place without any hint of romance.

Late May seemed quite a busy time on the farm and in Pembrokeshire in general. The county is famous for its new potatoes, and the picking season had just begun. On the Prices' farm there was also a pig killing, not the gory public spectacle of Thomas Hardy and Flora Thompson's time, but a more hygienic affair. Two pigs were driven to town alive, slaughtered by a professional behind closed doors, and then returned horribly cut into halves as if by a circular saw, nose to tail, straight down the middle, to be lifted carefully into the freezer.

'I never give the farm animals names, in case I grow too fond of them,' Mrs Price told me regretfully. 'I save my affection for the pets here, like Non and Satan the cat. Once I had a pet magpie, Maggie, who lived in a cage hung outside our door. I'll never hear a word against magpies now. Sharon's got a molly lamb she's very fond of, mind. That's a pet lamb that's been rejected by the mother and reared on a bottle. And do you know, I rather miss the duck with a humpty back. We heard an awful noise outside only a week ago, in the middle of the night. When we looked out of the window, we saw a big fox had snatched our poor duck. Davey sent a shot after it, but he must have missed, for all we found next day was a feather. There's a bounty on foxes yere, a pound a tail.'

For some time, everyone on the farm had been nervously scanning the sky, in case it rained before haymaking time. Mr Morgan, whose wife played the organ at Chapel, owned a hay-cutting machine, and would be arriving next to 'do the meadow'. He was to be paid partly in kind, and had already laid claim to one of the pigs.

'When the hay has been cut and cubed, it will fetch hundreds of pounds,' Davey told me, with relish.

At breakfast next day, postman Tom gave us word that Morgan the Hay was on his way. He also gave us a card from my actress sister, who would soon be arriving for a weekend.

Below a blue sky, Mr Morgan shouted a greeting to me above the noise of the machine. Just when I thought the haymaking was over, I was surprised to see Mr Morgan, Tim and Davey each take a scythe and cut vigorously at bunches of hay along the sides of the field and in the corners that the machine could not reach. From his workshop balcony – a former railway carriage joined on to the stables – Mr Price eyed me a trifle balefully, I thought. Everyone was working except myself.

My morbid fear of work of any kind stems partly from my helplessness and my instinct for doing things wrong. At least, that's the excuse I make for myself. I remember the incredulity of my fellow-workmen at a market garden where I pushed, in despairing zig-zags, a trolley which everyone else knew should be pulled.

After an enormous dinner followed by tea and bread and butter, Mrs Price declared that I looked 'as full as an egg'. 'Look at him, he's eating us out of house and home, and he never does a tap!' her husband joked. 'I bet he's not even going to help with the washing-up.'

Hastily I jumped to my feet.

'How terrible to have to wait to be told,' Mrs Price admonished kindly. As we worked, she chatted to me of events at Chapel. She went every Sunday, Yvonne went sometimes, and most of the women from the farms went while the men stayed at home. Mr Price loved to sing hymns and to listen to male-voice choirs, but doubted if there was a God. 'If there are no lathes in Heaven, I don't want to go,' he would always say firmly. As Joseph was a carpenter, it's possible something might be arranged, but for the moment Mr Price's workshop was a heaven on earth. He needed an extra-long blast of the hunting horn to bring him out of it at mealtimes, dressed in his grubby overalls and with the abstracted expression of one interrupted at prayer.

Farmers' wives, gathering every Sunday and at other times for flower-arranging, cleaning and 'emergency meetings', held the community together by the links forged at Chapel. Few, if any, husbands were militant atheists, but most smiled and labelled Chapel a woman's affair. If they had a message or a request to pass on to a neighbour, it would be done via the wives when they met in the little stone building with green railings and the words 'Ebenezer 1883' carved above the door.

It had not always been thus. Old men well remembered the days of Chapel glory before the war, when the men ran everything and chose hard, stern-faced ministers who would terrify housewives with tales of Hell. 'There's a meeting of the Sisterhood tonight — we're going to look over a "possible",' Mrs Price and many a farmer's wife would now tell the family before driving off, leaving a cold snack in the kitchen.

The Sisterhood! A power in the land indeed, more formidable in its way than the Brotherhood of Dutch Reform Church Boers in South Africa or the freemasons in an English country town. 'A possible' meant 'a possible minister', for yes, the Sisterhood now controlled the Chapel and chose the pastors. As a result, the ministers were usually handsome young men who looked like pop stars — well dressed, well fed, with chubby cheeks and a rather fatuous air about them. They received £5,000 a year and 'all found'. The latest recruit, picked by the Sisterhood, was named 'the woolly bear' by Mr Price, with an indulgent chuckle. This referred to his mop of brown curly hair which shook as he preached. This young bachelor had once given me a lift in his flashy new car with a blonde seated beside him who definitely did *not* belong to the Sisterhood. You could tell, as she didn't wear a hat.

'I remember Sundays when I was a girl,' Mrs Price told me. 'No one was allowed to do any work. There had to be a Sunday dinner, mind, so different people did different things. Some families cooked everything on Saturday and heated it up on Sunday, but at our house mother would do the cooking but leave the washing-up till next day. There, that's our own washing-up done. It wasn't so bad, now, was it?'

That night my sister arrived, and we had a merry social evening with songs and sea-stories. Mrs Price gave a recitation, 'Guilty or Not Guilty', which her mother had taught her. I was quite charmed by the sincerity with which she chirped out the melodramatic story. Everybody clapped. A busy weekend lay ahead, with a farm sale on Saturday and Chapel on Sunday.

As Mr Price, Tim, Davey, my sister and I squashed into the car and roared off to the farm sale, with Mrs Price waving at the gate, we caught a glimpse of a most unusual sight at the edge of the wood. A big ginger and black fox and a gaudy magpie seemed to be playing, the fox leaping in the air and patting the bird with its paws, and the magpie fluttering over the fox's head. Then they fled in opposite directions, the fox diving into a hedge with a whisk of its black-tipped tail. Perhaps in deference to my pet-loving sister, none of the men spoke openly of guns, traps or poison. Usually such animals were only seen from the car when it was dark. One night a badger had lumbered across the road just outside the farm gate, and on another occasion, when Tim's petrol-less van had been coasting serenely down the hill nearby, a startled fox cub had trotted across the road, looking very innocent.

'Sale', a big sign by the roadside informed us. His eyes gleaming at the thought of farm machinery, Mr Price swung the battered vehicle through a gate and into a muddy field with cars parked all over it. Tractors and a great variety of lethal-looking mechanical devices were standing in rows in an even muddier field nearby. Mr Price walked from one contraption to the other, discussing them with the boys. Yet another small farmer had gone broke, and his effects would now be spread among all the other fluctuating farms of this little England beyond Wales.

The farm had an air of dejection about it. From his pen, the curly-browed Charolais bull roared repeatedly, as if in desperation. Nearby, his many brownish white wives stared at us with strange, wondering faces. The Charolais, a French breed, had been brought into Wales as lean beef cattle, to suit people who leave their fat on the edge of their plates.

The local farmers, big men in dung-coloured clothes and slouch hats, had the grimmest faces imaginable, like stuffed, glass-eyed bulldogs who had heard bad news. It was hard to imagine speaking to them. An English back-to-the-lander, with glasses, long hair and an arty-looking wife, seemed infinitely more agreeable. Taken one at a time, as dinner guests of the Prices, the local farmers were not too bad, if a bit obsessed with their children's exam results. In a mass they were formidable. Whisking a stick and uttering sharp cries, a cloth-capped man drove the cows into a yard that acted as an auction room. Huge farmers sat on the wall in rows, their boots dangling. Most of them had left their wives at home. The auctioneer, a capable-looking man, began to sing his wares, going faster and faster as he got up steam, sounding like Lonnie Donegan skiffling his way down the Rock Island Line. Mr Price caught the flashing eye of a gypsy, the most volatile character there apart from the auctioneer. The whole gypsy family were present, down to the smallest baby. After a chat with them, Mr Price told us it was time to go.

'That's old man Lovell's son,' he mentioned, nodding goodbye to the gypsies. 'His grandmother died a while ago, and there were gypsies here from all over come for the funeral. She was their queen, I heard. The fires lit up all Haverfordwest Aerodrome, that's where they live. Old Lovell always comes to these sales and picks up what's left of the machinery afterwards for scrap. We get on very well, and he tips me off for bargains. Just now his son got me a hen-house for next to nothing. You ought to meet old Lovell, Porridge. He comes over for dinner sometimes, and he's full of stories.'

Next morning, Mrs Price, my sister and I, dressed to the nines, made our way decorously to Chapel, greeting all the wives at the door. A few young husbands were there, with neatly brushed hair, and the many young ladies and children were very brightly dressed. As the three of us were late we had to sit in the front row, below the pop-eyed gaze of the male choir – four angry old men in tight waistcoats who stared us straight in the eye as if defying the Sisterhood. They burst into the opening hymn, which was in Welsh, singing as if in outrage.

When 'Kill the Saxon Dogs' (or whatever the hymn was called) was over, 'the woolly bear' came on with some timely platitudes about love, peace and understanding. This restored the balance. Mrs Morgan the Hay, a slim, sensitive woman with glasses, played the organ beautifully. According to Mrs Price, she had been up at six that morning nailing slates on to her farmhouse roof. For the most part, the hymns were in Welsh and the Bible readings in English. Mrs Price knew no Welsh but was going to evening classes. She was having a race with a schoolfriend in Merthyr to see who would be a Welsh-speaker first. All the same, when there was a Bible reading in Welsh for a change, she looked as be-fogged as I did.

An English hymn followed, roared out by a short man with the face of an indignant terrapin. 'Now raise your Ebenezer!' he commanded in song.

All at once my sister was rocked with choking giggles, and I realised she was a victim of the television viewer's complaint, of seeing a double meaning in every utterance. Fortunately, she controlled herself and became ladylike once more. As we left, everyone shook our hands most cordially, even the men in the choir.

Back at the farm my sister oohed and ahed over the chicks, ducklings and piglets, and had a go at milking one of the cows. The boys seemed sorry to see her go. Soon I too would have to leave. Mrs Price would take no money for my keep. 'It's a pity you can't stay until Whitsun, mind,' she said, as she carefully paid Tim's wages and stuck a stamp in his book. 'We have a Cymanforoedd-ganu at our Chapel – that's a singing festival –

and all the children from miles around will be taking part, the little girls all in red ribbons. Never mind, why don't you take a bus to Haverfordwest Aerodrome and visit old Mr Lovell at the gypsy camp? Say you're a friend of the Prices.' I felt a bit dubious about this, as gypsies very seldom ask 'gorgio' friends into their caravans, let alone strangers.

When the bus had put me down, I found myself in a deserted concrete airfield, with weeds growing out of the cracks. Behind a hedge the permanent trailers of the gypsy camp formed a shanty town, but few Romanies were at home. The camp, an official gypsy site, had an attractive home-made gateway. A huge iron wheel formed the centre of the gate, with bedsteads, cycle wheels, pram handles and an amazing collection of scrap iron oddments welded on to it. Large boulders, painted white, formed the gateposts, in grand eighteenth-century style. 'Elvis is King' was painted all over the boulders in bright scarlet. I popped my head over the hedge and saw one of the Lovell family hammering at some wood, a little girl playing at his feet.

'Do you know if Mr Lovell senior is home?' I asked, and he gave a start. 'I'm a friend of Mr Price who goes to farm sales.'

'There's no one called Lovell here, sir,' young Lovell replied. 'You must want the hippie camp over the way.' Though respectful, he looked tough, so I decided to go and look at the hippies instead. Hippies are so hated among the Pembrokeshire farmers that gypsies stood in high renown in contrast.

'Poor gypsies, fancy having hippies on their doorstep,' people would say. Again and again, the council had towed the hippie caravans away, but the hippies always towed them straight back again. 'Thanks for taking us nearer the dole office!' they taunted the officials on one occasion.

Only a field separated the gypsies from the hippies, yet there was little contact between them. They were not hostile to each other and as ex-grammar school and polytechnic pupils seeking a natural life, the hippies were in awe of the Romanies. The hippie trailers, I noticed, differed from the gypsy ones by being covered in misspelt slogans, ferociously defying and libelling the prime minister and the government. Lurchers, indistinguishable from gypsy dogs (or 'jukels'), barked at me as I walked along reading the caravans.

'There's a man from the council, counting our caravans!' one hippie said loudly so that I could hear.

'No, I am writing a book on folk customs,' I explained.

At this they grew friendly, flattered at being thought to be 'folk' and I was invited to stroll around their camp. The small children gathered around me, eager and friendly, and showed me their parents' marijuana crop growing under glass and a wild polecat that someone had trapped and put in a hutch. 'We wish we could go back to school!' an earnest little boy told me. 'We used to go to a school at Roche, and we loved having other children to play with.'

I said goodbye and climbed over the barbed-wire fence just as a police car drove slowly and ominously past. Back on the main road, I began to hitch-hike, for no more buses would run till evening. A grey van stopped, and a friendly Scottish voice told me to jump in the back. I found myself crouching among straw litter, surrounded by young potato-pickers – men, women and children – who came down from Scotland every year. A cheerful crowd, they sang and joked as we bumped along the road and up a very steep hill to the village of Mathry. They weren't going anywhere near the Prices' farm, but Mathry seemed an interesting destination. Everyone climbed out at the potato fields and began to work straight away, but the driver continued up to the summit. While he went to see the farmer about his wages, I looked at the potato-pickers' camp in surprise, for their caravans were jammed between rows of disused but smelly pigsties. Clothes were hung out to dry on lines and over the pigsty railings, and a small girl was helping her mother with the washing tub.

That day Mathry was full of playful Welsh children racing around the rocks and cottages. The local pub had an enormous sign in capitals over the door.

No Potato-Pickers

Tinkers

Hippies

Tramps

Dogs

It seemed certain that I must belong to one or another of these categories, but the landlady served me without comment. Later I strolled down the lane, where linnets fluttered in the hedges, along with greenfinches, hedge sparrows and 'chinking' stonechats.

At ten o'clock at night I limped wearily into the farmyard, to be met by barking Non and an alarmed Mrs Price. 'I was terrified!' she said. 'I thought you must have been beaten up by hooligans. Come on in, I was just putting corks at the foot of my bed to keep off the cramp.'

In Search of Ancient Britain: Gypsies and Druids

'Retain Your Loyalty – Preserve Your Rights.' These proud words are inscribed on the town cross at Appleby-in-Westmorland. No longer a county town – the pomp and pride of assize courts and mayoral robes of office vanished with Westmorland itself – Appleby is now chiefly noted for its gypsy horse fair, held in the first week of June. The inhabitants view this fame, or notoriety, with mixed feelings.

'Appleby isn't itself this week,' I was told. 'We're normally such a clean, quiet town. Now with the gypsies here, I have to keep my twelve-year-old daughter indoors, and those pubs that are staying open have locked away anything that can be moved. Mind you, the *true* gypsies are all right, it's these others.'

Gypsies, Nature's rascals! The myth of the 'true gypsy' recalls that of the 'true Rasta' in West Indian lore. Very likely the 'true Gypsy', like the true Rasta, would turn out to be the worst one of the lot. Thousands of gypsies, true or false, pour into Appleby every year, by horse and wagon, car and trailer, cart or lorry, and set up camp on Fair Hill overlooking the town.

On the Thursday night, when I arrived in Appleby the town was full, but after much searching I found an inn, the White Hart, which wouldn't take gypsies but *would* take me. Thus privileged, I unpacked my carrier bag and set out on the town. The spiritual leader of the wild invaders proved to be an elderly swashbuckler·with a high-crowned hat, Facey Romford sidewhiskers, clay pipe, scarlet neckerchief, leather waistcoat, and a stout ash stick in his hand. Taking command of a local pub, he waved his vast tribe of horse dealers into every available seat and began roaring orders at the landlord.

'Drinks all round for everyone – a glass of water each! Come here, my mush, come here!'

Ingratiatingly, the landlord produced a mauve notepad and went from table to table taking orders. Conversation became general.

'A glass of mickey mouse for me, landlord!'

'That girl! I wouldn't let a dingler like you get within wagon shaft length of her?'

'Every year when I come here I see a magpie in the same tree.'

Many of the men resembled Smithfield meat-porters, in open-neck striped shirts and braces and with huge bellies and short bristly hair. Whether or not they were Romany by blood, they were gypsy by inclination: a good bargain their only religion, their pride was measured in dogs and horseflesh. Anxious policemen guarded the bridge over the River Eden. One year, an officer had been thrown through a plate-glass window. In the growing dusk, I crossed over the river and made for Fair Hill, already white with modern trailers.

Not all the caravans had arrived yet, but many horses were tethered in nearby fields and on verges. Most of the small boys were dressed as skinheads, a cult that has an enormous attraction for them. Three girls, two small and one large and round, stopped and stared at me.

'She wants to go out with you!' the small ones said in jeering, whining voices, pointing at their friend. Evidently they expected me to walk primly by, and when I made a bee-line for the older girl it created a sensation. 'Get back! Get back!' she screamed, trying to climb over the fence in natural panic at the thought of going out with me.

'I would be greatly honoured if you would let me buy you some chips,' I said, 'but if you'd rather not, never mind.'

This speech increased her terror, but the wire fence proved intractable. I would have to retrace my steps and walk past her if I wanted to see the White Hart again, and as I did so she broke into fluent Romany, probably calling for help from her friends. At that moment I was forcibly reminded of this rhyme, translated from Romany–Spanish by George Borrow, the nineteenth-century wanderer and friend of gypsies:

> Loud sang the Spanish cavalier,
> And thus his ditty ran:
> God send the Gypsy lassie here,
> And not the Gypsy man.

The prayer was answered in part, as no men appeared to defend her, and I reached my hotel in safety.

In the morning I climbed a wooden ladder into the upstairs dining-room, where I admired the many colourful framed jigsaw puzzles around the room. Outside in the hot sun I saw three old-fashioned caravans jogging by, each with a piebald mare in the shafts. The last one to go by had a bucket swinging from the rear.

How was I to get to know the gypsies? Notebooks, pencils and interviews have unfortunate connections for them, and would shut the best of them up completely and bring forth a stream of cadging lies from the worst. After due thought, I bought a sketch pad and a packet of cheap toys. Many more gypsies had arrived by now, some of them walnut-coloured with headscarves, others blond and in modern clothes, but all wild and foreign in appearance. Two small girls wore crimson velvet, with lace collars and knee-breeches. Cheers arose from the river-bank, where boys were racing piebald ponies from one side to the other, plunging and splashing. Other children swam or rode on a raft of plastic paraffin cans lashed together, and older couples sat on the banks and watched them. Holidaymakers sat on the other side of the river and watched the gypsies.

That evening I made my way to Fair Hill with my sketchpad, sat by a hedge opposite some caravans, and began drawing funny animals. As a boy I had greatly admired the animal caricatures of L.R. Brightwell, a popular illustrator in the 1940s. Brightwell had been influenced by J.A. Shepherd, the comic animal artist of the late-Victorian *Strand* magazine. Pretending to ignore the gypsy children who came out to watch me, I frowned severely and rapidly drew sub-Brightwells one after the other.

'What are you doing, mister?'
'Drawing pictures, twenty pence each. Want to buy one?'

Little eyes gleamed with joy at these gloriously commercial words, and soon I was surrounded by boys and girls, pressed ever backwards into the hedge till I looked like a goblin of the hawthorns. Shy as a deer, my nervous friend of the night before came out and stared at me from a distance. Chivalrously, I sent her a picture for nothing. It seemed hard to take the children's money, for I was soon busily changing pound notes, but I believe that if the drawings had been presents I would have been mistrusted from the first. As it was, those with permanent addresses, such as Andrew Miller of Cheadle Heath, Cheshire, gave them to me with instructions for future drawings. Their requests were always for horses, dogs, donkeys, rabbits and ferrets.

'I can't draw horses – only unicorns,' I admitted, and Andrew had to be content with a pastoral scene of grazing unicorns.

Just as it was growing too dark to draw, the men came along and stood over me in a body.

'What are you doing, master?' one asked.

I showed him, and he quickly pointed out several errors. The men, literal-minded to a fault, scorned cartoons and insisted on absolute accuracy. Their passion for dogs and horses was touching, and any reasonably good lightning artist could make a fortune at a gypsy camp and learn a great deal besides. I was surprised not only by their frequent use of Romany words, such as 'jukel' for dog and 'chav' for child, but by the way they assumed I would understand them. Luckily they were not the first gypsies I had met.

'Let's see you do a jukel, a good rough-haired juke, and a chav, a little mush, holding him.'

I tried to draw a lurcher, held by a boy, and added a rabbit diving into a hole.

'A shosho!' a man cried in delight. 'The back legs are wrong.'

'Here's my jukel,' a swarthy man wearing a slouch hat and neckerchief announced, holding up a she-whippet very like the juke I had sold to a gypsy after a hilarious bargaining session many years ago. ('Jackal' derives from the same word, apparently.) He held up the animal for me to draw and paid me ten pence for the result. All this while, the children, feeling backstaged, had been throwing leaves and twigs at my head, only half-consciously, while staring at me intently.

'These children are too rough,' I complained.

'If you think the chavvies are rough, you should see the fathers,' was the reply.

When darkness compelled me to leave, I found I was wearing a wreath of stinging nettles, painful to remove. While wandering along, rubbing my fingers on a dock leaf, I was accosted by two policemen and ordered into a Black Maria.

'What are you, an obvious non-gypsy, doing with the fair people?' I was asked.

My explanation that I was a writer sounded very lame. For half an hour I was asked every question known to man (or mush) save 'When did you last see your father?' It was my mother they seemed to be interested in.

'You're a middle-aged man, never married, living with your

mother!' one of them exclaimed. 'You know what that suggests, don't you?'

I didn't, so he enlightened me by asking if I had any convictions for child-molesting. I felt shocked and unclean! It's true I usually gravitate to the company of children, but it feels to me like water finding its own level. Being an old bachelor, especially if an uncle, as I am, had once been considered perfectly honourable. A fondness for mothers used to be thought a virtue. Now these states suggested perversion, thanks to the accursed belief that everyone must be having sex with someone.

'We're giving you all the time in the world to tell us anything you may have done to children,' my persecutors continued. 'If you lay a finger on the gypsy children, the men will murder you. They're a very volatile crowd.'

At long last I was turned loose and warned off the gypsies 'for your own good'. Buying some chips to cheer myself up, I found that every drunk gypsy wanted to 'borrow' one. Then a meat-porter type, granted permission to abstract one chip, seized and scoffed the lot! I grew belligerent.

'Right, that'll be twenty pence!'

He looked at me in surprise, his love of bashing people warring with his fondness for haggling.

'Right, I'll get my mate!' I shouted, nodding towards the mateless White Hart Hotel.

'Get my mate,' he repeated with an incredulous laugh at such an obvious ruse. 'Ten pence or nothing!' he answered.

'Done!' I snapped, and he paid up like a gentleman.

'Hello there, chav!' a boy greeted me next day.

'I can't stop,' I apologised, 'as I've got to call at a house beyond Dufton Wood.'

'You mean a caravan!' he protested. 'You wouldn't call at a house! Come back Sunday night as we're having a fire.'

He stretched the last word out in ecstasy, 'fi-i-ah', and caressed the air with flame-like gestures. No mere bonfire, but a revelry, was afoot. Another boy tried to sell me a cheap wire ring as 'genuine silver'. When I said I would take it to be appraised, he looked so wobegone that I gave him a pound for it. At once he ran leaping down the road, waving his arms in the air and whooping with joy.

After a long trek through some of the finest woodlands I have ever seen, where rabbits darted among the bluebells and sheep lolloped up into the hills, I reached Keepers Cottage and met Edwin Gospatrick, crag-faced guardian of a thousand pheasants. This good-humoured man had a strong local accent and a passion for fox-hunting, foot-pack style. We had a friend in common, so I was invited in. As the keeper himself was very busy 'watching the woods on account 'o the gyppos', he asked his fifteen-year-old apprentice to show me round.

Clearly fascinated by birds and animals, the boy ran from pen to hutch to incubator, showing me everything there was to be seen, from a tray of hatching pheasant eggs to a brood of blind baby ferrets who looked like grey sausages. One of the adult ferrets had been taken from a gypsy poacher. He opened an incubator drawer and helped a struggling chick out of its cracking egg. In some boxes nearby, striped baby pheasants, three days old, were running around.

'Every gate is barred against the gypsies, and we have to be on the watch all day,' he told me. 'This morning one got in with his lurcher, and wouldn't stop when challenged. Mr Gospatrick shot just above his head, and that changed his mind. He left quietly. Here's where we keep the hounds – here there, Ranter! See that Alsatian? He was thrown out of the police force for ripping out a man's stomach, so we keep him to scare off gypsies.'

'What made you decide to be a keeper?'

'Well, I started off as a poacher, but I kept getting caught, like. The magistrate sent me to Mr Gospatrick and I've been learning the job ever since, though I have to go back to school sometimes.'

Back in the kitchen, where I admired a fox mask mounted by the gifted keeper, little John Gospatrick, his five-year-old son, drew pictures of foxes and talked eagerly of animals and birds. Appleby children, resident or gypsy, thought little of television or pop music, it seemed.

Sunday was a big day for the gypsies, their last fling before the serious business of horse-selling began. It had rained heavily during the night and the horses swam rather than waded in the river races. With a great clattering of hooves, a youth galloped down the street, riding Romany-style, leaning backwards and holding on to the rope reins as if water-skiing. He was stripped to the waist, with enormous bare feet sticking out on each side of his mount. In a corner, on a tiny pony, a small boy practised 'leant-back' riding, and in the water a tinier pony was being scrubbed in a white lather of suds.

Up on Fair Hill it was open day for visitors, and stalls lined the various muddy tracks, selling horse tackle, cut glass, china ornaments and brightly coloured cushions. A farrier worked from the back of van, banging on the anvil and hammering on the shoes amidst clouds of steam and smoke. Men walked around carrying long whips. One had a parrot on his shoulder, a balding African Grey. Facey Romford took his ease among friends, sitting smoking on the steps of an old-fashioned barrel-top wagon. A buxom, dark-haired girl with pink cheeks, brown arms and a merry look about her, offered to tell my fortune. We stepped into her bright modern trailer, decorated with strips of chromium, windows with engraved and stained glass patterns and a bright chaffinch in a cage. I sat down, and the 'dukkering' began. She spoke rapidly and mechanically, moving my hand this way and that.

'Ah, you have luck in your face, sir, luck in your face. You've been going through a bad time, a very bad time, I know, but things are getting better, believe me. This time next year, sir, you'll be married and a family on the way. You have a son in your face, sir, I can see. If you give me five pounds, I can look into the crystal ball and give you an even better fortune.' This I declined, and she waved goodbye cheerfully. My face seemed as important as my palm in this 'dukkering', though no one's ever told me that my face was my fortune.

Going on my way, I counted several Original Gypsy Lees, but failed to beat my last year's record of eleven in a row at Nottingham Goose Fair. A gentle, elderly, brown-skinned Gypsy Lee, surely the real one, offered to read my palm, but I explained that I'd just had a 'dukkering.'

'You've got a head-piece on you, I can see,' she said, nodding sagely. 'I'll do your fortune another time. I'm not like those German gypsies in Scotland, who grab hold of people and frighten them with demands for their fortunes. A few poor German gypsies escaped from Auschwitz after the war, when Hitler put our people to death, and they got over to Scotland. I truly think our people can't be destroyed, as we live right. We don't believe in divorce, dear, or any business like that. When you're married, you're married. My old man and myself have come here straight from the Derby.'

I wandered away from the holdaymakers' track to a wilderness of caravans, new and traditional. Here I was offered chickens, goats, lurcher pups, canaries, ferrets and clothes pegs for sale. In one half-hidden corner I found a circle of barrel-top wagons, pioneer style, fenced round by washing lines. These belonged to humbler gypsies and Scottish tinkers, an open-faced, pleasant crowd with many children.

Hours later, the fire cancelled because of heavy rain, I sat upon the doorstep of a traditional wagon in the guise of a peddler of cheap toys, and told stories to the young members of the Smith family and their friends. The tinker children, or 'wains' as their mothers called them, were fair-haired and very well-mannered. Their parents too were remarkably courteous, while the darker Romanies cracked jokes and tried hard to get a camp fire going beneath a blackened cooking-pot. Some of the dialect was unfamiliar to me. I have known Scottish tinkers in the South of England to light Beltane fires on May Day and drive their ponies through them. In Sussex, these same red-haired and freckled tinkers offer to buy knives, forks and spoons. In Pembrokeshire they pick potatoes.

At length, wishing goodbye to Lavinia, Arabella, Lynsey and others, I walked straight into the arms of the same two waiting policemen, who soon released me with many a sardonic remark.

When the gypsies have gone, Appleby reverts to apple-pie order, a gem of a town. While I was reading the inscription on the town cross, a sprightly gentlewoman emerged from her cottage and asked me if I was looking at a bird. I said that I wasn't, so she said that I could if I liked, and asked me inside.

Rainbow-coloured parakeets squawked from their cages in a drawing-room that opened out on to a bloom-filled conservatory. Upstairs, Miss Molly Sprott, my new friend, showed me carefully into a room where birds flew freely around or perched on branches. All were casualties that she was nursing back to health. Finches fluttered around brightly, budgies sat impassively, and I was pleased to see a tame swallow and a dark-brown skylark with expressive black eyes. An expert had proclaimed it to be a Mongolian skylark, a very long way from home. Downstairs, over tea poured by the neat young maid, Susan, Miss Sprott told me of her younger days when she had had the time of her life doing good to the poor in north-west London. With treats and parties galore, she and the poor seem to have enjoyed themselves enormously. Now her kind heart was at the disposal of every sparrow that fell from its nest.

During a bus ride from Oxford to Wallingford in Berkshire, I was held in conversation by a talkative old lady of the type who goes to bingo and thinks that *everyone* else does, and who sees life with the bland cheerfulness of a television quiz-show compère. 'Look, that's where I live,' my persecutor said proudly, pointing out a particularly hideous council estate overlooking a bypass. She then went on to tell me of a lewd television series she admired, opened a magazine at a picture of a gondola tied to a stripey pole and said that she too was thinking of going to Paris. Finally we arrived at Wallingford.

There in the attractive old Town Hall, with its jutting-out top storey supported by pillars, was an exhibition of the town's past and of the findings of its archaeological society. Facing the hall was a cobbled square surrounded by small white houses, pubs and shops. Inside I found my former companion staring at a recently unearthed medieval skeleton. The skull stared back at her as if in derision. 'Why's he grinning like that?' she asked in genuine puzzlement. 'What did he have to laugh about if he was dying?'

Stupidity such as that must be Inspired. I looked at her in awe. She had rediscovered the idea of ancient sculptors who depicted death on tombs as a skeleton always having the last laugh. There is a smile in each and every one of us.

Just outside Wallingford the Thames lazily loops its way towards London, fringed by willows and meadows and frequented by swans and boats. On that glorious summer's day when I escaped from the chatty old lady, the place was bright with holidaymakers enjoying themselves. I walked on to the sleepy village of North Stoke on the edge of the Chilterns, where a stout, friendly man pointed out the steep hill path to Ipsden.

First, my walk was under trees, with cottages here and there by the roadside. Then, as the great hill rose in a languid curve, the trees were shrugged away and I walked along the narrow road, as free of traffic as any footpath, between fields of corn and beneath singing skylarks. Manor houses peeped from the beech woods that crowned the hills, and some fields were given over to plump, docile sheep. I passed Ipsden on my right and walked onto the hill's crest, where I looked down on what seemed to be half of England, the dusty road disappearing into it like a trail of thread.

Retracing my steps to Ipsden, I explored the sprawling village. The church, with its knapped-flint walls, stood with attendant cottages a field's length from the rest of the houses. I climbed one of the surrounding wooded hills, passing some girls on horseback in the sunken lane by an old red brick stables. Up on the hill at the other side of the dark wood was Ipsden House where the Reades live, descendants of Charles Reade who wrote *The Cloister and the Hearth*. One of my favourite books is Charles Reade's novel of the early days of the trade union movement, *Put Yourself in His Place*. An unusual blend of Gothic romance and industrial realism, it is set among the cutlery factories of a thinly disguised Sheffield.

Near Ipsden House, under the trees, I found a heap of strange stones, like a dolmen. I was convinced I had found a place of pagan worship, but in the village I was told that the stones had been brought there by one of the Reades, perhaps the author. Children played there a lot, I was told, so the site may have had magic of a kind. Down in the village again, I passed a cottage called 'Janets'. In the flowery garden, raised on a bank from where I stood, romped a lively highland white terrier.

'What a nice dog,' I said to its mistress, as she looked up from her gardening. This remark led to a conversation in which the lady told me a great deal about Ipsden.

'Yes, my house is called 'Janet's' after the previous owner, who lived to be very old. She was a well loved character, very fond of flowers, and she laid out this garden much as you see it now. All the older people here say how fond they were of Janet, but we only came after she died. This house was the post office then, and Janet was the postmistress. There is a happy atmosphere here, which may be thanks to Janet. Do you know the village ghost story? Just down the road there a young soldier appeared to his mother at the very moment that he died in India.

'We still have a squire, you know. The Reades own the village, which is part of an entailed estate, and all the houses are on lease. Unfortunately, the family only use Ipsden House in the holidays, but it's nice to know that they still have the old family home.'

'How enormous the stinging nettles are here!' I said, gesturing towards the five-foot jungle of menacing barbed leaves by the verge where I was standing. It's a curious fact which may be an omen, that when I grasp a nettle manfully I get stung, but if I brush one timidly I don't.

'Oh yes, this is nettle country all right. There's even a place near here called Nettlebed.'

I said goodbye and rejoined the main road back down to Wallingford. On the way I passed Ipsden's one small row of modern houses and shops, including a new post office. It was called 'Janet's Grove'.

Not far from Wallingford, travelling westward, is the market town of Wantage, where in the year 849 Alfred the Great was born. Now, it appears, Wantage is no longer in Berkshire. 'We've been demoted to Oxfordshire,' a middle-aged man told me sourly. From Wantage I hoped to walk, in easy stages, thirty miles or so along the Ridgeway, said to be the oldest road in Britain. My destination was Avebury, which may have been England's capital three and a half thousand years ago.

I found Wantage, on a Saturday evening, to be an agreeable red brick town, its streets surging with smart young people roaming from pub to pub in search of excitement. The whole town seemed to be given over to the young. Deafening disco music from the Swan drowned the chimes from the church opposite, and I wondered if these happy, seemingly unreflective youngsters were the unemployed youth of whom I had read so much.

Some months earlier in Newport, Gwent, a dockside town with very little work about, I had been almost trampled beneath roaring, revelling, red-faced hordes of young people in pursuit of their Grail of a better pub. They too had been dressed to the nines — by no means punks, skinheads or whatever, but a new, noisy aristocracy. However did they do it?

In the fading light the anguished features of King Alfred, depicted on a statue looking across Wantage market square, offered no clue. Beneath the monarch these words had been inscribed, over a hundred years ago:

Alfred found learning dead and he restored it.
Education neglected and he revived it.
The laws powerless and he gave them force.
The Church debased and he raised it.
The land ravaged by a fearful enemy from which he delivered it.

From the bottom of my heart there swelled a mighty cry: 'Come back, Alfred!'

You may say that no fearful enemy ravages the land, but having seen the ancient church of Wantage quail before the blasts of rock music from the Swan, I know otherwise.

On the bus to Wantage I overheard two farm boys with rich Berkshire accents describe English customs to a bemused American couple.

'Funny, Oi'm the only one o' moi family doant loike beer,' one lad of ten ruminated. He lived with his grandparents in a tied cottage, and boasted of his skateboard, BMX bike and the motor bike and tractor he was allowed to use on the farm. To his great pride, his mother was being married for the third time that very week.

'Moi mum's getting married tomorrer, but that's only the second toime,' his older friend chimed in a trifle jealously.

Smiling all over their plum-pudding faces, the two boys alighted near a farm track and waved the Americans a long goodbye. Perhaps this explained the prosperity of the Wantage yougsters — each may have had two or three fathers sending pocket-money.

Next day a fox paused and gave me a quizzical look as I toiled up the hill towards the Ridgeway, my pyjamas, alarm clock, towel and electric razor stuffed into my plastic bag. It was a hot day in the lowlands, but on the hilltops a cool breeze restored me, and I strode along, greeting other walkers and listening to the twitterings of meadow pipits and corn buntings. In pagan times, we Ridgeway travellers would have been pilgrims to the great temple at Avebury, with many sacred sites to detain us along the way. One of these, the White Horse of Uffington, I was eager to see, and made a detour down the hillside to do so. I was almost standing on the horse before I saw it, for the curving white scars on the hill suggest broken paths rather than the sacred beast of the Celtic Atrebates tribe, and the strange beaked head stretches on a long neck over the brow of the hill. The horse was visible as a whole only at a distance, but I made up for this disappointment by finding the head and standing defiantly in its jaws. The habit of putting beaks on horses and other animals is typical of Iron Age art. What would the Atrebates have made of a platypus? The connection between horses and dragons in English folklore may stem from the influence of fanciful Celtic art on literal-minded Saxons, for a beaked horse certainly does look reptilian.

Below me, the sudden stark contours of flat-topped Dragon Hill suggested a man-made earthen pyramid among the serene sweeps of natural scenery. Here it is that St George is said to have fought the dragon. Again, horse and dragon collide, not necessarily unseating poor George, for many unravellers of myths have decided that our national saint was once himself a horse. The knightly saint took the place of a horse-god when Christianity came, and we are a People of the Horse. Possibly the god's name resembled George's, and today's cry of 'Gee-up' may once have been 'Gee-orge'.

Despite these mysteries, the White Horse Hill had no eerie sense of Celtic twilight about it, but was a jolly spot, alive with weekend picnickers – Mums, Dads and children. The England it represented was that of John Bull, and the fact that this hill was chosen of all others as a place to sit in the sun and watch the youngsters play, attests to the potency of the horse-gods spell.

Uffington's Castle's circular earthworks mark the site of the Ridgeway, which I regained once more, and travelled on to Wayland's Smithy, a long barrow set in a clump of trees beside the path. This neolithic burial place became a smith-god's forge for the Saxons, just as Bronze Age hill forts became Saxon burial grounds. Latter-day Saxons told tall tales of Wayland and his Smithy until the modern era, when the overgrown mound with boulders tumbled round its cave entrance was tidied up by the Department of the Environment and the archaeologist Stuart Piggott. Although I admire Professor Piggott, who writes as well as he digs, I feel a tinge of regret that in future no awe-struck children will peer into the black depths between the brambles, ready to run at the first sign of a spark from the smith's fire or the 'chink' of his hammer (perhaps supplied by an obliging stonechat).

Far from being an open track, showing my silhouette on the skyline, the Ridgeway rolled up and down between hawthorn bushes hung with late-flowering May blossoms. Now the path grew wilder, corrugated with grown-over tractor grooves. Walkers returned to their cars, and the trail became a grassy, shadowy lane. A gypsy trailer stood at an angle to the deep ruts I was hopping along, but nobody was home. Later I met the swarthy incumbent and we exchanged long, suspicious stares. So gloriously white had the hedge now become that I felt I was walking among snow-laden Christmas trees. Where the Ridgeway became a thorny, flowery rabbit tunnel, difficult to walk along, I came across a weathered wooden sign reading 'Wiltshire'.

Hours later, having crossed a motorway, I was still walking, now up the side of Liddington Hill, where some say that King Arthur defeated the Saxons. Just as each age reads its own preoccupations into Stonehenge, from amphitheatre to temple to computer, so King Arthur has ranged from medieval monarch to a Dark Age freedom-fighting guerrilla leader.

The sun had set long ago, and in the failing light I shushed my way through the long grass away from the Ridgeway to the haunted Iron Age fortress of Liddington Castle. Looming battlements of earth and stone rose above a grassy moat and enclosed a weed-covered circle where, if myths are true, the dragon standard of the Celts once flew.

The young Richard Jefferies, a great hero of mine, used to sit dreaming under the rim of this earthwork, gazing down at his parents' farm. The sun's last red gleam across the horizon was reflected in the glow of Coate Water, the reed-fringed lake that appears in so many guises throughout his works. Jefferies must have lingered on the magic hill until far later than I, knowing every stile and footpath of the countryside, even in pitch darkness. In his day, the lights of Swindon would have seemed further away and of a more wholesome hue than lurid orange.

Over my hazardous descent to the insensitively placed M4 motorway, my confusions of direction, my succession of lifts from tipsy teenage motorists and my eventual arrival in Swindon Old Town, where I knocked up a surprised guest-house-keeper and demanded admission, I will draw a veil. Suffice to say that the helpful youngsters of Swindon seemed to regard me as a quaint old Wiltshire character, and one insisted that I ask for a cell in the police station for the night, 'or else you'd only have to pay money'. But I had tried this ploy once in Huntingdon, only to be told that the cells were full of drunks.

Never for a moment doubting that Jefferies' old home would be sacred ground and Swindon's pride, with scarcely a blade of grass altered since the author lived there, I unwittingly rode past it on a bus next day and had to walk back through the featureless housing estates it had become. Coate Water was now 'Coate Water Country Park Barbecues and Mini-Golf', and abounded in asphalt and notices such as 'No Access Except for Yachting Personnel'. Jefferies' farmhouse home, now the Jefferies Museum, was a place of empty whitewashed rooms with neon lights and shining pine floorboards. A woman sat at the souvenir stall reading a magazine entitled *Goofy Puzzles*. Jefferies' old attic room had been 'restored' by some unfortunate bureaucrat. I stepped over the guide-rope for a closer look, but the creaking floorboards gave me away and the woman rushed upstairs to see if I was stealing something. As she followed me everywhere after that, I soon left. It would have been a far better tribute to Richard Jefferies' genius to have let Coate House remain a working farm, amid unspoilt countryside, leased to a farmer who had never heard of the author of *Bevis*.

Not only did a poster advertise the 'Richard Jefferies Dance Orchestra', but an advertisement in that week's *New Society* ran as follows: *Richard Jefferies Adventure Playground, Swindon*. Two Workers Required. The Challenge is to Revitalise this Facility within the Community.' So Jefferies, who died in poverty, is remembered in his native place at least by name – but no one who had actually read his work could have associated him with council playgrounds. Well, *almost* no one . . .

'. . . it's my turn to be playground leader,' Bevis told Mark. 'You are only my co-worker or junior liaison playground co-ordinator, and if you don't do just as I say, I'll tie you to a tree and let the natives gnaw you. The natives of Swindon are known to be especially ferocious.'

Mark bit his lip, thought for a moment and agreed.

'This playground we have discovered is every bit as mysterious as New Formosa, and we won't let any of the others near until we've made it really special, revitalizing facilities like anything. How they'll stare when they see it!'

'Yes, and praise us and wish they'd thought of it.'

Within seconds the pair of them had erected a sturdy hut with a palisade around it, made a bow and arrow and a spear, dug a moat, filled it with water and constructed a raft and a canoe.

'Here come the Guv'nor and the Jolly Old Moke now – how surprised they'll be!' Bevis exclaimed as two men approached the playground. Pan the spaniel ran towards the newcomers, barking joyously.

'Get that dog on a lead before a car hits him!' snapped the Jolly Old Moke, who had been surly and irritable ever since a six-lane motorway had been built across his farm, forcing him to work in local government under the Guv'nor, now Chief Environmental Executive Officier, Grade 1.

'Aren't you ashamed of yourself, sir?' the Guv'nor addressed Bevis, his face darkening. 'Do you call *this* an adventure playground? Why, there's everything here a boy's heart could desire, perfectly made and a pleasure to look at! Don't you know the first principles of playground revitalising? Adventure playgrounds are meant to be official replicas of the derelict sites children used to play on before things got organised. You should have scattered bricks around, thrown in an old tyre, made a flimsy climbing-frame out of old planks, painted a space monster on the wall in the style of a cheap comic, and in general respected the play culture of the individual within the community, both in a full and also a very real sense.'

'What stupes we've been!' cried Bevis.

'Most awful stupes,' Mark agreed.

Swindon left behind at last, I was soon high on the windswept downs, with all Wiltshire to my right and left, and Liddington Hill standing in the distance like a green Table Mountain. Two walkers approached, and to my delight one of them proved to be the editor of *Private Eye*. At once I began to hector him about the non-appearance of my contributions to his paper, while he good-naturedly fended me off with his stick. He went on his way, and I on mine, but two great forces such as these (Ingrams and Kerridge) cannot meet without causing apocalyptical changes in the temperature, climate and atmosphere. As it happened, in London the Queen suddenly prepared to open Parliament, the pound fell and two-headed calves were born, while on the Ridgeway a strange fog descended and a light drizzle sprayed across my spectacles.

Now I appeared alone in the universe, walking for ever along the Ridgeway, with Wiltshire invisibly below me. I nearly trod on a crow, which flew from beneath my feet to join another on a wire fence ahead. I felt as a character in *Pilgrim's Progress* might, on a path through the air leading towards two crows who sat by two signposts pointing in opposite directions. As I walked on, the crows flew ahead, leading the way. I heard traffic, but instead of a road I found two shepherds rounding up their sheep by driving tractors at them and honking. Soon all the flock were pressed together, without casualty, within wattle hurdles. The rain lifted and I walked down the hill to Avebury.

To my surprise, the road ran through a gap between tall Celtic defences spread with buttercups. The village was inside the fortress, as in ancient times. Rings and avenues of great stones jutted lopsidedly here and there, and I found a bed for the night at Hollis Cottage, where kindly Mrs Jane Lees takes in visitors. This delightful old house was full of unexpected corners and ingle-nooks; it had a minstrel's gallery of sorts, where a staircase had replaced the old ladder and trapdoor.

'Where did I get all these old ornaments? They're things we used when I was a girl and this was still a farm,' Mrs Lees told me. 'There's our old bellows, and that's where we used to put the cheese. It was lovely growing up in Avebury, as you could climb on the stones and slide down the banks. But then, before the war, Mr Keiller bought the manor and had lots of cottages pulled down because they got in the way of the stones. We were a much bigger village before, and there were plenty of hotels for visitors. But nowadays the National Trust has taken them over for their officials. When I was a girl we had knowledgeable ladies and gentlemen come to see the stones, instead of just school parties who only go and see them because they have to.'

The day I was there, the manor house – built by Sir William Sharington from the ruins of a Benedictine monastery on the proceeds of an embezzlement from the Bristol Mint – was closed to a grumbling bunch of tourists because the present lady of the manor had gone shopping. One sacred site stands outside the main ring of stones – the village church. Here, to my annoyance, I found the Jerusalem Bible was in use, and Jehovah was referred to as Yahweh.

I daresay the Hebrews of old *did* call God 'Yahweh' as the moderns insist, but in the English language the name merely suggests 'Yah-boo!' the cry of 'with-it' clergymen rebelling against authority without realising that *they* are Authority. 'Jehovah', on the other hand, suggests Jove-like majesty, a nod to the pagan past by no means out of keeping with the beauties of Avebury. That evening I walked along the turfy ramparts looking down at the strange grey boulders on the other side of a moat where in the Bronze Age water might have gleamed, making Avebury a sacred Isle of Avalon. Medieval castles appear to have evolved from such ancient forts and temples. In the distance, the man-made pyramid of Silbury Hill presided over the birth of the River Kennet, a weed-clogged stream hurrying on its way towards Newbury. In its shallows I watched a water-rat, a round-faced miniature beaver, felling water plants at the stem and then munching them up leaf by leaf.

Old England and its ways and waywardness have all but vanished, though its outward appearance is preserved by the National Trust and the Department of the Environment, with labels to tell us what everything means. Soothed, we look at it and then go home. Only as night falls and we glance up at the darkening hills and the misshapen long barrows, do we feel that somewhere there is something more. The old gods may have the last laugh, or Jehovah, or, I hope, St George.

Back at Swindon, I accepted the invitation of a 'Moonie' acquaintance, a red-haired woman named Joan Langrick, to visit her at Stanton Fitzwarren a few miles out of town. Here the Church of Unification (as Moonies are officially called) have been given a large country estate by one of their followers. One function of this 'Moonie village' is as a retreat for those interested in the faith. While there, I was able to explore the woods and fields with their wealth of animal life, both domestic and free.

My first surprise was to find in the farmyard a tame fawn of most unusual appearance. It was a young Père David's deer, a rare Chinese species named after a nineteenth-century French Missionary, the first Westerner to observe this strange marsh reindeer with its splayed hoofs and heavy back-to-front antlers. At that time, in 1865, the deer was already extinct in the wild state, but preserved in the Imperial Hunting Park at Peking. Floods, followed by poaching, wiped out the Chinese herds in the nineties, but a few had been brought to England by the Duke of Bedford.

Three hundred or so are now kept in captivity throughout the world, descendants of those bred at Woburn. The Unification Church have established a breeding herd on their estate, and the fawn had become a popular pet. I was not told why it had been removed from the main herd, nor why three other deer had been put down, but it was in good condition and had a hearty appetite for dandelion leaves.

The fluffy ginger fawn – the size of a new-born colt and just as leggy – had a rather calf-like head and dark, melting eyes, already showing the black, slit-like line from the eye to the nose which gives the species such a Chinese appearance. A patch of dark hair marked the shoulder blades, but there were none of the white spots so familiar on young European deer. With a loud squeak the fawn clicked away on its shiny outspread hooves, and I went in search of its grown-up relatives.

I crossed a stile, and on the other side of a small wood I found a herd of nine animals in a large field with a high wire-netting fence. The

Moonies had warned me that the stags were in rut, three months earlier than our native red deer, and a guttural choking roar told me that this was correct. A great king stag with a dark-brown mane and a white face with Chinese eyes lorded it over the russet-coloured females and young, while another, smaller, harried-looking male moped in a corner. A wreath of torn-up grass adorned the first stag's brow tines, or rather what would have been his brow tines had they not pointed over his back. He threw back his head, opened a jagged mouth, and bellowed once more in Cantonese. (Choi Ying, a moonie convert from Hong Kong, referred to the animals as 'Cantonese deer'.)

I entered the field but stayed near the gate, although my experience with red deer suggests that rutting stags charge at people in a spirit of bluff, like male gorillas, and veer away at the last moment. This information has been dearly bought!

Lowering his head, the stag paced towards me, looking like a prehistoric moose with his humped back and thick, wide-spreading antlers. I fancied I was a spear-wielding nomad on the waterlogged plains of ancient China, before the paddy fields were made. As I had expected, he soon wheeled aside and began chivvying his wives to a place of safety. The herd seemed in very good condition, and I was pleased to see that water was being pumped into the field so as to form a swamp. Split hoof prints showed that the deer had voted for this arrangement with their feet. Behind the herd a hare raced in circles, obviously under the impression that it was still March. Perhaps inspired by their aggressive lord, a pair of hinds reared up and began a boxing match with their forefeet.

I spent that night at the farmhouse with an idealistic batch of converts. Early next morning I walked past the deer once more and into a long belt of woodland. When I rounded a corner, there sitting on the path before me was a sandy animal with a splash of white on it. A fox! I stood quite still, and the fox, who didn't seem to see me, stood up and craned his neck towards the undergrowth, his ears erect, graceful as a doe. Another fox appeared and scanned the undergrowth on the other side of the track. Both animals were long and lean. They flinched every time they heard a noise, for a rook-scarer went off every so often and someone was banging crates about on a nearby farm. To my surprise, one of them began trotting purposefully towards me, his tongue out, a grin on his face and the dappled light rippling over his back as he ran. Suddenly he appeared to notice me and bounded away through the trees, his long, white-tipped brush streaming out behind him. His friend sat and watched me with relaxed interest, well aware that I had no gun. I could see the white hair inside his dark bat-ears and the foxy black moustache on his white muzzle as easily as if he had been in the zoo.

Suddenly I glimpsed a dog-like flurry: a third fox cannoned into my new friend, and they rolled and tumbled around like big puppies. The new arrival trotted straight towards me with a cat-like gait, and then vanished between the trees, a mere ten paces from where I had been standing. Another moment and I was alone.

'Yes, the woods here swarm with foxes,' a Moonie farmworker told me later. 'The best place to see them is from up in a tractor, as they know tractor drivers can't hurt them, and you can get quite close. The Vale of White Horse hunts over this land, and I'm a keen supporter, as I know what damage a fox can do.'

This man, who had been brought up on a farm in Dartmoor, took a party of us guests on a tour of the estate, and threw clods of earth into a cornfield to try to drive out the hares. One of the Friesian cows had given birth two hours earlier, and stood by patiently as we admired her calf. At first curled up like a sleeping fox, the calf soon staggered to its feet and tried to find its mother's udders, aiming its mouth too low. Gently, the tall Devonian Moonie guided the wobbly newcomer's head. Shula, a spirited maiden from Singapore, took photographs all the while and as we walked back to the main building I was kept busy telling the Oriental visitors the names of such plants as I knew. They were particularly astonished at stinging nettles, and at the table that night the snapdragons in a vase entranced them, and they happily poked their fingers into the dragons' mouths.

Afterwards there were hymns, sung in folk style, very bright and breezy.

> You know, dear Lord, we're happy now to sing.
> We'll be your puppets, Father, we want you to pull the string.
> For ever in your debt we know we'll be,
> But thank you Lord for guiding us into Your family.

Number 136 was based on a protest song popular in the 1960s, the words changed to suit the Moonie family outlook on life:

> Come all you folk with riches in business and land,
> And ask yourselves why you can't lend a hand.
> What you spend for the good of the world will stand
> As your eternal merit.

'It's wonderful on a matching day!' Joan enthused. Her Church believes in arranged marriages, and sometimes she helped with the introductions. 'Ideal partners' are found for unattached members; often a boy and girl are 'matched' from different ends of the earth. Oriental beauties hold a great appeal for Western men.

'But when a couple are "matched", can they always speak the same language?' I asked.

'No, it's hilarious!' Joan replied, laughing heartily. 'We get interpreters where needed, but mostly they just look into one another's eyes. The language of love does the rest.'

Shula, who was a nurse at a Norwich hospital, decided not to join the Moonie family.

On the eve of the midsummer solstice, I crossed Wiltshire from Swindon to Salisbury. At dawn – which would be at twenty to five – the Druid Church of the Universal Bond was to meet at Stonehenge to carry out their mystic rites.

I took care not to arrive at Salisbury until ten to midnight. At three in the morning, by arrangement, a taxi was to take me to Stonehenge. Meanwhile, I had three hours in which to explore the ancient market and cathedral town, alone, by lamplight. A small red light in a black sky showed the top of the cathedral spire. The Close, a gracious city within a city, was locked up for the night. Cats ran from alleys, between creaking, top-heavy timbered buildings, then along silvered streets, and ducked under the great cathedral gate, set in an archway at the road's end. A Scotsman, the only other person abroad at that hour, asked me if I would put him up for the night. He was neatly dressed and said he had a letter for 'the cardinal'. No one had told him about the Reformation.

'I've got nowhere to go myself,' I explained. 'The railway station is open, so we can sit there.' He shook my hand. 'My name's Keith,' he said. 'If I had the money I'd put you up in a good hotel. It's man's *inhumanity* to man, that's what gets me! If I was in Glesga, anyone wud put me up.'

At the station he grew irritated with me for sitting on a bench within sight of a clock. A great one for rooting out officials and asking porters, he found that a waiting-room was open. 'You'll never get anything if you don't ask!' he told me. 'Already you're causing me problems. The porters were asking me who you were.'

We stretched out on waiting-room seats, but to his mystification I arose before three and met my taxi. The driver was impeccable in a peaked cap and uniform, and seemed surprised to see me. Evidently he had believed that writers were grander than they are. At Stonehenge, a place I had never been to before, I followed the crowds and stood staring into the darkness across metal barriers drawn up around the great stones.

'No one can go inside except the Druids, unless they've got written permission,' a police officer told me. The air was loud with electric guitar music from the pop festival below the Henge, a row of lights with a shining red tent in the middle. As dawn approached, the music grew louder and more frenzied. 'It's like a scene from Hades,' a wise-looking man with a pipe remarked. 'I remember when scarcely a soul came here on midsummer morning.'

Soon we were discussing Geoffrey de Monmouth and other authorities on Stonehenge. As we spoke, a line of Druids dressed in white sheets walked silently past us into the stone circle. Some of them were young girls; their leaders carried trade-union type banners with mystic signs. Soon the Druids could be seen standing in threes around various fallen pillars, meditating over cut roses laid on table napkins. As a background to their solemnity, the pop music raged on, and some hippies around the barriers played an insistent rhythm on bongo drums. The Druids pretended that nothing was the matter.

All of a sudden, black figures could be seen flitting like crows across the field towards Stonehenge. Pop fans surged over the barriers and invaded the pitch. I was to find that many of them regarded the Druids as rivals. They, the 'alternative society', were the true heirs of the shamans of the Bronze Age when Stonehenge was built! As at Pentre Ifan, I was a witness to the youthful quest for a barbarous religion, a religion suitable for the 'rock generation' and for our times. I prefer a faith in something *better* than our times, but mob belief seems to yearn for the lowest common denominator. The neo-Druids were but the genteel precursors of the hippies.

The police were turning a blind eye, so I too climbed over the railing and ran towards the stone circle. Almost everyone from the festival had the same idea, and we were packed too tightly to move. Most of the crowd weren't bald beardies or Guinevere folk-damsels, but ordinary young roughs, scruffs and polytechnic students. It could have been a football match or a night on the beer with the lads. One or two youngsters leaned their foreheads on the Herculean pillars, or placed their palms on them as if feeling for mystic vibrations. But they might have just had hangovers. It was impossible to reach the centre of the stone circle, from which frenzied bongo-drumming could be heard. The

Druids seemed to have been swallowed up in the crowds. But no – there were three, a little way off, still meditating around a slab of rock, while derisive pop fans stared at them rudely. Their faces were as impassive as those of guardsmen surrounded by tourists. A wizened, red-haired girl tried in vain to heckle them. Eventually all the Druids gathered together, forcing their way in single file through the crowds.

'Let us open with the contemplation,' one of them suggested, in an upper-class female voice. The rock music reached a manic pitch as they contemplated. They then squeezed their way through the amused crowds, some holding bunches of oak leaves, and formed a circle around a grassy hummock.

'Why do we stand at this ancient mound?' a hooded Druid enquired in ritual tones. It seemed a good question, but the answer was drowned out by the music and catcalls of the festival folk. More pushing and shoving, and soon we found ourselves pressed around a sacred slab. Here the Druids found it hard to part the crowds. When they reached their slab they found it defiled by a hippie in a top hat and white shirt-ruff, an idiotic caricature of a Hollywood drunk, empty bottle in hand. With mock solemnity he greeted the dismayed Druids, who were too unnerved to ask him to leave. While they stood reeling, the unpleasant red-haired girl and her small, scruffy daughter sat down on the other end of the slab.

At this, a Druid who looked like a trainee accountant asked her politely to leave. His voice shook and he seemed close to tears, but she was unmoved. Evidently a feminist, she declared she would never take orders from a man. The crowd seemed divided in their opinions, and debated among themselves if the Druids should be allowed to perform their ceremonies or not.

'Asking her to move – that's a violation of her freedom!' someone said accusingly, glaring at the Druid.

'Freedom!' someone else chanted nobly.

'Why not let the Druids mess about if they want to?' a third put in, reasonably.

I was surprised to see that the festival-goers treated the Druids – a pathetic group of solemn eccentrics, apparently unworthy of police protection – as Authority with a capital A. Perhaps the hippies had been hoping for a confrontation with the law, and had to make do with neo-Druids instead. Making the best of a bad job, the Druids fumbled on, carrying out their ceremonies. One swung a smoking censer around, a great bronze globe on a chain, while another emptied drops of water over his own head.

'This I do in reverence to my mother!' he chanted.

'Let us make our way to the dwelling of light,' another suggested.

By following the line of hooded white figures I was able at last to penetrate to the very centre of the Stonehenge circle of gigantic stone pillars and cross-beams. It was a cloudy morning and a mystic half-light prevailed, the rituals taking place through Nature's smoked glass. I was so squashed by the crowds that I could scarcely move. A punk girl with spiky hair and a complacent grin sat in the middle of the circle the Druids formed, mocking their gestures. His drunkenness a pose, the top-hatted hippie shouted encouragement to his soulmate above the tousled heads. Tough young men stood with legs apart on top of the mighty stones, thumbs hooked into jean pockets in classic attitudes of insolence. Thousands filled in the gaps of Stonehenge, giving the stone circle a compact, unruined appearance. Like Inigo Jones before me, I fancied it a Roman auditorium, the young men who looked down sneeringly from aloft representing the invading barbarians. An atmosphere of danger hung over the proceedings.

'Why do you bear the branches of the sacred tree in your hands?' the Druids continued.

'As an offering to the Ineffable One.'

A fat bearded hippie king in a headband seemed to have some authority over the rest of them. Perhaps he was the man who had organised the illegal pop festval in the first place. His speeches won cheers, not jeers, from the crowds, and he appeared to consider himself a true Druid, unlike the figures in sheets. Now it was time for the Druids to expound their philosophy to all who would listen. An uncouth, gum-chewing Druid took this task upon himself, and in defiant Midland tones tried to appeal to his ribald listeners.

'Look, think of this circle as a womb, right? The sun pierces into it like when you have sex with your girlfriend. You can understand that, can't you? Just as the sun penetrates the womb, so thought can penetrate the mind, from the power like the sun and the sex force.'

'He's making it up as he goes along!'

'I'm not! Shut up! I'm not making it up! Shut up saying that!'

'Preudo-Druids!' a voice jeered from the stone-tops.

Then an Arch-Druid who resembled a refugee from *the Desert Song* produced a black telescopic device from his robes, pulling it open in three sharp jerks. It was a mystic foghorn, and he blew four sonorous blasts to north, east, south and west. Somewhere behind the clouds, the sun had risen. Rising also, the cheerful hippie king took his cue. 'Children of Albion, behold the Sun!' he announced. 'Happy solstice!'

This mumbo-jumbo, unlike the Druid variety, won respectful acclaim. If you want to make a hippie into a patriot, say 'Albion', not 'England'. If you want to create hippie monarchism, say 'Arthur' not 'Elizabeth'. Drowned out by the hippie Blimps, the Druids tried to conclude their ritual.

'I don't believe this! I don't believe it! They're all black and evil inside!' a scrawny woman remarked of the Druids. 'Talk about authoritarian!'

'This ceremony is now ended,' a Druid chanted rapidly, and amid laughter and swearwords the sheeted mystics fled back to their coach. Producing trumpets, bongo drums and guitars, the hippies began their unseemly revels, and I departed.

At least the amplified music from the festival site had ceased. Thanking the god of the Druids for small mercies, I hurried to the coach before they left. Now quite cheerful and brisk in their ordinary clothes, they seemed normal compared with the hippies. Many of them, including a striking-looking white-haired woman who had fainted during one of the rituals, were visitors from America.

'Why do the festival people dislike you so much?' I asked the trainee accountant.

'Basically, they want to occupy our space.'

Druid literature was on sale, all rather nebulous stuff until their 'history' reached the year 1717. Then it was that modern Druidism had been created by one John Toland of Londonderry, who set forth its principles in a Cheapside tavern. One of his disciples was William Blake. William Stukely, clergyman and antiquarian, helped to form neo-Druidism by dogmatically proclaiming his theories on Stonehenge as proven facts. Just as today, folklorists and enquirers on ancient ways could not resist the temptation of pretending to be not only researcher but also object of research. Thus an investigator into the ways of Celtic priests would be led into proclaiming *himself* a pagan priest, and fake folklore would be in the making. Not Celts but Bronze Age men built Stonehenge. Though there is no proof that Druids ever used the site, they may well have done so, for in our time we see Protestant priests in former Roman Catholic churches.

With the departure of the Druids, the pop fans streamed back to the site and the police barred all further entrance to Stonehenge. From the road overlooking the festival, both civil and military police looked down on rows of expensive blue and red tents and shining motor-cars. A disturbing mixture of pop music blared from a variety of transistors, and one of the military police raised his field glasses in search of Army runaways from the many camps on Salisbury Plain. The civil police were relaxed and unconcerned. None entered the site, an intrusive piece of modernity amid peaceful cornfields and strips of ragged woodland. A lark sang overhead and I strolled into the festival.

'Arrest me! Arrest me!' a bearded baldie implored, shouting at the top of his voice in mock anguish. 'Won't somebody *please* arrest me?'

From what I saw of the police, they wouldn't have cared if he had declared himself a Druid and performed human sacrifices in front of the rows of tents. Over a mile in length, the festival had divided itself into avenues of makeshift dwellings. The tents were rough tarpaulins hauled over branches, planks or oil drums, and each one of these advertised on roughly scrawled placards the wares sold within. 'ACID – microdots £1.50, Red hearts – £2.50, Blue microdots – £2.00', I read, each pill able to cause permanent insanity. Hell's Angels manufacture them in Amsterdam, I believe. Marijuana or 'hash' nearly all seemed to come from the Lebanon, a troubled country with at least one flourishing major export. I was in the middle of an enormous drug fair, all business carried on quite openly. Groups of hash-smokers sat blearily around camp fires. No pop performers seemed to be present at this market-place.

'Lebanese Hash', 'Leb', 'Black Leb', Finest Moroccan', 'Coke', 'Speed', 'Lines of Coke', 'Hot Knives of Black Leb', I read in clumsy capital letters. The Druids' sun had risen, it was a hot day, and lone motorcyclists roared between the tents in clouds of dust. Many of the festival-goers had brought their dogs and small children. Some of the tents were quite ingenious – one man had made an Eeyore stick-house and then hung it with cool bunches of grass tied together at the stems. Their night of orgy over, the pop fans lay in heaps inside their shelters. 'I'm sick of hearing about your bad trip,' a girl told her companion.

A large wood near the camping ground resounded with the ring of axes. Fine young beech trees had been clumsily felled, leaving fresh, jagged tree stumps everywhere. Stripped to the waist, four young men were building a hut from trees bent in a circle. All over the site, flags hung from bowed saplings that swayed over the sweaty tents. What was England coming to? If it were gypsies instead of hippies camping there, every tree in the forest would conceal an armed gamekeeper, and volleys of shots would ring out whenever anyone carved so much as a clothes peg. Shocked, I walked away from Stonehenge towards Amesbury.

On the road to the village I fell in with a French girl who also felt upset at the sacrilege done to Stonehenge – not by hippies but by the Philistine road-builders and fence-erectors. We cheered up at the view before us, of stone cottages basking in the sun, a lazy river with cows and, on the hills ahead, a vivid band of red formed by thousands of poppies. A tree-lined drive led to Amesbury Abbey, a magnificent stately home that gave the impression of a Greek temple placed carefully across the front door of a English mansion. Saying goodbye to my new friend, I met an old one in the 'fifties-style village coffee bar. This was Liam, a young Irishman whom I had known from my days in the Liverpool YMCA. He seemed pleased to see me.

'I've hitched all the way down from Liverpool and now I'm going to hitch up again,' he said cheerfully. 'I've never seen anything like the way drugs are sold openly here, before. Adverts for 'Hot Knives' everywhere. What does that mean? Well, you take your piece of Leb and hold it between two knives you've heated in a fire. Then you hold a plastic glass over it, with a hole in the bottom, put your nose in and inhale'.

Geoffrey de Monmouth wrote of the Night of the Long Knives near Stonehenge, when Saxons massacred the Britons. Now we had the Night of the Hot Knives. Thankfully, I took a bus to Salisbury, booked into an hotel and slept for six hours. Awaking refreshed, I stepped out into the cool of the evening and at once was approached by a young gypsy, who looked me straight in the eye. Another fat, unshaven one stood nearby staring into the distance.

'Pardon me, sir,' the young man said with a slight bow. 'Think it no shame on my account that I must ask you this, for though once a working man like yourself, I now have no roof to my head. I would take it most kindly, sir, if you would give me some of your small change. You too, sir, one day may want for shelter.'

Delighted at this recitation, which might have been handed down from father to son, unchanged over the years, I gave the young man a pound.

'Thank you, sir! God bless you! God bless you, sir! (to his friends down the road) Hey fellows, that was a good one!'

My round trip in search of Ancient Britain was almost over. Next day, I took the coach to Oxford. At Amesbury it filled up with worn-out ill-looking festival-goers. All the 'normal' passengers, except myself, huddled together in fear of a hippie neighbour. My hippie, when he came, promptly fell asleep with his head on my shoulder. I wouldn't have minded, but he kept on dribbling.

While looking for a room in Oxford, I was approached by another young man — this one resembling a Cockney crook.

'Could you give me some money, please?'

'Not until you phrase your request more poetically. I met a gypsy in Salisbury who puts you to shame.'

Unabashed, he carried on begging from one person to the next, up and down the High Street. He seemed to be doing very well for himself.

Two Irelands:
the Orange Parade
and Londonderry

I was on my way, by plane, to Ireland. Entranced, I forgot to be frightened and looked down, seeing patches of ice-green creamed with foam upon the blue, where the water was shallow, with rocks protruding.

All too soon, Ireland, my next destination, came into sight. We passed a few islands, then flew over the Irish countryside: a patchwork of fields, every one a different colour – emerald, pease-pudding, in fact 'Forty Shades of Green'. There is an Irish ballad of that title, composed by an American. I guessed that he had been inspired by just such a plane's-eye view. A native Irishman, his feet on the ground in an Irish lane with high banks hiding the fields, would never be able to see the forty shades.

A bus waited at the airport and soon I was speeding on my way through the Northern Irish countryside to Belfast. There I hoped to see the colourful Orange Parade held on 12 July, the anniversary of the Battle of the Boyne. I had no idea where I was going to stay, but a friendly taxi-driver took me to a clean and cheerful boarding house near Lisburn Road. After I had unpacked, I hurried down to the Presbyterian district of Sandy Row, not far away. There I had spent many happy days in the spring of 1969, on the eve of the Troubles, among the spotless dolls' house terraces. 'Dolls' Houses' not only because they were miniature, but because dolls so often graced their windows – Spanish ladies in scarlet ruffed dresses and Action Men labelled 'B' Specials', the armed guards of Ulster Presbyterianism. Magnificent paintings of King Billy at Boyne had graced the house-ends, preserved from being 'folk-art' by their anti-socialist message. Those who admire the hardy Scots and the Scottish virtues should appreciate also the descendants of Scots in Ireland. Patriotism to Britain seems inexplicable to the English governing classes, and Ulster Loyalists seem born to be betrayed.

All my musings exploded into horror as I saw that Sandy Row had been demolished! With broken walls and gutted interiors, it was a sad ghost of its former self. Where dolls and maidenhair ferns had stood proudly between net curtains, the windows were now filled in with ugly, grey concrete blocks. Although condemned and evacuated, the houses still stood, with an occasional elderly couple in residence. The maze of terraces still served as a film-set-like strolling-ground for the Presbyterians and Orangemen. It was the Saturday before the Twelfth, and there was an excited holiday atmosphere in the Row, where one or two streets of tiny, dark shops remained, full of Union Jacks, King Billy rosettes, maces for twirling, orange lilies and Orange records. The old songs seemed more popular than ever, and some new ones had been written in praise of the Ulster Volunteer Force, to which, though it is an illegal counter-terrorist organisation, many Orangemen give tacit approval. It is prevented from becoming as powerful as the IRA by its politics, which have little international appeal. So banishing the qualms of unease caused by occasional UVF slogans on walls, I bought an ice-cream and began to enjoy myself.

Indeed, carefree innocence, bonfire-building and ice-cream-licking seemed to be the order of the day. (How the Orange Order has come to be so closely associated with ice-cream is a mystery to me, but I had noticed it before in Liverpool.) Young rogues in skinhead haircuts, the small boys of Sandy Row were busily building and guarding enormous bonfires, which would be set alight as the chimes of midnight ushered in the Twelfth of July. Bonfire gangs abounded, one for every piece of waste ground, and all out to steal wood from one another or set a rival's mountain of planks and tyres alight before the proper time. Small huts were built alongside the pyres, and one or two boys stood guard every night. One hut I saw had a real carpet inside, boxes to sit on and National Front and UVF slogans on the walls. The wall facing the bonfire was missing. Numerous tales were told of boys who crawled into the unlit bonfires to ambush possible wood-stealers, only to fall asleep on guard and be burned alive.

'There used to be competition in Sandy Row, to see who had the cleanest step or the best decorated window,' my landlady told me. 'But nowadays people want a bath in every house, and the young people are never happy unless everything is being pulled down around them.'

Shankill Road, rising steeply up from Peter's Hill, was bustling with shoppers. Oldpark Accordion Band, with nine accordions, drums and maracas, played in the Graveyard, the Shankill's main pleasure-ground. It is a real graveyard, which says much for the Presbyterian temperament, a mixture of dour solemnity and light-heartedness. Doris Mackay, the band's blind singer, gave powerful renditions of hymns and old ballads. Her elderly husband sat proudly on a bench nearby, along with her patient guide-dog, a golden labrador named Topaz. 'Doris and Topaz are well-known figures on the Shankill,' he told me.

A broken tombstone told the story of a man who had died while hurling a friend from the path of an assassin's bullet. Outside the gates, stentorian-voiced evangelists roared through loudspeakers on the eternal suffering of the damned in the fires of hell. Everyone listened with complacent enjoyment, but no one stepped forward to be 'saved'. They seemed to be looking forward to their fate.

After a drink in the crowded Elephant pub, with its strange plaster statue of a pachyderm over the door and its high-backed settles, brown paint, stale smells and cloth caps nodding over the racing results, I returned to Lisburn Road. Outside Queen's University, a magnificent building at the safe end of town, I saw two students sitting on the wall. They looked an appealing couple and I lost no time in introducing myself.

'I'm a Protestant atheist and she's a Catholic atheist,' the young man said, gesturing towards his friend. 'You're Protestant and Catholic here for ever, no matter what you believe, even if you never go to church. Do you mean to say you're just going up and talking to people? I'd be careful if I were you. Not far from here, a policeman shot a man dead for painting on a wall. He claimed he thought the paintbrush was a gun.' A tall policeman stood by the university gate, in dark-green uniform with the polished wooden handle of a pistol poking from its holster. I gave him a wary glance, but his nerves seemed to be steady enough.

'The best graffiti are in the Falls Road where the Catholics are,' said the girl with spirit. 'Marvellous paintings of hunger-strikers starving to death — wonderful.'

'You Papists!' the boy joked. 'My grandfather was a farmer in Tyrone, and he said you could always tell a Fenian by the small squinting eyes close together and the greasy locks of black hair.'

'Steady on, atheists!' I cried for a tiff seemed imminent. However the Protestant atheist and the Catholic atheist walked off fondly, arm in arm, and vanished into the dusk.

Next day I made my way to the Falls Road, where I had never been before. On my last visit to Belfast, names like 'Falls Road' and 'Shankill' had not reached their present notoriety. Now, without the reassuring presence of the patrolling soldiers, I felt mildly apprehensive as I approached the Provos' stronghold.

'Smash H-Block' appeared in hugh white letters all over the grim, grey flats that act as a gateway to Belfast's Republican quarter. Then, just before council tenements and burned-out houses destroyed by the Army gave way to decent terraced streets, I spied an enormous painting of Bernadette Devlin in triplicate. Each Bernadette, pink on a loud green background, seemed to be bawling with all her might and shaking a knobbly fist in the air. 'Have Strength, But Never Forget Tenderness' was the motto. From then on, paintings of every kind abounded on the terrace ends, with signatures such as 'Junior Sinn Fein' and 'Broomfield Street Youth-to-Free-the-Blanketmen'. Many of the paintings were too allegorical for me to understand, or showed politicians I was unfamiliar with. Some displayed elaborate Gothic texts, others showed the Virgin hovering above a dying hunger-striker, or Christ looking down on a ragged wretch in a dungeon. Most showed a vigorous barbaric talent. The art department of the IRA must be the envy of many an advertising agency.

Only the young men lounging around the paintings looked menacing. Everyone else seemed to be quiet and easy-going, the small girls bright in party dresses. Despite the religious paintings, the Falls Road atmosphere was intensely political, with communist slogans everywhere. When I reached a Catholic Church, I felt instantly relieved, the sacred statues outside offering a soothing contrast to the rough, angry folk art of the streets.

A poster on a wall showed a nondescript man wearing a suit superimposed over a picture of a soldier in uniform. It had been issued by the Provos, and the caption read: 'Beware! This Brit Could Be The Man Standing Beside You. Loose Talk Costs Lives.' 'I'll drink to that,' I thought, and kept my mouth, with its English accent, tightly shut.

Suddenly I received a terrible shock, for ahead of me stood a pillar-box painted green! No greater symbol of Republican rule could be imagined, not even the tricolour itself. South of the border, this emerald fate has befallen all the pillar-boxes. As I approached the People's Republic of Andersonstown, at the top of the Falls Road, I noticed another pillar-box in trouble. This one had been burnt out and only a stump remained. Why do Irish Republicans pursue this insane vendetta against the Post Office? Perhaps it represents British efficiency and order to them, in which case they are sadly out of date.

Andersonstown, on the edge of Belfast, with views over the hills, had a tall fence of sagging corrugated iron around it, surmounted by a police observation post. My impression was that both wall and post were as much for the convenience and use of those inside as of those out. When I entered, passing several bombed or otherwise demolished houses, the road check-point was unmanned. However, a small, sealed-up Army vehicle cruised cautiously up and down, with a gun poking out of a narrow slit. It was a hot day, and the only people I could see were a stout, kindly-looking old man holding the hand of a little girl.

I walked past all the street-corner paintings again, weaved in and out of the grey council flats, and stumbled across the Catholic Pro-Cathedral. In its cool, holy depths I sank into a reverie before the statue of a Virgin Mary with a neon-lit halo. The Orangemen should be cursing the Kremlin, not the Vatican, I decided.

Back at Sandy Row, I noticed a stream of chromium-decorated tinkers' trailers moving through the narrow streets, watched with some disgust by the elderly passers-by. A camp was set up, eventually, near the railway station, complete with flapping washing-lines and eager little yellow-haired children. The bonfire boys waited expectantly for the witching hour. At midnight it would be the Twelfth of July.

Midnight on Sandy Row brought forth great scenes of jubilation. I was sitting in a little café crammed with soldiers eating beefburgers when I heard a drum and pipe band striking up. I hurried outside, where a tipsy crowd thronged the narrow streets. A circle had formed around a small band who were playing in the middle of the road, where men and women danced and laughed boisterously. A boy of twelve repeatedly sent a large red, white and blue mace spinning high into the air over our heads, to everyone's admiration. He caught it every time. Beer-peddlers bore tin-laden trays, and young couples carried small children on their shoulders. Ice-cream vans were out in force. Worried-looking policemen in flat caps tried to control the crowds and keep them back from the street bonfires. Each blaze seemed four times as high as a Sandy Row house – roaring towers of flame, sparks and black, tyre-fed smoke, that illuminated the Row with a fitful orange glare. A group of hollow-eyed preachers screamed of hell and damnation in front of one enormous blaze.

'If they curse the Pope, don't argue with them,' a friendly soldier had advised me. 'They'll think you're a (here he stamped his left foot and whistled, to signify a Catholic) – and you could be a dead man.' The crowds looked friendly to me, but I didn't put them to the test. Instead I went to bed in readiness for the Twelfth itself.

Next morning I found the Lisburn Road, once taken by William of Orange on the way to Carrickfergus, to be lined with household chairs. Two thousand Orange Lodges from all over Ireland, Scotland and the dominions would soon be pouring out of their temporary bases in Sandy Row, and marching and playing all the way to Edenberry, several miles out of town. There is nothing sinister about most Orange Lodges, and the fresh, freckled faces of the visitors brought a breath of country air to tired Belfast. If James had defeated Prince William at the Boyne, England might have been made Catholic at the cost of a civil war that would probably have destroyed what remains of our medieval Catholic churches. Orangemen would then be radicals, not Conservatives, and no doubt much admired.

This was an innocent, happy occasion, and I felt the same sense of anticipation I had known when the Pope visited Britain. Then the killjoys had been Protestants, but now the boot was on the left foot, for the Provos had promised a 'blitz'. Higher barriers than usual were raised to keep out the awkward Catholic presence, and the day went off safely enough.

Dashing to and fro amid the crowds, and climbing up on walls to see above their heads, I soon glimpsed the bands approaching, their colourful silk banners adorned with ribbons and orange lilies, rising in waves one above the other, as they emerged from the Row and marched uphill. Excited children holding Union Jacks ran up and down singing to the tunes played on pipe and drum – 'The Sash My Father Wore', 'Derry's Walls'. 'The Green Grassy Slopes of the Boyne' and my favourite, 'The Lily-o', with its rousing, thumping chorus. I asked a fourteen-year-old boy what being a skinhead meant to him. 'Having short hair and listening to this marvellous music!' he replied with a friendly grin.

Young people, many dressed in jeans and punk fashion, seemed ecstatically happy as they chanted traditional songs and waved non-satirical Union Jacks. Perhaps the Orange way of life was exciting enough for youngsters to be both rebellious adventurers *and* dutiful, much-praised children at the same time.

Invalids were brought out of the City Hospitals for two hours of pageantry, the time it took for the parade to pass their roadside chairs. There were several Indians and Africans among the crowds who stood oohing and ahing at each new wave of colour, music and spectacle.

Here came the Shankill Road Defenders, the Whiteoak Temperance Band and the Saracen Truth Defenders of Glasgow! I followed the bands up Balmoral Avenue, past a country estate, the Barnett Demesne, and over Shaw's Bridge in glorious summery countryside and parkland. Then on to 'the Field' at Edenberry, where gangs of scampering young skinheads looked out of place among country lanes. The bands began to separate, taking different routes to various little halls amid the trees, where feasts were laid on for them. In festive mood, the Orange folk sat down on the grass, opened picnic baskets and cider bottles and listened to preachers telling them how damned they were.

I slipped into one of the halls, and enjoyed the sight of two hundred or so decent-looking men and women doing justice to heaps of ham sandwiches and cakes. Silver instruments and banners lay propped against the walls. Here I mused on the colourful orange and purple spectacle I had seen, on the Wishaw Purple Defenders of Scotland, on Cromwell's Ironsides riding again, and on the banners so beautifully illustrated with Biblical themes. Enormous talent had gone into this festival, which is to Belfast what Carnival is to Trinidad or Mardi Gras to New Orleans.

Garry, a raffish-looking young man, his arm around his sweetheart Laura, had this to say: 'You can't put it into words, it's so fantastic. Unless you're born in Ulster, you won't understand. We wouldn't miss this for the world! Yes, we have Catholic friends, and although they don't want to know about the Twelfth, they're all right as they have their own festivals.'

Another of my favourite tunes, 'Cock o' the North', struck up, upon which the bands marched all the way back to Sandy Row, ceremonial swords and pikeheads flashing in the sun. A troup of girls in red tartan skirts, the York Street Accordion Band, played Scottish airs. A middle-aged couple strolled along behind me, the man's sash proclaiming him to be a Past Master of the Loyal Orange Lodge. When I asked him about his beliefs he seemed alarmed at first – so used are Orangemen to finding themselves misrepresented.

'The essentials of being an Orangeman are these,' he replied. 'Faith in God, upholding Protestantism, honouring the Queen and living up to what an Orangeman should be – kind, helpful, humble and unselfish. There is one mediator between God and man, and that is Jesus Christ. We would like to convert Catholics, Hindus and others. I was elected as Past Master by my Lodge, after gaining several degrees and learning the various signs and codes. No, I did *not* have to ride on a goat, that's just a story some lads tell outsiders for a joke.'

That evening in Belfast, big swag-bellied men, singing along to deafening UVF records, rolled about in the cobbled yard of a pub among the kegs that their beer had come from. All the well-behaved Orangemen, women and children, had gone home in their thousands long before; some, like aesthetes, holding lilies, others carrying chairs. I remembered the words of the kindly Past Master of the Loyal Orange Lodge, and hoped that his views would prevail. Litter piled the streets and Sandy Row's day of glory was over.

Much of Belfast seemed to be peeling and shabby, for as someone said, 'Houses get painted and repaired, and then get blown up again. After a while you just lose heart.' However, the streets around the university were clean and tree-lined, and the main shopping streets compared favourably with London's West End. These streets had become 'precincts', open only to buses. Barred at each end with elaborate gates, they were guarded by soldiers (mostly Ulstermen) who searched shoppers one by one in little shelters. So, theoretically, once you were in the shops you were safe. Within a week I had become a familiar figure, frisking *myself* at checkpoints, patting my clothes and saying, 'No, there's nothing on me', to smiles all round.

Some corners of Belfast had quite a nautical flavour, and outside a shop called 'Sea Chandlers and Sail Makers,' I asked an old merchant seaman the way to the bus station. He was in the middle of an argument with a younger man who was drunkenly jeering at the merchant fleet. 'It was us lads with the red duster who brought the food over during the war', the youth was admonished. 'As for you, sir, just carry on down the road and steer to the port side.'

So I left Belfast by bus, riding up the coast, through the Glens of Antrim to the village of Cushendun. There I dismounted at the grocery-shop-cum-post-office and looked around uncertainly. The coast road scenery had been breathtaking, and Carrickfergus Castle would be the making of any resort in England. I had passed sugar-loaf mountains with bright Alpine meadows, and white cottages among the firs and oaks.

Cushendun proved to be a small, hospitable village on a bay, and on the far side of the Dun estuary I could see a strand with three hotels upon it. This was no case of 'eeny-meeny-miny-mo', for when I saw the Cushendun Hotel, redolent of old-world prosperity, it was love at first sight. A mild-mannered manager greeted me in the hall. I paid him the

110

equivalent of a small boarding house fee in England and went up to my room.

From my window I could see swallows flitting across the river, and gulls over the sea some yards further on. Boats skimmed by, and children on a jetty cried out excitedly as they caught one miniature eel after another. Near the hotel door, the mascot, a sturdy brown goat, stood chewing enigmatically. My room was furnished like a cabin in a luxury liner, and later I learned why. During the Great War the Belgian Royal Yacht, having been pressed into service, had been sunk in Cushendun Bay, and the furniture from the wreck had been installed in the hotel. Fishermen could sometimes glimpse the yacht on the sea-bed, I was told. Another wreck helped to furnish the downstairs, and an old mill had been transformed into a country house hotel, first opened in 1926.

On my visit, the waiters were well mannered sixth-formers from Belfast, and the only other guests were Nancy McCullough, also from the capital, and a permanent resident, Mr. Walsh. We all got on very well, but I regretted later that I hadn't joined Miss McCullough for a 'crack' and a sing-song in the village pub. 'When I went in, they all began to sing the old ballad 'Where is the Ring I Gave to Nancy Spain?' she told me later, as she is a regular visitor to Cushendun.

However, in the nearby Bay Hotel, I enjoyed 'family night' where children danced to the music of an accordion, watched by their parents who had motored in from outlying villages. Near here, the shore erupted into large rocks, ideal for children to climb, and there were caves in the cliffside for realistic games of pirates and smugglers. These weird rock formations had indeed erupted, as the lone, grass-capped pillars reeling groggily towards the sea, as well as the caves and grottos, were all formed by long-ago volcanic activity. Dangle a spoonful of syrup over a plate and imagine the sticky loops to be molten lava which could suddenly cool and turn to stone, and you can picture the scene at Cushendun.

Some man-made architecture also interested me in Cushendun – the almshouses designed by Sir Clough Williams-Ellis in the thirties. They were larger than most almhouses, resembling luxury villas of the period, white with slate roofs. I once worked for the Williams-Ellis family engraving slates at a quarry they owned in North Wales. Clough and his authoress wife Amabel were fellow-travellers of the Communist Party at one time, but as they remained a remote lord and lady of the manor to me, I never met them for a political argument. Sir Clough, a very colourful character, designed the Welsh holiday village of

Portmeirion, which was later used as a setting for *The Prisoner* television series. It is said that when he died, he left instructions for his ashes to be shot up in a rocket to explode over his beloved Portmeirion. As he had been an atheist, this might be interpreted as a last-minute wish to blast his way into Heaven. In his heyday, bohemian parties were held at the village, and one Welsh taxi driver refused to drive up to the place, saying simply, 'I will go no further. For it is the gates of Hell.'

Most of the villagers and holidaymakers at Cushendun were Catholics, but nobody asked me what I believed. Mr. Walsh, a dignified, scholarly man in his nineties, was a great favourite at the hotel, where many visitors would call in for a meal before driving off into the glens.

'So you've just come from Belfast! I remember the bakers' vans they had there – it was wonderful how the horses always knew where to go. They would go on to the next house ahead of the man who was delivering. I'm sure animals can think as we do. I've seen dogs meet one another to go hunting, as if by appointment.'

In his younger days, Mr Walsh had been a salesman in the West of Ireland. His sporting activities there, with dog and gun, led to a great interest in natural history, as so often happens. He described to me how an otter would take one bite from each salmon and then leave it by the water's edge, for the crafty passer-by to cut up and sell to an hotel.

'Men used to put a badger in a barrel and then pop a terrier in as well, and bet on the outcome of the fight,' he told me. 'One man had a very good terrier, but he boasted about it too much. When he next put it in the barrel, it shot out like a rocket, in such terror that it jumped clean through a window-pane to get indoors. Someone had put *two* badgers in the barrel, and after that the man never boasted.'

Such cruel sports belong to the long ago, yet not long before, to Mr Walsh's indignation, someone had shot a seal which had befriended bathers, and which used to play ball in the sea with the children. This was not at Cushendun, where no one would do such a thing. There are two Northern Irelands, the tear-gas and bullet-infested Ulster of the newsreels, and the glens and beaches of such places as Cushendun.

Another bus took me on to Portrush, a cheerful Protestants' Margate, where I thoroughly enjoyed myself. Nevertheless, Northern Ireland has shown me the flaw in the fairy-tale medieval peasant ideal. What is Ulster if not a place so saturated with folk customs and traditional songs that people are killing one another? As I explained in the Introduction, the medieval ideal falls apart if there is heresy. Then an idyll becomes a scene of carnage. The peasant world of folklore can evidently be based on only *one* view of life. In Northern Ireland, there are *two* sets of folk customs and *two* ways of life, both conducive to happiness and fulfilment if kept apart. Together, they appear to destroy one another. Catholic Cushendun and Presbyterian Portrush seemed wonderful places to me, where everyone appeared confident of a bed in Heaven at the end of life's road. Catholic-and-Protestant Belfast was less of a success.

Portrush was still hung with red, white and blue bunting from its Orange Parade as my bus moved on towards the city of Londonderry.

A large yellow hoarding greets the visitor to Londonderry. Expecting a message of welcome, I was disconcerted to read instead that information on murders and explosions would be treated confidentially if a certain number were dialled. The bus rattled on, away from the army barracks and Protestant terraces, over the Foyle bridge and into the walled city itself. Clutching my bulging plastic bag, I disembarked and wandered uncertainly towards the Guildhall. Already I had been unnerved by a glimpse of a truckload of soldiers, whose defiant, angry expressions differed greatly from the good-humoured or calmly resolute features of the soldiers I had seen in Belfast.

Bars and metal shutters covered every shop front, and before the fenced-off Guildhall, an imposing Victorian pile with a tall clock tower, more soldiers stamped about, waving guns wildly. One soldier stood near a bus queue, and the passengers averted their eyes as he clapped loudly. Perhaps he was applauding the ghosts of the city wall, where cannons presented by Elizabeth I and the London companies who had financed the city still pointed their barrels at friends and foe alike. Away from the bus stop, I found the city to be empty and ominous. Where was I to go?

'The hotels have all been blown up long ago,' a woman told me briskly. 'Some houses do bed-and-breakfast, but they have no signs up. Just ask the children playing in the street.' There were no children in sight, and the city coat of arms, shown on such buildings as were still standing, seemed to mock me. It consisted of a seated skeleton resting its skull on one bony hand in a fed-up attitude, as if to say, 'That's another fine mess you've got me into,'

An hour later, I knew how the skeleton felt. By now I had found plenty of children, all very polite, who directed me hither and thither to houses where nobody answered the door. My bag had burst, and was spilling souvenirs of Belfast's Orange Parade, King Billy rosettes and postcards showing Dr Paisley at home, on to streets covered in bloodthirsty IRA slogans. Evidently this was the notorious Bogside. I retraced my steps to a door marked 'Samaritans. Open ten a.m. to ten p.m.', and threw myself on their mercy. My good Samaritan was a middle-aged man who seemed surprised at my English accent. He sat me down in an easy chair, made a telephone call and then drove me straight to Logan's Lodging House.

On the way, I noted that Bogside had been rebuilt along the main road. A ruined house with the neatly painted sign, 'You Are Now Entering Free Derry', remained as a memento of the brave old days of the early seventies. High above us, the city wall lined the crest of a hill, covered in slogans about H-Blocks and hunger strikes.

'Have you any advice for an Englishman in Derry?' I asked the Samaritan.

'Stay out of Bogside,' he replied, and delivered me to Mrs Logan.

A spirited seventy-two-year-old, Mrs Logan welcomed me with a mischievous smile and a curtsey-like bob. The lodging house was musty and Victorian and resembled boarding houses for migrant labourers I had known twenty years ago. 'You won't even have to share a room!' she announced proudly.

At midnight I was disturbed by a young man holding two bottles of Guinness, but I found his proper room for him, declined one of the bottles and went to bed. Outside I could hear soldiers shouting fiercely.

'Good morning, sirree!' Mrs Logan greeted me next day. 'A beautiful morning it is, surely, surely! Those soldiers? Och, they were shouting at each other, as they keep falling asleep! They wouldn't dare shout at anyone else. In this town you must not talk to the soldiers. Informers here have come to a very sad end. But sure, the soldiers are only poor boys who've been driven into it by sheer want. So what I do, I bid them the time of day and good weather, but don't get into conversation.'

I admired the many watercolours of country scenes around the breakfast-room walls. Mrs Logan came from County Donegal, she told me, from a village in the mountains. She loved to look at mountain scenery. One picture showed Tory Island, whose pirates gave the name to my favourite political party. 'There's a reel called "The Waves of Tory",' she said, and for a moment I thought that she was going to dance it.

Other lodgers came downstairs, and soon we were animatedly discussing the pubs on Kilburn High Road. It was a Catholic house, and while murders were deplored, the Provos were referred to affectionately as 'the boys'. This ambivalence seemed to pervade Derry as a whole, for it is now a Catholic-dominated city. In Belfast the soldiers had the goodwill and co-operation of the majority of citizens:

hence their high morale and exemplary behaviour. Here it was different. I saw few older officers, but plenty of young boys in uniform, in what must be as popular a posting as was Hadrian's Wall in a previous era.

'The boys get hold of some bombs and don't want to hurt anyone,' Mrs Logan explained. 'They leave them somewhere and go and 'phone the police, who don't go near for fear of booby traps. But eventually they explode them all right. While you're here, you must visit the Bogside!' she urged me, heaping bacon on to my plate. 'Such nice people, and St Eugene's Cathedral up on the hill is beautiful. They're all good musicianers on Bogside, and they'll be practising now for Our Lady's Day on the fifteenth of August. You've no need to fear anyone. It's only the men in hats, police or soldiers, the boys are after.'

Encouraged by good Mrs Logan, I felt myself warming to Londonderry. By the end of my five-day stay there, I felt a strong affection for the city. I began by visiting St Columb's, the Church of Ireland cathedral. While I was inside, the roof of the courthouse opposite fell in and killed a man. This was not directly due to a bomb, but as the building had suffered an explosion before, the fabric may have been weakened. Not realising the extent of the tragedy, I left the police, ambulance men and firemen at their work, and went to the bank. It had very obviously been bombed recently, but business was as usual. 'It's the third time we've been bombed, but we never let it get us down', the manager told me as he let me out and locked several doors after me.

Unlike Belfast, there were no security checks or friskings in the streets or shops. Perhaps the public would not have stood for it. The Derry men and women seemed, on the whole, as kindly a bunch as you'd meet anywhere.

Beautiful wall paintings of the Boyne and the Siege of Derry decorated the council-flat gateway to the Fountain, the only Protestant estate on this side of the river. A single Gothic tower, remnant of the old city gaol, loomed over the menacing new flats of the Fountain. 'This tower is an affront to the Catholics.' one of that faith told me later. 'The patriots at the time of the Rising were imprisoned here, and the Protestants treasure the tower so as to gloat over their sufferings.'

Londonderry's walls resemble those of medieval England, with ramparts on top and gateways below. They were made, however, in 1618 or thereabouts, shortly after the city was built as an English base in a wilderness, beside the crumbling ruins of St Columb's monastery. Ulster Protestants are settlers, akin in character to the pioneers of New England and Canada. Like Americans, who feel they 'began' in 1776,

Protestants feel that their proud history commenced in 1688 with the Siege of Derry. If the Protestants are somewhat two-dimensional through denying their medieval heritage, the 'original Irish' suffer from a lack of Imperial Roman discipline. So honours are even.

Thus I mused as I walked along the top of the wall and looked down at the Fountain estate. As well as advertisements for the Ulster Volunteer Force and the National Front, a coalition which worried me, the wall messages read: 'Build More H-Blocks. May the Hunger-Strikers Rot in Hell.' Just then a stone flew over the wall and narrowly missed my head. I backed away in alarm, as further missiles followed, and I was about to leave the wall when I saw a stone hit a boy of about five, who began to cry. I took him to his mother's door in a tiny wallside cottage, but he didn't seem to be badly hurt. His injury was partly my fault, as I had provoked the Fountain skinheads by looking over the wall at their estate. 'They're rough, that lot!' the boy's mother told me. 'See, that's the house they bombed, and the lady is still in hospital.'

A corrugated-iron fence with a small door in it separated the Fountain estate from its Catholic neighbours. Here the battlements were barred to visitors, and I rejoined the wall a few streets away, where it towered over the deep valley of the Bogside.

Imagine yourself on the walls of Conway, in Wales, finding the ramparts looped about with barbed wire, and the camps of Welsh chieftains outside equipped with modern weapons. Then you will realise how strange I felt along this stretch of Derry's walls. Not long ago, this too was a tourist attraction. Now I looked down over the Bogside and saw the Irish Republican flag flying from the roof of the highest block of new council flats, above the slogan 'This is Provoland'. Nearby, on the wall, stood the stump of a blown-up statue, surrounded by barbed wire. From a school below came the sound of 'musicianers' playing martial airs on drums and flutes, very similar to Orange music.

Outside one of the shirt and collar manufacturers that once made Derry famous, girl machinists sat lazily in the sun enoying their lunch break. They greeted me in the cheeky manner of factory girls everywhere, but ignored the scattered party of five armed soldiers who prowled below them on the city side of the wall. The soldiers obviously resented their mission, and spat and looked surly. Ruined and blown-up houses and narrow alley-ways offered perfect cover for snipers, and the men's lives were at great risk.

Near Hangman's Bastion, at Butcher's Gate, the historic entrance had been walled up, but a small door had been let into one side to allow Bogsiders through one at a time. Although I more properly belonged at

Coward's Bastion, another ancient site, I stepped through the doorway and into the council estates and Victorian terraces of Bogside. Wall paintings were everywhere, mostly in flat orange and green, their messages spelling doom to British soldiers. Names of 'Bloody Sunday' victims were commemorated as if on a war memorial, but religious messages were lacking. Nevertheless, St Eugene's Cathedral, which towered above the far side of the valley, facing the wall on the opposite bank, was full of worshippers. Some splashed holy water on their foreheads as they left, others knelt on the gravel path outside, before the Virgin's grotto. I presume that a bog once lay between the two hills, where now an ugly new road shimmered in the sun.

Children played happily in the streets near the cathedral, bumping their tricycles or toy tanks over kerbstones painted in orange, green and white, the Republican colours. These may have been copying the far more prevalent red, white and blue kerbstones of the loyal Presbyterian estates. Far from looking war-worn, the children seemed merry enough. Only the pavement chalkings were odd. One showed a tombstone with the inscription: 'RIP to commemorate Curly. Killed in Action. Hit by a Banana from Outer Space'. A few steps further on, however, a reassuring 'Curly Lafferty OK' in the same handwriting, showed that the self-penned obituary had been premature.

Traversing the Bogside was no ordeal, but a pleasant journey through streets of laughing children and gossiping neigbours. Mindful of the Samaritan's advice, I asked no controversial questions, but instead enquired the way to a variety of destinations. I met with great helpfulness wherever I went. Talking to soldiers was out of the question, as there weren't any. Although 'Operation Motorman' supposedly opened the no-go areas, the Bogside was patrolled from the sky, helicopters rising vertically from the riverside barracks and buzzing slowly over the valley. On my fifth day in the city I saw one armoured vehicle, sealed so tightly I wondered how the driver could see his way, passing swiftly along the road.

Only one corner gave me cause for unease – the house whose message proclaimed 'Free Derry'. Here a flagpole and tricolour had been planted, and shaggy-haired youths stripped to the waist sat glaring on the low walls. An official-looking sign over a garage read 'Provisional IRA Arms Depot'. 'A trick!' I reasoned to myself. 'I bet the arms are *really* hidden somewhere else.' Perhaps this was what they wanted me to think. This unpleasant spot apparently represented the Ireland the Provos were fighting for. Nothing less like the easy-going South could be imagined. Here were no jolly nuns, no shops opening whenever the proprietors felt like it, and no drinks going downwards or prayers upwards in the familiar leisurely sequence.

Back in the city centre, I suddenly noticed the five soldiers emerging from a dark alley with expressions of terror on their faces, guns at the ready. Their exaggerated caution seemed comical when contrasted with the relaxed mood of the shoppers around them. I was reminded of the inconsequential humour of a television sketch where big game hunters emerge from the palms in an hotel foyer. But there was nothing funny about a soldier's life in Derry.

A bomb scare at the Strand Cinema proved to be a false alarm. To avoid the police cordon, I cut through a backstreet where I was much amused to see a fat man in his socks angrily chasing a puppy with a slipper in its mouth. At dusk I returned to Mrs Logan, through streets patrolled by police officers with rifles.

'Oh, it's yourself,' said Mrs Logan, letting me in.

'Yes, it's myself.'

'Hear that noise? It's the helicopter. There's trouble on the Bogside tonight.' she remarked sagely. 'All I've seen all my life, is fighting and killing and strife. Sometimes the boys rest on their laurels, and it stops for a year or two, but then it always starts up again. You see, when a young lad grows up, he rebels, and here it's only the IRA and the UVF to rebel into.'

That night I looked through my window at the red brick lamp-lit street outside, and pondered on my mortality.

Next day in the flowery shrubs of the 'good' side of the river, I met a Presbyterian doctor and his wife who invited me in for tea. We were interrupted by a house call, and my host dashed off to the Bogside in his car.

'I was worried when I first moved here,' his wife told me, passing the home-made cakes. 'The boys on the Bogside have a way of waving down cars and taking them for their own purposes, either to transport arms or to plant bombs in and park somewhere. When they do this, they wear black hoods on their heads. But my husband has lived here all his life, and even with the hoods on he could recognise their voices from when he'd treated them. Twice he was waved down, and each time he'd say, "Is that you in there, Willy? Oh, and hullo, Pat, I nearly didn't recognise you." "Sure, Doctor, we didn't know that was you," they'd reply, and stop the next car instead.

'It was the Bogside's big day when Bobby Sands the hunger-striker died. Everyone ran up black flags, tied strips of black plastic bin-liner on to everything and marched and sang in the streets, thoroughly

118

enjoying themselves. The Bogsiders aren't so bad, really. Once my husband was called out during a riot, and the boys waved him through to the patient's door, waited outside and waved him back. Mind you, when Free Derry was declared, all the doctors said at once that if they were interfered with, they would stop going into Bogside altogether. One doctor *did* have his car taken, so he went straight up to the IRA headquarters and kicked up such a fuss that they gave it back again. Some money he had left in it was missing, so he went back to the IRA and shouted at them until they returned it.'

'Wait a minute,' I broke in, 'Do you mean to say that you can call on the IRA at a known address, as if they had an office?'

'Of course,' she replied. 'It used to be over a row of shops in the Creggan, but I don't know where it is now.'

She gave me an address in Bogside of a man said to be a friend of both the IRA and the Catholic bishop. However, when I saw him he denied the former charge and welcomed the latter one. When I suggested calling on the IRA he turned pale and told me what would probably be the outcome. Whereupon I turned pale too.

Before I left kindly Mrs Logan, I gave her a small box of chocolates as a farewell present. 'Sure, I'll see you again, all being well,' she declared cheerfully. 'Everyone always comes back.'

Now I walked far into the countryside, in search of peasant wisdom. At last, near Claudy, I found an old man scything. He proved to be a Catholic, and at once turned the conversation from the weather to a recent killing in Derry – the case of a supposed burglar who had been convicted by an IRA kangaroo court and shot in the legs. 'Imagine bleeding to death in that way!' the greybeard exclaimed. 'Sure, that's going entirely too far! They should have just shot him in the knee.'

One summer's evening I went for a stroll by the shores of Lough Erne, just outside the city of Enniskillen. Swifts and swallows patrolled separate strands of midge-covered water as if divided into Catholics and Protestants. Gleaming in the twilight, the gospel tent stood in a field beside a full car park. A small poster on a telegraph pole proclaimed a 'Fundamentalist Convention, Preacher: Dr Ian Paisley.' The event was scarcely publicised, and few people in Enniskillen knew that Paisley was on their doorstep.

Now at last I had the chance to hear the man whom Dervla Murphy, a courageous traveller in Ulster, had described in her book *A Place Apart* as 'the presence of pure evil', radiating sinister and 'powerful emanations'.

119

Nearly every bench in the tent was full, but at last I managed to
wriggle in beside a housewife in a summery hat. Most of the Paisleyites
were young couples of a meek appearance. I hoped that the emanations
of evil would not annihilate them. A big jolly man took the platform,
cracked a few jokes and then announced a hymn.

> There is a fountain filled with blood
> Drawn from Emmanuel's veins,
> And sinners plunged beneath that flood
> Lose all their guilty stains!

'Some of these meetings may be timed a bit awkwardly for you,' the big
man continued, 'but the cows won't know the difference if you milk
them a bit earlier or later than usual. Now I would like you all to pray
for our friends the McFaddens, supporters of the Democratic Unionist
Party, whose lonely farmhouse was burned down last week by the IRA.
And as for Tim McFadden, the crippled lad who died in the blaze, we
may rejoice, for we know he is in Heaven.'

After the prayer Paisley himself appeared, passed along the aisles
between the benches and took his stand, wearing a large pair of
black-framed spectacles. He was an enormous man, and he gripped his
Bible with massive hands. To my surprise, he too began with a boyish
joke or two.

'D'ye see this tent? D'ye like it? This is my tent! They had to ask me
along here tonight, as it was my tent. Twice after I have spoken in this
tent the IRA have burned it down. Each time the insurance company
have paid for the damage. Now nobody will insure this tent any more,
and I don't blame them. While we are holding these meetings here, the
tent is guarded night and day.'

Suddenly forgetting the tent, Paisley began to speak of sin and
sinners. His face had already darkened when he had briefly mentioned
the Pope, whom he apparently regarded as the brains behind the IRA.
Now his brow grew thunderous, as did his voice. Savagely he roared
about degraded sinners, dead sinners and sinners of all kinds; about a
'Niagara Falls of Hell with churning, turning torrents of souls.'

A black cloud seemed to hover above his head, but all of a sudden the
sun came out. He took off his spectacles and looked the better for it.
The bellowing bull was replaced by a cooing dove, as he spoke of the
Salvation that can rescue the most abject of sinners. His change of voice
and manner had the effect of a fatherly copper replacing a sadistic bully
in a police station. Everyone felt relieved and seemed to seek his

approval. Although there was a technique in this, his sincerity was beyond doubt.

Years of attending West Indian churches in London have given me immunity to so-called 'emanations'. Very many evangelical churches have ranting, screaming or bellowing preachers, and their congregations seem all the better for it. Paisley was a great deal more restrained than another Doctor I have heard, the egregious Billy Graham. West Indian pastors frequently rant to the point where I fear an epileptic fit will ensue, and then end the whole service suddenly with a gospel song. Paisley's altered and friendly tone was an agreeable surprise. Even his belief in the Satanic origin of the Catholic Church was traditional to chapel preachers the world over. It only took on a new significance because the behaviour of the IRA seemed to confirm it. My mother, as a girl in the Elim Church in Worthing, often heard Rome described as the Scarlet Whore of Babylon. The man before me in the gospel tent was no villain, but merely a heavy-handed kirk elder, rather fond of having his own way. In the immortal words of Lonnie Donegan:

Now you might think it's Satan that's coming down the aisle,
But it's only our poor preacher boy that's putting on the style.

Paisley's style quite suited me. When he read from the letters of St Paul to the Ephesians, he stated that the Ephesians were Presbyterians, but this might have been a joke. 'My friends, the Gospel never changes. Should the moon weep blood and the stars be extinguished the Gospel will remain the same.' His voice resembled that of W.C. Fields at times, while at others he sounded like a medicine-tent showman in the American South. His Ballymena accent, his flourishes and his cries of 'My friends!' were extremely American. I had a vision of an America pioneered by Ulstermen – not entirely a false one.

'My friends, when I make you this unique genu-wine offer, the Dr Killumkwik's Infallible Indian Snake Oil Remedy, guaranteed to cure all ills known to man and grow hair on a billiard ball, I do not ask for five dollars, not for three dollars, but, my friends . . .'

A fairer comparison would be with the frontier preacher who waves the Bible to Heaven as he swears vengeance on the Sioux Indians for the bloody midnight attacks on the little settlement – a non-Christian approach, but a very understandable one. On this occasion, however, the real Paisley spoke only of sin and salvation, and saved his political wisdom for the interminable sittings of the Northern Ireland Bill. A Catholic friend of mine, a former navvy from County Mayo, speaks of

Paisley with a twinkle in his eye as 'th'owd rascal', and relishes his tangles with authority. Just because the IRA have no figurehead, we should not blame 'the troubles' on Paisley. Many do so, misled by television, which juxtaposes scenes of IRA carnage with Paisley shouting angrily about them, in confusing cross-imagery.

When Paisley had finished and the faithful had filed away, some to see Mrs. Eileen Paisley in a caravan and invite Jesus into their lives, I approached the man of the moment and asked for an interview. The Doctor leaned back, chuckling hoarsely over a joke with his friends.

'I never give interviews on a Sunday, friend,' he told me.

'Well, do you think I could have your autograph? It's not for me, it's for my sister.'

He agreed to this, and at last I was able to extort a message from him: 'Believe, that you might be saved.'

Leaving the old charmer in his precious tent, I went outside and found his wife Eileen beside her caravan. She came of the long and honourable line of women in hats, along with Mrs Thatcher and the Queen. In her case the hat was ornamented with bobbing dark-blue feathers. She agreed that her husband was somewhat disliked in England.

'They know he's defending Northern Ireland, so they just see a soldier as a soldier and not a husband and a human being,' she told me sadly.

'A soldier? Does your husband have any connection with the Ulster Volunteer Force or any of the unofficial Protestant armies?'

'None at all!' She was shocked. 'The UVF are wild, irresponsible young boys, banned by the government. They are nothing like Carson's UVF, and my husband has nothing to do with them. He never handles weapons. All he did was tell folk in outlying places that as the army couldn't defend them they would have to defend themselves. That's only natural. If you had seen the sorrow of bereaved wives whose husbands had been killed by the IRA, you would know how we feel. You might say, "Just another death" and pass by, but their grief remains for ever. I'm sorry for the poor soldiers. They could do better than this, as they did in the Falklands, but their hands are tied. Mrs Thatcher helped the Falkland Islanders – why won't she help us?'

'Now there's Direct Rule, do you think England might betray you, as she betrayed . . .'

'South Africa,' Mrs Paisley ended, although I had been going to mention Indian princes. 'I do hope not.'

'Well apart from these political themes, I'm afraid I can't quite agree with your husband's views on Rome. For instance, think how many Latin countries there are, along the Mediterranean and in South

America, to say nothing of all the Catholics who lived in England in the Middle Ages. It seems incredible that they should all go to Hell.'

'Yes, doesn't it?' she answered sorrowfully.

'No, I mean it *is* incredible. In England many people assume that Catholicism is a Christian religion.'

'Well, some Catholics are Christians,' she replied doubtfully.

Not so long ago, say twenty years, the Catholics and Presbyterians of Ulster could laugh at one another's differences. I remember hearing a very funny song, surely composed by a Protestant, played and sung in a pub by a Catholic ceilidh band in 1965. 'That song's sung by both sides,' the fiddle-player told me. So what better way to leave Northern Ireland than with a song, 'The Old Orange Flute', sung to the music-hall tune of 'Villikins and His Dinah'?

In the County of Tyrone, near the town of Dungannon,
Where many a ruction myself had a han' in,
Bob Williamson lived, a weaver by trade,
And each of us thought him a stout Orange blade.
On the Twelfth of July, as it yearly did come,
Bob played on the flute, and we banged on the drum;
Ye may talk of your harp, your piano or lute,
But there's nothing can sound like the old Orange flute.

But this treacherous scoundrel, he took us all in,
For he married a Papist named Bridget McGinn.
Turned Popish himself and forsook the old cause
That gave us our freedom, religion and laws.
The boys in the townland made some noise upon it,
And Bob had to fly to the Province of Connaught;
He fled with his wife and his fixings to boot,
And along with all others the old Orange flute.

At Mass every Sunday to atone for his deeds
He said Paters and Avers and counted his beads,
Till after some time, at the priest's own desire,
He went with his old flute to play in the choir.
He went with his old flute to play in the Mass,
And the instrument shivered and sighed 'Oh alas!'
As he blew it and fingered it made a strange noise.
For the flute would play only 'The Protestant Boys'.

123

Bob started and jumped and he got in a sputter,
And he threw his old flute in the blessed holy water.
For he thought that this charm would bring some other sound,
When he played it again, it played 'Croppies Lie Down'.
And all he could whistle and finger and blow,
To play Popish music, he found it no go.
'Kick the Pope' and 'Boyne Water' and suchlike 'twould sound,
But one Popish squeak in it could not be found.

At the Council of Priests which was held the next day.
They decided to banish the old flute away.
For they couldn't knock heresy out of its head,
So they bought Bob another to play in its stead.
So the flute was condemned and its fate was pathetic
It was fastened and burned at the stake as a heretic.
But out of the bonfire there came a strange noise.
The old flute was still whistling 'The Protestant Boys'.

Tailless Cats, Coracles, and the Green Children

One day I took a ferry boat to Douglas in the Isle of Man, where I had never been before. I dragged my heavy suitcase from the boat, through a hall and on to the clean white jetty. Crossing the road, I looked around bewilderedly, seeing a criss-cross of crowded shopping streets near a clock tower on a traffic island.

'Do you know where I can find somewhere to stay?' I asked a middle-aged man.

'Aye, you see those yellow houses there? That's where the boarding houses are. You can't go wrong.'

Nor could I, for within ten minutes of entering the narrow street I had found a place and lugged my case painfully up a steep staircase to a tiny room. The vivacious landlady owned most of the tall house, and the ground floor was a confectioner's and saucy postcard shop. Like every house in that street, it was of jaundice-yellow brick, picked out in red around the windows.

I set out to explore, just as it was getting dark. Neon lights and raucous crowds were everywhere, for Douglas is very much a working man's resort like Blackpool, and caters to holidaymakers from Liverpool and Glasgow, among other places. Knowing Glasgow's young men as I do, I am not surprised that Man retains the birch.

One long street running parallel to the seafront was crammed with bright little souvenir shops, chip shops and pin-table arcades. The swaggering young and stout elderly people, moving restlessly along it in groups, reminded me of a fairground crowd. Facing the prom were musical pubs both rough and grandiose and, out on the blue—black ocean, a castle tower on a small rocky island was outlined in fairy-lights.

125

Near my boarding house was a Yates' Wine Bar almost like the one at Blackpool – nothing could be *quite* like it – and not far away was an Irish pub with draught Guinness and a country and western group playing.

Later that night I saw chains of northern grannies, some seven-strong and all fat with bleached curly hair, stagger along arm in arm. Between laughs and screams they were trying to sing 'If You were the Only Girl in the World'. Hovering harassedly on the flanks of this invading army were a few little bald husbands.

Next morning I found the dining-room at breakfast to be as crowded as the night-time streets had been. I sat at a little round table, among scores of others, and a flustered girl popped what looked like a three-tiered silver cake-stand on the cloth, and rushed off. This contained breakfast for three – bacon and eggs, toast and bread and butter. Cereals in packets and tea ready in a pot were already on one side of the crowded table. My breakfast companions were an elderly couple from a small town in Lancashire. From the hatch into the kitchen, a record-player filled the room with Scottish songs by the Alexander Brothers. As we took turns with the teapot, the Lancashire man felt it incumbent on himself to give me a lecture on the origins of the breakfast.

'It's a plant is that, is tea,' he told me sagely, pronouncing 'plant' to rhyme with 'ant'.

'Oh yes?' I said, as if in polite wonder.

'Aye, it's a plant. Folk pick that, out in them hot countries.'

'Will you pass the su-u-ugar?' his wife bleated in a high, pathetic voice.

'Aye, it's a plant too, is that, is sugar.'

'Yes, I had heard.'

'Aye, it comes from a plant. Some from sugar beet, like, and some from sugar cane. Both plants, them. Aye.'

He drank his conglomeration of plants with evident relish. How mistaken was Orwell, I reflected, to suggest that in the interests of friendship between classes, everyone ought to drink their tea noisily. There is enough noise in the country as it is, what with Concordes and transistor radios. If everyone were to suck their tea noisily at the same time, the sheer wall of sound would cause buildings to collapse, and it might well be the end of Civilisation As We Know it.

Outside, among the fresh sea breezes by the prom, I met the man who had shown me where the boarding houses were. We got talking and he told me that he was of old Manx stock, as was shown by his name, Skillycorn. I complained that all the cats I had seen had tails.

'You won't see a pet cat wi' no tail here in Douglas at all, you'd have to go out to the farms in wild places. The Manx cats come from the Calf of Man, a little island where the cats interbred wih the wild hares. That's why the Manx cats have got long hind legs and bobtails like a hare. There's a cattery in Noble's Park, above the town, where you can see them in wire pens.'

He directed me to the cattery, which stood in a delightful park, with bowling greens and aviaries with peacocks. However, the tailless cats were kept inside a small building, rather like an old-fashioned monkey house in a zoo, with no outside runways. They were lovely animals, mostly tabbies and a few white ones. Both cats and kittens were very friendly, and rubbed themselves against the wire mesh, purring loudly. I tickled them between the ears, and twiddled a pencil through the wire for them to play with. It seemed a shame to keep the cats prisoners in the interests of racial purity. Their hindquarters rose a bit higher than other cats', but I noticed no bobtails, only wisps of fluff, and no hare-like back legs. In spite of both being called 'Puss', hares and cats cannot cross-breed, and Mr Skillycorn's tale was simply a legend. Later I heard another Manxman say that the cats came from the East. Inasmuch as all tame cats came from Egypt and thereabouts he was right, but there can be little doubt that centuries of inbreeding caused the Manx cat to lose its tail. Without the cattery and artificial breeding, the tails would have returned with the introduction of pets from the mainland.

That afternoon I walked up the cliffside road above the quay where the ferry came in, to green turfy country with views of the whole Douglas promenade, blue sea and hills. Soon the lighthouse was before me, and the keeper showed me round — and round and round and round, for there was a spiral staircase. At the top, I was much impressed by the lamp and the beautifully gleaming brasswork. The original lamp of 1892 was still in use and working as well as ever, run on paraffin.

Descending to the prom, I took a jog-trotting horse-tram along the whole of the seafront, another very Blackpool touch. There was a variety theatre, a 1920s shopping arcade, open-air evangelists near the beach, and happy visitors everywhere. At the terminus I changed straight on to the mountain railway that goes to the peak of Snaefell. The railway too, was made in the 1890s and was still going strong, although there was a slight delay up among the hills when a wheel came off.

It was delightful riding through the Manx countryside, along the narrow track, by woods and gardens, Victorian stations and gracious hotels, with stone walls and the blue sea for company. Before long we crossed open green fields on the flanks of the hills, with little farmhouses and at one point an immense water-wheel in the middle distance. The huge red wheel, made in 1854 to pump water from the lead mines, is one of the sights of Man. Although the mines are now disused, the wheel, 'Lady Isabella', remains – the largest in the world.

Snaefell is over two thousand feet in height, and as we neared the top the cables grew taut and the scenery became wild and tussocky, with a few sheep grazing. At the station on the peak, everyone got out and scrambled up the last lap. It was very windy, and I found that the highest point on the Isle of Man was the top of a small boy's head, as he sat on the marker stone.

Everyone had told me that from the top of Snaefell the four kindgoms could be seen – England, Scotland, Ireland and Wales. so they could, but the last two were very faint. Snaefell seemed to be the entire Isle of Man, surrounded by a softly gleaming glass-like sea, with faint grey lines on every horizon. I could make out the hills of Cumberland very plainly; a Manx eye-view of England shows us to be a mountainous country.

On the beautiful moors of Man covered in dark-purple heather, red grouse whirr and golden plovers fly. A late coach tour from the prom took me that evening to a rushing waterfall by a litle wooden bridge, set among ferns and trees; nearby, a lane wound its way among the woods. It was a mellow summer evening, just before dusk. On the way back to Douglas, the driver pointed out Tynwald Hill, with its steps of turf and flagpole on top. According to ancient Norse tradition, the laws passed in the House of Keys parliament have to be spoken aloud on this hill.

Earlier that day I had walked along the twisty lane used for the TT races, a peaceful place when the races weren't on, with flowery banks and hedges, the fields growing steeper as the lane sank between the gnarled roots of tall, dark fir trees. All along the way, little culverts poured clear stream water from the banks on to the side of the road, or into stone troughs once used by horses.

At the coastal town of Peel I was surprised by the Viking boats with dragon heads, moored casually in the harbour among the fishing vessels, in readiness for next year's pageant. They looked other-worldly, lying lopsided on the shore, yet as if great beast-headed boats were nothing to get excited about – just part of the workaday scenery.

I found an excellent zoo deep in the North Manx countryside, the Ballaugh Wild Life Park. It was in a wild and lonely spot among rugged hills and black forestry plantations, on the far side of Snaefell. Creating a zoo from the creeks and tangled undergrowth must have been hard work, and sites for new cages were being hacked from the bush when I was there. It was pleasant walking around in the as yet animal-less places, where paths had been cut through a swampy jungle that looked almost Amazonian. However, the Brazilian tapir lived not here but in a windy paddock. It seemed to suit him, and he galloped around like a pony.

I liked the wildfowl lake, with its beach of grey stones at one end and cafeteria at the other, ducks waddling on to the terrace and pink flamingoes wading disdainfully not far away. One sloping paddock bordering on a stream and wood had a footpath through the middle, and there I walked entranced, among curious wild geese, bill-clacking white storks, and jumping wallabies. I felt like Uncle Remus in the Walt Disney film.

But my favourite bird was a pelican, back near the entrance. He and his friends had only a small pool surrounded by wire netting, but this pelican could fly! Spreading his great wings, he was soon high up in the air, a brilliant white against the dark conifers on the mountainside. He looked like a gigantic prehistoric egret with his head and neck rolled back and his long bill pointing forward. Then he was overhead, higher still, and I looked up in amazement to see so huge and so graceful a bird, his pointed wings making him look like the king of all seagulls. A fanning of the air with long pinions, webbed feet poised in mid-air with toes outspread, and the pelican was back in his pen once more, the envy of his earth-bound comrades with their clipped wings. He must have been an expert at landing, to pick out his tiny enclosure from so high in the air.

Later, in a Welsh zoo, I saw a pelican dive for fish like a cormorant, into a large glass tank. The pouch under his bill opened out like a yellow balloon as it filled with water. When I was home again, I opened a newspaper and read that a pelican had flown away from a zoo on the Isle of Man.

Away from the prom at Douglas, below the lighthouse cliff, is an old-fashioned fishing harbour on the estuary of the River Glass. On one side of the water are woods and quaint grey houses in the Gothic style, and on the other is a quayside with moored fishing boats bobbing up and down and waterfront pubs looking like illustrations to a sea shanty. The dockside is much higher than the river, and even at high tide there is a bird's-eye view of the decks and hatches, fish and fishermen. Not far from here, up a hill to the right, I found a railway station where a small steam train with tiny red carriages puffed its way through the countryside to Port Erin. The station had a red brick archway with miniature gold domes on top, like something out of Portmeirion, the fairy-tale village in Wales.

Port Erin stands at the very tip of Man, near the Calf, the little island where the cats are supposed to come from. It boasts some cafés and prim seaside architecture, a sandy beach and a long stone harbour walkway, with a saltwater aquarium at the shore end of it, the Marine Biological Station. It seems to be one of the aims of most marine biologists to farm fish and establish great dover sole ranches, with breeding-pens, round-ups and the full Wild West treatment. Perhaps, when this is underway, sea fishermen will be replaced by fishboys or land-bound fish-farmers. Imagine the adventurous life of fish-hands at the Speckled Gurnard Ranch, fighting off Icelandic and Russian rustlers who dare to rope and brand our British fish. Or life at Seawillow farm, with the old varmer leaning on the wooden rail of a murky tank, scratching a great turbot's back with a gnarled stick carved from driftwood, and saying 'Arr, I calls un Daisy. Reared un from a speck o' spawn, I did.'

To return to reality – I admired the baby soles and other fish in their tanks, at various stages in development. Flatfish are not born flat, but flatten into adulthood, their eyes moving across their heads slowly but surely from the sides to the top until flatness is complete.

At the other end of the bay I could see a cliffside walk to Bradda Head, a high, jutting cliff with a glorious view over the sea from the top of a strange castle tower. (This tower, I was told, was built as a memorial to the man who invented Yale locks, so it can't be as old as it looks.) I walked up to it one fine day, among the yellow gorse, lichened rocks and sea pinks, with the metallic chink of stonechats from the seaward side. These bold orange, black and white patched birds fluttered ever before me. At the Head I dutifully climbed the tower, then descended and sat on the grass. It had clouded over where I was sitting, but out at sea the sun sent shafts down through a gap in the heavens to form a glow on the ocean, brighter and brighter, through which a battleship slowly cruised. It was a dreamy, not a dazzling, light, for it came through a thin mist.

Realising that I would miss the bus, as the last train had gone, I rose at last and went up to the tower for a last look around. A crisp white envelope lay on the grass at my feet, with 'To the Finder' on the outside, and the flap tucked in, unsealed. I opened it and read: 'Girl of Outstanding Beauty Needs More Pocket Money. Donations to this Worthy Cause should be sent to Room 4a'; then followed the name and address of a boarding house in Douglas.

Thoughtfully I put the missive in my pocket. Probably it had been cast to the winds from the top of the tower and the outstandingly beautiful girl had imagined it would be blown across the sea to one of the four kingdoms. Feeling lightfooted and excited, I ran down the inland path to town, a steep track among the fields, by a crumbling dry-stone wall with turf growing from its cracks. Stopping for a moment to take breath, I caught a glimpse of two black-faced sheep, scrambling to the top of the wall to get out of my way. As always when I run for a bus, I ended up having to wait for a quarter of an hour, but this time I had entertaining company.

Two bright eyed young Manx girls, with strong local accents, were flirting and joking with two cheerful public school boys on holiday. After a minute or two I found myself included in the conversation, and said something about going back to England.

'You're in England now, surely,' one of the boys said.

'No he's *not*,' the taller of the two girls replied indignantly. 'This is the Isle of Man, it's our own country by itself.'

'I don't believe in countries,' the boy told us. He was spectacled and brainy-looking, with dark curly hair, while his schoolfriend was fair-haired and looked like a cricketer. 'I am an anarchist.'

We at once began a heated political discussion which utterly bored the two girls. The other boy occupied his time profitably by studying my accent, and when I had argued myself out he told me the name of the exact town I had been brought up in. This impressed me no end, and then the bus came.

Chivalrously, I let the young people go upstairs and sat downstairs myself. At Douglas, the brainy boy went off with one of the girls, but his friend was left alone, as the tall blonde girl belonged to a village on the way. To interest him, I showed him the letter I had found.

He asked if he could have it, and when I agreed he took out all his change, put all the silver coins into the envelope and sealed it. Then together we set out for the address. It turned out to be an elegant guest-house on a hill at the top of the town, and one especially catering for cyclists, according to the board outside. You could see all the cyclists having their dinner through the ground-floor windows. My new friend walked in, and I waited outside to see what would happen. Two minutes he walked out again, looking quite pleased with himself.

'I knocked at the door of Room 4a,' he told me airily. 'But there was no reply – she must have been in the dining room. So I went in, and found myself in a room with three beds, and books and comics everywhere. Quite a happy family, and one of them seemed to be a girl of thirteen, judging by the books and things. So I put the envelope on her bed and tip-toed out, seeing nobody. How surprised she'll be! I daresay she threw the letter off the tower this afternoon, as the envelope looked so fresh and clean. If she's cycled back from Port Erin, she'll have come back tired out and famished, gone straight in to dinner, and then, when she goes up to her room afterwards, there will be her letter, full of money. She and her family will talk about it for the rest of their lives – I've given them a whole new interest in life! Well worth the money, easily.'

'You shouldn't be allowed out without a keeper,' I said, but he just smiled and strode away. Now, if the girl should happen to read this, the mystery will be explained.

Next morning I had to leave Man, and so did my table-mates, the Lancashire couple. In readiness for taking the ferry across to Liverpool, the man was wearing a smart nautical blazer with a gold anchor on the pocket and a yachting cap. He was smiling from ear to ear, and clearly saw himself as a modern Sir Francis Drake. His wife was worrying about being seasick.

When I said goodbye to the landlady she gave me some good advice – to sit at the rear of the plane, where the wings wouldn't spoil my view. It turned out to be quite a small plane, and when I took my seat at the rear I noticed that the young man opposite me, who looked like a salesman, was praying fervently with his hands together. We began to move along the ground, but I felt no lifting sensation. I glanced at a paper, then looked out of the window, and to my utter amazement, I saw that we were airborne! A peninsula of Man seemed to jut out, with tiny grey houses aslant upon it; and then the plane levelled itself and we were flying calmly above an azure sea.

Cardigan Castle, which overlooks the River Teifi, is surrounded by brambles. One tower has been converted into a manor house, but any Welsh Sleeping Beauty inside would catch her death, for the windows gape vacantly on the world below.

'Yes, the owner's in hospital now,' my landlady told me. 'The council have been trying to get her out for some time, as they want to get their hands on the castle. It's their own fault – they were offered it for nothing years ago and turned it down. Now they're offering the lady a council caravan if she'll move. A caravan! Did you ever hear of such a thing? They hate her for keeping them out of the castle, you see.

She's on social security now. People say that there's a tunnel under the castle, leading to the other castle at Cilgerran.'

Cilgerran, a village further along the dark-green river, is well worth tunnelling to, as I found next day. Perched on the edge of a gorge, where primeval forests of oak and ash grow on sheer slopes between the river and the fields above, it is the scene of the annual coracle races and aquatic sports, held at the end of August. Crowds were hurrying down to the banks as I arrived, their way between the cottages barred by sturdy fishermen selling tickets. Others climbed on to the battlements of one of the most romantic castle ruins I have seen, built straight up from a crag that towers above the trees, the masonry seeming to grow naturally from the jagged rocks. For myself, I retired to the cavernous depths of the medieval Pendre Inn, where the flagstone floor shone with soap and water. Two men at the bar were discussing coracles, so I introduced myself. They proved to be the announcers, Mr Davies and Mr Griffiths, both eager to tell me all about the races.

'The coracle is one of the oldest boats in the world', I was told earnestly. 'It's been used for salmon fishing yere for over two thousand years, before the Romans came. Only three rivers in the world have coracle fishers on them now – the Teifi, the Towy at Carmarthen and the Severn at Ironbridge. Our Teifi coracles are heavier boats altogether than those on the Towy, and they're harder to handle. We make them in the same way that we've *always* done, out of willows and hazel, only now we stretch calico covered in pitch over the frame, instead of animal skins. These aquatic sports began in 1951, the year they had the Festival of Britain, and we've kept them up ever since.

From the castle walls I admired a view that had scarcely changed since the first Welshman had paddled down the river in his coracle, past wolves that prowled among the sessile oaks. Then I stopped at a cottage door to chat to a friendly old lady, Mrs Bevan, who advised me to marry a local girl but didn't say which one. She tried to teach me Welsh pronunciation without much success.

'Yes, I've lived in Cilgerran all my life,' she said. 'You people drove us all into Wales, you know. Your ancestors did, I mean.' Judging by their descendant, I doubt if my ancestors could have done anything so decisive. In their place, I would have settled at Cilgerran and chased anyone who objected into England.

'A pack of wolves escaped from the wild life park not long ago,' Mrs Bevan continued. 'We all hid indoors until they were shot. The last wolf stayed loose for ever so long. They were starving, people say, and leaped over the fence.'

From the river, a starting-pistol was heard. The first two events were children's swimming races. It was a hot day and the crowds of families sitting on the grass and eating sandwiches made a colourful sight. Welsh cakes, tea and other dainties were being sold from a stall in a spot where the rocky gorge had been broken by a stretch of grassland, forming an ideal setting. From his platform, Mr Davies commanded a powerfull loudspeaker. The coracles were off!

Two ropes had been stretched above the river, a starting and a finishing line. Three black coracles, each with an affable Welshman inside, bobbed about alongside the starting rope. Other coracles lay on the bank like turtle shells. When their owners picked them up, the effect was of a giant tortoise on its hind legs. A coracle – a deep, elongated pudding basin of a boat, five feet long – is carried on the back. The calico sides are bendy, and the oval shape is slightly blunted at the bows. One wooden seat spans the craft, and only one oar is used. Salmon fishermen can dart across rock-pools and shallows with ease, hopping out to lift the boats over sandbanks, boulders and tree trunks when necessary.

Holidaymakers from England watched in fascination, as the pistol cracked and the boatmen charged forward, stabbing the water in front of them again and again, their heads down, teeth clenched and eyes popping. Three abreast, they buffaloed through the water, leaning over the bows like furious figureheads as the oars plunged up and down. Roars of triumph greeted the winner. I made my way to Tough Egg Corner – as I named the stretch of bank near the starting line, where gnarled fishermen and their families sat cracking jokes in Welsh beside their boats. As race followed race, money changed hands, and bets of ten to fifteen pounds were made. These were the ribald Welsh, the ones who don't go to chapel.

Nobody I spoke to was a full-time salmon fisherman, and I doubt if such a breed exists nowadays on the Towy or the Teifi. 'I'm a sea fisherman, and the coracle fishing is only part-time,' one man told me. 'Coracles are a hobby now, as the salmon-fishing has declined so terribly.'

However, a salmon was being raffled, and ticket-sellers were walking up and down the bank. Standing apart from the crowds and flanked by her royal attendants Sharon and Beverley, Tracey Williams, the Coracle Queen, smiled elegantly at her subjects. She told me that she was thirteen years old and had been chosen at a special beauty contest. Her coronet sparkled in the sun, and she wore a patriotic sash of red, white and blue. Mandy Davies, a boyish girl in shorts and blue denim, with shark tooth earrings bought at Cardigan Market, was equally adept at swimming and coracle-racing. She seemed to win every event she entered, and did so every year, I was told. Her father was a fisherman. Races followed one another with such rapidity that the results were announced as the next event was in progress. Twelve-year-old boys and teenagers swam and steered coracles alternately. On the far bank of the river, a long greasy pole with a balloon on the end protruded from the forest and over the river. Small children in swimsuits shrieked and giggled as they tried to walk along the pole to the balloon and fell in the river instead. Everyone here could swim, but a rescue boat patrolled in case of accidents.

Coracles are not built for racing, and I preferred to watch them skim carelessly back to shore at their own speed when a race was over, rivalling the nearby swans in gracefulness. A rowing-boat overloaded with twelve teenagers hovered about on the edge of the proceedings for a while, until the diving competitions began. Then one by one the youngsters hopped into the Teifi and disappeared, to rise minutes later a long way downstreams. Sometimes the soles of their feet broke the surface during these salmon-like streaks along the river. The races lasted for nearly four hours, the halfway point marked by a ceremonial glide-past of the royal party.

One race, 'for licensed coracle fishermen only', aroused great excitement at Tough Egg Corner. 'Come on Bill! I've got a pound on him, five to one,' a bearded young man shouted. 'It's a steward's enquiry!' he exclaimed in disgust, when the race was over. However, Bill *had* won, and the crinkled notes were paid over grudgingly by a stout man with an equally crinkled face. The punter kissed the money flamboyantly, not knowing that when you kiss money, you kiss it goodbye.

'Thieving bastard,' the other man muttered.

'Note the superiority of the Cilgerran coracle,' the announcer declared. He seemed highly conscious of the difference, invisible to me, between the Teifi coracle and the lesser Towy article.

A surprise item came next.

'And now, ladies and gentlemen, we are having a dummy trawl to show you how the Teifi fishermen catch the elusive salmon. This is only a demonstration, for no salmon has ever been caught on this stretch of the river. However, if by chance they *do* catch one, it will be the prize in the raffle instead of the one we've raffled already.'

Two fishermen, one red-faced and excessively ribald, the other craggy, carried their coracles to the bank, grimacing broadly. When the announcer repeated that no salmon had ever been caught here, they began to laugh. Now, for the first time, I should see coracles used as the Ancient Britons intended them to be. Each man paddled along the river by the bank opposite his partner. One hand held the oar, the other clutched one end of a long trawl net. So between them they could sweep the Teifi. 'Here they come, slowly, painstakingly, hoping against hope,' the loudspeaker crackled melodramatically.

Suddenly there was a splash, and both boats flew like minnows towards one another. The net was raised, and there was an enormous salmon! Crowd and announcer went wild, as the men triumphantly held the great silver fish aloft by the tail. It was at least three feet long, and had died with surprising suddenness. On shore, a photographer from a local paper went into a frenzy of picture-taking, posing a small girl beside the sheepishly smiling men and their trophy.

'How much does the fish weigh?' I asked in admiration.

'Ten pounds,' one fisherman answered promptly.

The sports ended with displays of trick coracle-riding by local youngsters. Towing an empty boat, one boy could somersault from coracle to coracle and back again, and finally lift the extra boat over himself like a clam in a shell. Another balanced three empty coracles on top of each other at the back of the one he was paddling, and reached the shore untoppled.

Finally, the gleaming cups were handed out from the judges' table. There was the Alan Sambrook Memorial Cup, named after a Teifi fisherman who had recently died. The Tanganyika Cup had been named after one of 'the Brothers' who settled in Africa. Everyone was expected to have heard of the five brothers of Cilgerran, two of whom had been fishermen. Mandy Davies's family were so laden with cups that they could hardly stand.

I left the festive scene and wandered the shore until I stood directly below the looming castle. A rod, unattended, lay across a pebble bank. Then came the owner, a boy of about ten, who leaped nimbly from rock to rock from one cliff side to another. While he expertly played at ducks and drakes with flat stones, a piercing whistle came from high up in the village.

'Dinner!' I could hear his mother shout.

The boy's bearded father appeared, stepping evenly from log to boulder above the swiftly-flowing river. Without a word, he strode straight up the cliffside on a path that would have puzzled a mountain goat, and his son silently followed. I felt I had seen Ancient Britons in their prime.

Late that night, at the end of a country lane outside Cardigan, I encountered the other sort of Welshman. A brightly lit-up tent outside a water-mill throbbed with song. I slipped inside, to find a Pentecostal camp meeting in its final stages – everyone crying, their arms in the air, as a grey-haired man bellowed hymns. When it was over, a kindly Welsh farming family drove me back to town. Baptist and Methodist churches in Wales are now self-consciously conservative compared with the 'Pentes', and take care always to say 'converted' instead of 'saved'.

Next day I took a bus to the Cenarth Falls, a spot well known for coracle fishermen until protests by anglers caused them all to lose their licences in one swoop. Now, in a vast pool scooped from the rocks as if by giant spoons, one of the Cilgerran fishermen was demonstrating his skills for the benefit of holidaymakers. At least, that is what he was meant to be doing. Instead, with roars of pleasure, he had become engaged in a water fight with two teenage girls, also Cilgerran racers. The big, burly man now looking so ribald as to be positively Irish – splashed his adversaries until they were soaked. Then the girls fought it out among themselves, with oars flying, until both were upset. The fisherman recognised me and grinned, showing two yellow teeth.

'Wasn't it wonderful how they caught that salmon yesterday!' I cried.

'Aye. But I'll tell you something. No one would *dare* catch a salmon there in broad daylight with the season ended. Don't tell a soul, but it's a hoax! They do it every year, just put the salmon in the net before they start. That's how they catch the salmon at Cilgerran.'

Zig-zagging about Wales as usual, I stopped at a bed-and-breakfast house at Llangollen, a town where George Borrow had been before me. Someone pointed out the cottage where he had stayed, near the banks of the River Dee.

'The last coracle fisherman in Llangollen retired in 1940, I think it was,' Mr. Roberts, my landlord, informed me. 'I remember, you'd always see him walking with his coracle on his back. It's a funny thing about salmon. The season starts in April, and on the very day it starts the shops are full of them. Poachers have caught them and kept them on ice, you see. At one time the salmon used to leap up the weir, near the water-mill. There was a one-armed man here then, and he was an expert fisherman. He would "snatch" the salmon. We call it "snatching" here – it's not legal, mind. He had three metal prongs on the end of a line, and he would whirl them round and round and then let them strike at a salmon, and haul it in. He once took twenty-eight salmon in a day by "snatching". You know how boys used to empty horse ponds when the farmer was away, and take the fish? Well, here I've known poachers who would empty the canal for the same reason!

That night it rained heavily, and in the morning the River Dee was in a mud-brown fury. Dead trees, torn from their moorings, flew below the fine stone bridge that dominates Llangollen. White breakers, row upon row, swirled around both bridge and flotsam. 'It's the water that blows from Lake Bala comes here to Llangollen,' a fellow bridge-leaner told me.

In one of the back gardens that faced the river, I admired a tame raven in an aviary. As the sun came out, coaches pulled in and soon the shops in the pleasant little town were filled with bemused-looking Americans and Australians. The owners of the trashy souvenir shops ('Crefft') rubbed their hands and glowed with servile greed. Nevertheless, I liked Llangollen for its Victorian-picturesque holiday atmosphere.

On the far side of the bridge, at the top of a steep incline, boats on the canal glided above the town. With cheerful holiday families, I paid for a ride on a horse-drawn barge. The leisurely clip-clopping along the towpath was wonderfully soothing, and I gazed in a dream down at myriad unpoached fish, then up at young trees dappled by reflected ripples. High above the town, haunting and strange, loomed the castle of Dinas Bran. The high, broken walls, curving in all directions, like outlandish plants, clung to the top of the hill. The first sight of the castle struck me as so wild and romantic that I vowed at once to climb up to it. However, the sun had set before I began my ascent, and when I stood at last beneath a tower seemingly halted in mid-topple, night was almost upon me.

'Dinas' signifies a fortress in Welsh, and here a medieval castle had been built, as usual, upon an Iron Age foundation. When I had made a tour of the Grand-Canyonesque ruins, I noticed a man walking with a collie dog. I greeted him, expecting him to be a shepherd. Instead, he turned out to be an Arthurian scholar who lived in an old house halfway down the hill. Discoursing all the while on Gildas and the legends of the Dark Ages, he step by step guided me down the wavering track through the bracken. My 'conqueror of Everest' pride was sadly dashed when he told me that in Victorian times there had been a tea shop on top! Today's holidaymakers either climb hills one after the other, with knapsacked backs, or leave them alone altogether.

To my surprise, my companion proved to be an Irishman from a strongly Republican family in South Armagh. This recalled one of the nightmares of my Ulster trip a month before, when one of 'the boys' from South Armagh had angrily questioned me in an hotel one night. I had gone to my room and waited for a midnight knock on my door. None came, and in the morning one of the guests congratulated me on still being alive. When I told this story to the man on Dinas Bran, he shied away in genuine alarm. 'How do I know you're not from Intelligence?' he asked. How indeed?

In the morning I shook hands with my landlord and left Llangollen, with the hope that I might return. 'Two men meet sooner than two mountains,' he said.

The village of Woolpit, in Suffolk, is named after the curious man-made pits once found there. 'Wool' is thought to be a corruption of 'wolf'.

One blazing summer day, I wandered through Woolpit towards the village church. Children amused themselves on the swings and slides of the playing-field. A young farm-worker I spoke to told me that he had been shown a pit in a field, where, it was said, wolves were once trapped. Be that as it may, the wolf pits at Woolpit are supposed to have been the scene of a strange incident in the Middle Ages, at the time of Stephen's disordered reign. Two children were found, dazzled by the sunlight, in one of the pits; they were green all over, and wore clothes of the same colour. Astounded, the villagers ran and told the lord of the manor, Sir Richard de Cain, who ordered that the newcomers be cared for. Every kind of food was offered to the children, but they ignored it all until green beans were shown. These they fell on greedily, and would eat nothing else. Taken into Sir Richard's house, the children settled down, and were beginning to learn English when the boy died. After a while the girl forgot her own language, learned to speak good Suffolk and to love the sunlight, absent from her native land. As the sun's rays shone on her emerald skin, her vegetable hues faded and she became a normal pink, pretty Woolpit girl. Eventually she married, moved away and was heard of no more.

Her story, which she told long after she had been found in the pit, was as follows. She and her family had lived contentedly in a green world beneath the ground, in St Martin's land, where sky and sunlight were never seen. Farms, houses, animals and men, all green, dwelt in a green half-light. One day she and her brother were exploring some tunnels they had found when they heard enchanting music – the bells of Woolpit church. Following the happy sound along a winding passage, they emerged at last into the open air, nearly blinded by the unknown sun. Unable to find their way back, they had remained there until discovered.

After centuries had passed, in the year 1613, someone wrote the legend down, and it is now Woolpit's pride. Sir Richard de Cain really did exist, but it doesn't take a very astute student of mythology to find parallels with tales of green men, green knights and ladies in the greenwood, dryads, sprites, tree gods, and Robins Hood and Goodfellow. The Company in Green are the fairies who live underground, beneath the hill. Mary Magdalen, once as wanton as a fairy lass, is traditionally shown on stained glass windows as a Wearer of the Green.

Musing on pagan tree-worshippers, I reached Woolpit's churchyard gate, with its iron sign depicting a wolf and two children. A funeral was just ending. Everyone looked most genial, particularly the undertaker, who wore a tall shiny top hat. A horse and cart did duty as a hearse, and a young red-eyed widow suddenly brushed past me, a veil draped over her black hat. So it was in a pensive mood that I wandered around Woolpit church, admiring the wonderful pew-end carvings, mostly of grinning dogs, brimful of character. One dog held an otter in its wooden jaws, another seemed to have wings. When I looked more closely, I found that it had stolen a goose and had slung the bird across its back. The seventeenth-century version of the Green Legend hung framed upon a wall, and I noted the address of the man who had copied it out, Mr Jones of Mill House.

When I called, only Mrs Jones was at home, a helpful woman who asked me into her cosy mill home with its orchard garden. Her husband, she said, was something of a village historian, and anyone interested in the Green Children always contacted him. Why, only a few weeks ago the Earl of Clancarty had called. Under the name of Brinsley Le Poer, his lordship had written books to prove that outer space was really inner space, and that the world was hollow, filled with flying saucers steered by little green men. So the legend of the Woolpit children tied in with his theories.

'People sometimes write to us saying that they feel sure they're children of the Green Woman, as they feel as if they don't fit in to the world,' Mrs Jones continued. 'Well, it stands to reason the Green Girl would have lots of descendants by now. She settled in Lowestoft, I believe. Last week a woman called here whose husband was her own son.'

'How could that be?' I asked.

'Well, she was a middle-aged woman and her husband was a very young man. She aged in a natural way, but he stayed the same as on the day they were married. Green Children age slowly, you see. His wife said he was four hundred years old, and quite unhappy about it, convinced that the Green Woman was his great-grandmother.'

'Four hundred years old! That seems most unlikely.'

'Well, why did they say so, then?'

Any amount of good reasons, mostly involving the phases of the moon, flooded into my mind, but I held my peace.

'Another theory,' Mrs Jones continued, 'is that the Green Children were foreigners of a sickly green, pallid hue, who had fallen out of a boat somewhere. There's a Dane Hill Road not far away, so they might have been Scandinavians.'

'Do you mind! My grandmother was Danish, and she wasn't a bit green.'

When Mr Jones returned, I spent an enjoyable afternoon sitting at a wooden table beneath the apple trees and poring over his collection of books on the Green Children. The Earl of Clancarty's treatise, *UFOs from Inside the Earth*, took the form of a lurid paperback with a cover depicting space-craft buzzing in and out of hive-earth like bees. Strange how UFO fanciers take their inspiration, so often, from the mythology of imaginative medieval peasants.

Among the many wonders of Bury St Edmund's, where I was staying, I found the smallest pub in England, 'The Nutshell'. The sign showed a blue-tit hanging on a half-coconut. The barmaid told me that ninety sailors from a submarine at Ipswich had recently managed to get into the miniature bar, squashed one on top of the other. 'The Yanks are going to try for a hundred,' she said. If they reached the ceiling, they might be able to read the jokes on the matchboxes that lined it, from one corner to another.

'I work in that monstrosity over there,' a woman told me, after directing me to the monastery ruins. She pointed to an enormous sugar beet refinery, with a silo tower. 'Packing the cubes is my job. We're lucky to have work here in Bury, as the refineries in most other places nearby have closed down. This isn't a bad old place. In the old days, Mormons would come here looking for wives to take back to America.'

Still thinking about the Green Children, I remembered how travelling stand-up comedians like to add a homely flavour to their act by learning one or two names of local places and personalities to drop into their patter for an easy laugh of recognition. Wandering story tellers in times past did the same, entrancing their listeners by declaring that a traditional story in their repertoire had 'really happened, right here!' Now and again a tale would stick to a locality, to be repeated by the inhabitants for ever afterwards. The same traditional story is often stoutly held to belong to thirty or forty widely scattered places, from Cornwall to Scotland. As far as I know, this Green Legend is unique to Woolpit, near Bury. Different Green Legends are told around the world, and in parts of France our own St George's Day is known as Green George's Day. The unsainted Green George is associated with oak leaves. If I ever meet St George in the hereafter, he may have some sharp words to say to me for comparing him first to a horse and then to a tree.

'. . . Are you sure you're not going to say I'm a damsel in distress?' he might add, with withering sarcasm.

'It's funny you should say that, as the man–woman figures in old mummers' plays . . .'

'George, George!' St Peter would interrupt. 'Put him down at once! Please try and remember where you are.'

A *Sheep Fair,*
an *Alternative Eden,*
and *Pagan Relics*

In the stockbreeder's calendar, September is the month for sheep auctions, as by then the spring lambs are big and fat. Such auctions, in hill country towns, often occur weekly. The Sussex Downs, once sheep country supreme, have long been ploughed up for wheat. Barbed wire fences now divide the old sheep-runs. Yet one vast sheep auction remains – the Findon Sheep Fair. Thousands of sheep are bought and sold on that one day (the second Saturday of the month).

My favourite walk to Findon, an opulent village of great beauty, is from the town of Steyning. From there I enter Mouse Lane, a green, mossy tunnel under the trees that leads to Wiston House. A footpath skirts the mansion, then runs under a crumbling old bridge, along a tree-root jungle of high banks, and joins a track through the woods to Chanctonbury Ring. It is always cold inside the Ring, a prehistoric hill fort planted with beech trees. Followers of Wicca, a revived pagan witch cult popular among Brighton antique dealers, sometimes dance round bonfires here at midnight, in the buff. Lone walkers, 'pixie-led', often get lost around the Ring. The clump of beeches, which can be seen from miles away, *does* look very ominous.

On the day I set out for the sheep fair for the first time, the Chanctonbury beeches reminded me of a giant, hairy, black caterpillar, brooding astride the hill for a while before humping and galumphing away across the Downs. A village girl who had always lived at the foot of the Ring seemed horrified when I told her where I was going.

'I've never been there in my life – the trees are full of murderers and rapists!' she cried. Like thousands of other walkers (for the Ring lies on

143

the Southdown Way) I survived the horrors of Chanctonbury, and set off down the other side for Findon. Before me was a view of the Downs so wild, steep and wooded as to suggest an unusually verdant and haunted part of Cumberland.

From the corner of my eye I glimpsed a dark-red animal spinning round and round in a playful fashion. For some reason, I thought at first it was a colt. When I looked more closely, I saw it was a large fox with a white muzzle, entertaining a mesmerised flock of guinea-fowl who had gone wild and were living in the hedges like partridges. Before the act could reach its climax, the fox caught sight of me and loped away. At once all the grey-blue guinea-fowl began to gobble excitedly, obviously crying, 'Come back! Come back!'

To prevent such an encore, and to save the audience from themselves, I sat on a bank and looked out for the fox. Sure enough, he reappeared further up the hill, and prowled along the edge of a belt of thorn scrub. Then he vanished, and I went on my way. Halfway down the hill I came across a turkey farm, with hundreds of noisy Norfolk birds in pens, each with an expression very like an indignant Bertrand Russell. Then past some abandoned pigsties and into Findon itself.

Years before I had heard an old man say, 'When I was a lad, the field at Findon was white with sheep,' and from this I gathered that the glory of the fair had departed. To my surprise, when I reached the fair at Nepcote Green I found the field was *still* white with sheep, which were crammed into wattle pens. Flocks already sold were being driven up ramps into three-tiered stock lorries. Some of these were already moving away down narrow lanes; sometimes the upper deck had an open top, with the bleating passengers peeping over the edge.

It was a great trouble to get the sheep up the steep ramps against their will. Farmers, shepherds, helpers and girlfriends whooped and shouted at their unfortunate charges, sometimes cajoling and occasionally rugby-tackling them. The whoops and shouts came in a variety of accents, for the buyers and sellers had come from as far afield as the Welsh border. Cosy Dorset burrs contrasted with the hoarse Londonised shouts of Young Sussex ('Get up there, mush!'). Occasionally Shropshire–Welsh accents could be heard around the pens of Clun Forest sheep. The sheep were diverted into wattle channels by men holding wooden gates and by a sheared Old English sheep dog who looked like a polar bear.

On the other side of the field, the sheep about to be sold were packed into smaller pens. Apart from the Dorset Horn and Oxford Down breeds, the rams' horns had been nipped in the bud in early lambhood. Only their sheepskin purses distinguished them from the ewes.

Whenever fencing came loose, a young man with a sledge-hammer banged the posts back in.

It began to rain, so a canvas pavilion was raised over the auctioneer's throne-like chair. This gave a tournament-like effect to the fair. One ram at a time was released into a pen, with farmers crowding round, poker-faced and silent. Bids were made by grim nods, some from formidably practical-looking women in boots. '. . . And here's a Dorset Horn and he's got them on to prove it . . .'

Oxford Down rams, with their high, rocking-horse heads and proud demeanour, were the most expensive, and the cheapest were cross-bred Leicesters. Rams were knocked down at only a few pounds over their starting price. Findon Sheep Fair has been held since 1790, though Findon had a medieval fair hundreds of years earlier. Before the last war, shepherds drove their flocks down to Findon over the hills.

Still in Sussex, I called on John Bickle the pigman. Harvest was only just over at his village, and near a rather old-fashioned harvesting machine I found the man himself, with his son, gathering bundles of straw. 'I'm rethatching my pighouse,' he explained. 'Come and see how they're getting on,' Of the nineteen tiny pink piglets I had seen huddled together earlier in the year, fourteen had survived and grown strong. John scooped up some meal from a trough, added water and fed the hungry pigs, who ran to greet him with squeals of joy. 'Eat up, lads! They like that, see – curly tails mean good health. It's a barley meal mix I make myself.'

Indoors, more home-made food was served by Mrs Bickle, and I told the family about the fox I had seen.

'There was a vixen yowling away behind the house and keeping us awake,' John Bickle told me. 'I passed the word on to the warrener; he put a finger to the side of his nose and said nothing. But he got rid of her all right! That reminds me, the hunter trials are on today.'

After tea, my host let me out of the back door and pointed the way towards the Big House on the other side of the woods.

'You take the Green Lady – that's the name of the lane – and turn right at the main road. I've let you out of the back door, as you're a guest. In the front and out the back means you'll always return. In the front and out the front is reserved for tax inspectors and nosey parkers. You don't want to see *them* again.'

Although possibly the nosiest parker of them all, I was glad of the compliment. So I followed the Green Lady until I came to a glorious white mansion in a terrible state of disrepair, with battered columns and flaking cherubs. A goat was tethered to the porch. Nearby, I met little Julie Bickle who pointed out the owner of the house to me, in a loud whisper. He was a dukish-looking man, in tweeds and cap, who sat silent and alone on a log, keenly surveying the horses. Horse-girls, horse-boxes and children were everywhere, and the trials were in full swing. Horses and riders cleared gates, hedges and pairs of logs in turn as they galloped across the course. I'm not a very horsey person; on the other hand, I was delighted to find a Nissen hut full of young French partridges, running around on sawdust under bright electric lights. The warrener (or gamekeeper) knew his stuff, for I had seen no less than five wire traps for stoats and weasels along their runways in the woods.

Just outside the village of Coolham in West Sussex, I met a man who restored and sold old gypsy caravans. He and his wife seemed glad to show me round. They had a smallholding with cows, and some modern gypsy trailers to trade for wooden wagons. The trailers came complete with sinks, stoves and pantries. The old wagons were usually sold as garden summer-houses; each had a tiny bed built in crossways at the rear, a fretworked interior, and a black stove and grate. They resembled the homes of the Scottish tinkers I had met at Appleby. The caravan-restorer's cottage was as quaintly decorated as a gypsy wagon, and he had a parrot in a cage.

My success at Appleby made me resolve to walk boldly into a gypsy camp that had long interested me, set on a Sussex roadside. Here the trailer-dwellers seemed to be ruled by a very forceful middle-aged couple of pure Romany stock, who lived in a highly ornamented, horse-drawn, barrel-top wagon. Every trailer in their camp was guarded by a dog, each animal sitting in an old crate lying on its side.

Along the bushy, overgrown roadside I passed one or two 'daughters of Egypt' coming and going, so doubtless my visit was announced long before I arrived. As I approached, the chief and chieftainess came out and stared at me with fierce hostility. The latter wore a long, red silk dress and a headscarf, the former a dusty black suit with bulging pockets. Both were brown-skinned with Mongolian cheek-bones. I felt like a Victorian traveller in some uncharted land.

'What magnificent specimens!' I said to myself, eyeing the couple and feeling some of the awe with which Europeans one approached Zulus. Primitive people often exude a strong force, akin to a wild animal of great character. They can be admired as Blake admired the tiger, even as they rush at you with spears or, as in this case, with tent pegs. A tramp or madman sometimes seen in Notting Hill Gate has this quality, with his ox-driver's slouch hat, his iron-hard bare feet, his belt hung with empty Coca Cola tins and a habit of tearing at bread with hands and teeth in angry ferocity. To me he represents the terrors of the Dark Continent, and makes civilisation all the more valuable.

Meanwhile the gypsy couple stared at me almost incredulously, in growing rage that a house-dweller should have the temerity to enter their domain. With relief I noted that their dog was chained up. My glance seemed to confirm their wildest fears. I was going to steal their dog! The man shouted, 'Go near that dog and he'll eat you!' Then he broke into a run, pulling a sharpened tent peg out of his pocket as he did so, and holding it like a dagger.

I sized up the situation. Evidently it was a case of 'Feet, don't fail me now!' My instant retreat startled him, for he expected a man-to-man fight, and he stopped.

'On your way, sonny boy!' he jeered.

George Borrow, my hero would either have pulled a poisonous snake from his bosom or felled the man with a blow. Or possibly he would have done neither, but merely *claimed* that he had, writing furious appendices denouncing all critics and doubters. Cowardice is my weapon, and I use it every time; no gypsy needs to tell me that my feet are my fortune.

One bright afternoon a few years ago, a friend was driving me along a mountain road in North Wales when suddenly he stopped and told me to look. When I did so, I could scarcely believe my eyes. In the middle of a field near a line of fir trees was a thirty-foot-high Red Indian wigwam, with a smaller one a little further away. I could have been in Canada. As I ran down the slope towards the wigwam, I was baffled by the fact that it seemed to have no entrance. At last I found a flap, pulled it open and five tiny black puppies tumbled out, licking at my hand. Poking my head inside, I found another tent and inside *that*, as something of an anti-climax, were a circle of dopey-looking hippies sitting among filthy rags in a haze of cannabis smoke.

'Greetings to the Big Chief, and to his squaws and warriors, and may the buffalo herds ever prosper,' I said, tossing them some small pieces of chocolate. They scrambled for these eagerly, and as I left, seemed to be trying to smoke them.

Thus my host and I became aware of the hippies in Wales. The hippies would lurch about in drugged stupors, stealing, assaulting people and alarming the postmistress who handed them their dole. But the story has an unusual sequel, for, when finally, they were visited by mystery men in flashy cars, my friend who was on the Bench, called the police. Arrests were made, and the evidence collected was of some use to the 'Operation Julie' investigation into drugs. Later, Pembrokeshire farmers spoke of losing lambs to the hippies, who presumably stole them under the impression that this was living off the land. In North Wales, one hippie couple living rough made a herbal stew, and as they included hemlock among the ingredients, the girl died. It seemed as if Wales had to bear the brunt of the hippie exodus from the mainstream of English life. Those who could not get jobs in education, or arts council grants, simply headed for the hills in search of Utopia.

Yearning for natural man, living and loving in the Garden of Eden, is an essential part of the hippie myth. As I understand it, we cannot re-enter the Garden, for a cherub with a flaming sword stands at the gate, and our attempts to evade him only land us in Hell, Soviet Russia, Jonestown, Guyana, or the preachers' community of Llanaba, North Wales (see page 152). Most hippies deny the doctrine of original sin, and say that human shortcomings are merely conditioning, caused by 'capitalism and the nuclear family'. In their mountain retreats they hope to rear unconditioned children – which can mean children who are either neglected or stringently conditioned by their parents' ideas. Ideas which seem to run counter to human nature are forced on helpless infants, who are cut off from normal life and ordinary playfellows and forced into a caste of their own. In towns, the children of hippies – often very earnest, worthy youngsters in their early teens – seek one another out with difficulty, and can neither mix with non-hippie children nor make any sense out of a bewildering world.

Hippiedom keeps pace with the sixties and early seventies generations, some of whom are themselves trapped in a teenage cult world as they approach middle age. Teenage cults seem to be a shelter from the unknown and unnerving life of adult experience. Cult members' ignorance is never exposed because the rules preserve it. Tortuously, hippies are now trying to invent an alternative society which may turn out to be a slipshod copy of the real world they have never understood, with different tasks allocated to different people, plenty of hard work, and the recruitment of Hell's Angels as an unusually dreadful 'police force'. Eventually goods may be handed out as a reward for labour, in return for tokens with an impression of the leader's head on.

I recently went to look at one such new society in Tepee Valley, near Aberystwyth. Here the wigwam-dwellers and many others in tents, caravans and buses had set up home on a stretch of river-bank outside the normally peaceful village of Pontrhydygroes. (There is another Tepee community near Carmarthen, and the wigwams, or tepees, are made for the hippies by a commercial firm.) The Aberystwyth settlement was called into being by badly printed circulars which found their way around the hippie flats and squats of Britain. People who still had an interest in drugs were invited to a psylocobin festival to begin on 5 September, the start of the fungi season. Psylocobin mushroms (or liberty caps), when eaten raw or boiled for their essence, have an effect similar to LSD, though are probably not quite so harmful. More to the point from the hippie point of view, they are legal. A walk through a Welsh wood in autumn reveals a fairyland of toadstools and mushrooms in a great variety of shapes and colours.

Tepee people still believe in drugs as a mystic road to salvation, unlike most communards, who now regard narcotics as part of the capitalist world they reject. Evidently the authors of the 'free festival' pamphlet, one of many groups seeking to organise hippiedom, hoped to antagonise the real world by choosing a site where camping was forbidden. When the hippies arrived they found that the landowner, Alun Davies, a twenty-two-year-old carpenter, had, with council aid, dug a moat to prevent their expensive cars from getting through. After a fight with the police, the hippies and some tough motorbike boys managed to fill in the moat, using logs stolen from a local timber yard. Instead of just putting on a short festival, the hippies set up a township and stayed and stayed. For all I know, they are still there.

I walked over the hills to Pontrhydygroes from the Devil's Bridge, down by Moel Arthur and its forestry plantations, to an enchanted spot where the Ystwyth River gleamed through the trees and buzzards soared over the hills. Here I met with a police road block, set up to prevent drugs getting to the hippies. Putting on an expression of moonstruck innocence, I walked by unmolested, and then ran into a more formidable hazard – rain. Grey sweeps of rain, like giants from the *Mabinogion* marching the forested slopes, drenched me to the skin. Glared at by the neo-barbarians, I sloshed my way around the mud-filled moat and into the settlement.

Cars and soggy tents were everywhere, and near a shelter of branches a cheery fire crackled. Two young men, a bit shaggy about the ears, kindly invited me to sit there with them until the rain was over and I was dry. They came from Clacton, and like half the people there, had originally only come for a week or two. Dry at last, I set out to explore.

Eerie in the half-light – for a yellow sunset glimmered over the hills, river, tents and water-filled tyre furrows – Tepee Valley looked rather like a Victorian oil painting on a grand scale. Crows hopped along the stony grey shallows of the river, perhaps looking for mussels. The variety of vehicles (including buses) gave some hint of hippie wealth, and the variety of hippies was no less interesting. There were my old friends in their wigwam, now surrounded by fellow-members of their tribe, while in tent doorways brawny, whiskery young men watched me in amazement, for I wore a shirt, jacket and tie, and might have come from outer space for all they knew. Some of these young men still possessed the fierce arrogance of the first wave of sixties hippiedom, if a little more embittered, while other, milder souls played fondly with their children. Inside the tents, lank-haired girls drooped over pots of soup. At least my blatant lack of disguise prevented me from being mistaken for one of the 'police spies' they so often talked about. Still the object of everyone's mute stares, I stumped around Tepee Valley poking my nose into tents and tepees, and finally, to universal cheers, fell flat on my face on the slippery grass. But the cheers changed to alarm when an Alsatian dog attacked me. With rough courtesy I was then rescued, and invited by a punk-looking youth with scarlet hair to stay the night. When I explained that I preferred to hitch back to Aberystwyth, I was told that I would never get a lift.

They were wrong, for a collar and tie works wonders. Not only did the police ignore me as I passed them, but a kindly Welshman offered me a lift of his own accord. I have never met a Welsh hippie, and most Welsh fear them as real brigands, not realising that the newcomers are mostly grammar school boys at heart. It is a shame that a beautiful country like Wales has been chosen as Utopia. Why ever did the hippies defy authority with their camp? Nothing outrageous went on there: I saw no drugs, heard no music, noticed no mushrooms. Were it not for the delight of all being hippies together they might as well have gone to an ordinary camping site. This would at least have been on higher, dryer ground.

Some miles away on the Shropshire border is a commune farm whose prospectus runs as follows:

We aim at self-discipline and integrity for people of all ages within an anarchic structure. We wish for relationships between people to be free and not based on possessive couple, parent/child or other dependent relationships. Our continual hope is that we will grow into a larger group of people who care for each other and wish for total communality – a communal group marriage. Some people have interests in providing work, rest and rehabilitation for ex-prisoners and others in disadvantaged children. . . .

Abolition of the monasteries left a gap in Protestant life that the new communards may unconsciously wish to fill. At this commune, where no drugs were allowed, I was greeted in a weary off-hand way by a tortured-looking well-spoken intellectual with long grey hair. He showed me around the farm, which seemed well run, with the animals in good condition and a few unusual features, including the large tobacco crop and the smiling Spanish vet who was breeding worms. He said they were for the hens, but I think he was really keeping them for his own scientific pleasure. It was odd to see people who would have been more at home with books forcing themselves to be farmers and making heavy weather of it. They were in debt, and worried continually about money. A blackboard in one of the few heated rooms outlined the daily jobs, but left them to whoever would do them. Some individuals there looked work-worn to a shadow, hardly capable of speech — yet full of hidden passions, for feuds and love affairs simmered and there was no sign of a 'communal group marriage', whatever that may be. If only they could take the magic step into the real world, where, comparatively speaking, all is light!

This commune was in an Edwardian country house; the furniture had been acquired from jumble sales and there was a great scattering of mattresses and blankets on the floors. There were plenty of books, and a piano, and some of the rooms appeared to have been furnished as private bedsits. As nothing had been done to the fabric of the house, a glimpse of Edwardiana remained in the full-length mirrors and the green baize doors that separated the servants' quarters from the larger rooms. When the former owners, returning from Rhodesia in old age, had looked in, they had been surprised at the lack of change.

What I liked about this commune were the healthy, high-spirited children, who had toys galore and seemed unusually bright and articulate, although they had never been to school and some could not read or write a word. Contrary to the aim of most communes, these children seemed to know who their parents were. Being brought up by a clearly defined mother and father, some hippies believe, is the cause of all human ills. One mother, who lived in a room on her own, had taught her ten-year-old boy and eleven-year-old girl particularly well, and they knew more than do most state scholars.

'Our Mum's given us all these books on bird-watching, and our Dad in America sent us these model-making kits,' the boy told me. He looked like Huck Finn, with his knees poking through his ragged trousers, and an eager smile on his face as he prepared a commune newspaper. 'I want to live on a Commune when I'm grown up, so I don't have to be in a nuclear family.'

Soon two camps were made, as the boy and girl established rival papers, the *Weekly* and the *Bugle* and recruited staff who spied on one another with dramatic zeal. Grown-ups threw themselves into the game with zest, although their own contributions to the well written papers were in questionable taste. As midnight approached, after momentous discussion, the two papers merged! One hippie grew so excited that he kept the children up finishing the paper until half-past two in the morning, long after I had crawled up to my mattress. So I left this commune in an agreeable frame of mind. The farm, the intended source of wealth, could never be self-supporting – which reflects another hippie ideal, for the benefits of trade have yet to be explained to them.

Half a mile away was a delightful village that feared its hippie neighbours, although a shopkeeper conceded that they were not drug addicts. On the day of my visited there was a bring-and-buy sale on in the village hall; I also discovered a pub where beer was served not from a bar but from a back parlour, a cup of tea for the postman on the post office counter, an old lady selling papers from a cottage window; and a smile and word for everyone. On Sunday morning, churchgoers hurried from their cottages. I found the service a little too high, and someone had messed about with the Creed. All the same, here was the paradise the hippies yearned for, but they were locked within their alternative society and could not see it, except as the enemy.

Some hippies who are greatly respected by the education-conscious Welsh are the Preachers' Community, as I shall call them, of Llanaba, North Wales. 'Barry of the preachers' is a formidable local figure, a magnetic-eyed shock-haired man in his forties, with a young flock of awestruck disciples, mainly female, who parrot his ideas with passion. These ideas, to judge by his pamphlets and conversation, owe something to Gradgrind and a great deal to Hitler, for he has carried the new hippie puritanism about drugs and the virtues of hard work to terrifying extremes. As well as running an educational shop full of toys that aim to teach facts, and exclude fairy-tale charaters, Barry dabbles in computers, printing and bookbinding. His commune, on a hilltop farm overlooking the town, is unique in making a profit of £120,000 a year, or so he says. This may be because it has abolished money internally and runs on a wageless Southern plantation economy. Barry also seems to be seeking an ascendancy over all other communes, who loathe him heartily. He advertises extensively in almost every left-wing periodical, but has less than twenty adult members.

Here is an extract from his prospectus:

You will be expected, on joining to declare and to donate all your resources to the community. This is a tough community. Should the child member behave irrationally, recourse to one form of force or another is necessary. The Preachers support 'trial' by peers. Members are required to answer any non-trivial question put to them. Triviality and ritual in relationships and in conversation will be discouraged. [I was berated soundly for saying 'thank you' for a meal.] Members are discouraged from getting overweight.

I pretended I wanted to join, and was at once set to work on an infernal paper-folding machine that kept breaking down. When I suggested that I fold the paper by hand, I was given a lecture on efficiency, and when I sat down to rest I was told 'We tend not to do things like that here, we work a sixteen-hour day every day of the week.'

Here is the egregious Barry in conversation: 'We're called the preachers, but I'm the enemy of all religion. Capitalist society is basically inefficient. Hitler was a necessity, if you let society get as run down as it is today. The Welfare State has set the thick people breeding, and so the leaders will have to start a war to wipe them out. It should be a crime to protect the sick and weak. I'm the only one who can see a way out. I must take power of some sort – power over the child – it begins with children . . . What do you mean, "Is that my little girl?" We have no mummies and daddies here. That's irrelevant – the ten children here have their own school, are kept free of all fantasy and superstition, *and* they have to help with the work! Everyone here works, spending ten years with computers, and that's why our commune is a success while others fail. You agree, don't you, Melissa? She was down and out in a squat when I found her, and now, like the other girls here . . . but why are you asking me all this? Who are you? You've got a lot of confidence, barging in here. Tell me about yourself!'

This put me in a spot, as I didn't want to say I was a writer, and so could not explain myself. He swiftly concluded that was an ex-convict who hoped to live on him 'parasitically' and I wondered, stuck as I was in his hilltop farm on a dark night, how I could get back to Llanaba. For a moment I thought I might be the lone victim of a Dai-Jones-town massacre. Pity for his wan child victims, for he could clearly run rings round any NSPCC Inspector, changed to pity for myself.

'I don't mind criminals as long as they're not murderers,' one of his girlfriends remarked, and this seemed to ease the situation. He detailed this girl to drive me down the mountain, and on the way a bat intent on chasing a moth hit the car – an omen if ever I saw one. Perhaps it heralds the end of the hippie idea, the closure of the communes and freedom for Wales.

Wales is a magic country. Twice when walking in her hills I have seen Merlin, or at least the small sharp-winged falcon who bears his name. If I were a merlin, I would build my nest on Wolf's Castle, a craggy hill in Pembrokeshire. Columns of reddish rocks rise from this hilltop, pointing fingers to the sky. The rocks can be seen for miles – a touch of the Arizona badlands. From there I would fly out to the wooded Sealyham Estate, where the Edwardes family were the first to breed the famous badger-digging terriers, and here I would strike at songbirds with my talons. A small bird myself, I could live on chafer beetles in season, and fly out over the headlands and the azure bays to Porthgain. This is an eerie little village with a half-derelict harbour wall, a ruined red brick industrial castle and artificial caves. There was once a quarrying industry here, with lime kilns, boats going to and fro and the sound of workmen's shouts where now only the seagulls cry. The tiny ridge-backed row of two-room cottages, made of mud, slate and stone, have recently been bought and 'poshed up' by their former tenants (whose fixed rent had been ten bob a week).

Not being a merlin, I had to walk up the cliffside path, the wheat stubble almost reaching the edge of the precipice. A combine harvester, with two sunburnt men on board, swung around with a few feet to spare and made for home, the men talking loudly. I turned and made my way back to the village, where the vistas of headlands stretching out to sea, the caves and the ungainly harbour, began to look more homely as I descended, exchanging my merlin's-eye view for my more usual one.

Mrs Price was waiting in her car to take me back to the farm, for I had recently descended on her family once again.

'You again, Porridge?' her husband had laughed as I fended off Non at the gate. 'At least while you're here you can read some good books for a change.' Reaching among the books on guns and shooting, brought so frequently by Tom the postman, he handed me a Victorian tale of adventures among savages in the South Seas in the days of sail.

Next morning I was feeling like a few adventures of my own, so I put on a pair of Davey's gumboots and went for a walk in the woods. Two enormous brown birds with speckly breasts flew across the lane just in front of me. Buzzards! I pushed open a rickety wooden gate and walked along a narrow path between blackberry bushes, stopping to eat a berry or two as I went. White skeletons of oak trees rose from the brambles and bracken, with rows of young dark, firs behind them, and a thick beech, ash and oak wood rising up the next hill. Somewhere to my left, a mansion stared reproachfully with one window-eye peeping between the trees. I could hear the gurgle of the river. Sweeps of bare, grey–green hills made a haunted horizon. Part of the woods had been taken over by the Forestry Commission, who had poisoned the oaks and left them to die. A few conifers had been planted, and then the Commission had lost interest and the land reverted to the estate. Jungly undergrowth now rose up to my shoulders; it was alive with small fry – snails with curious patterns on their shells, six-inch slugs, and beetles and spiders of every kind. Small birds fluttered in and out of the brambles, and a beating of wings revealed the buzzards. The bare oak branches provided them with a look-out perch and a chopping-block for their prey.

Disturbed once more, they soared up, hitching a lift on an air current, wheeling and circling away over the hills like cinder-specks. Two ravens, rare in Pembrokeshire, played happily on the same current, sometimes closing their wings for a few seconds and pretending to fall. Their spirals around one another may have been the corvine equivalent of walking arm-in-arm, for they seemed a fond, teasing, flirtatious couple. Perhaps the legends of ghost-hounds in the sky had been inspired by their aerial 'barks'.

Descending into the woods, which closed over me in a green Amazonian half-light, I splashed along the muddy path, the brown waters of one of the Teifi tributaries flowing underneath me as if through a tunnel. Ahead, the path climbed among giant rhododendron branches. I ran down a mossy bank towards a shore of grey pebbles. There I found that the path I had taken was really an overgrown bridge, the stone walls hidden by undergrowth. Creepers swayed over the edge, almost touching the water. From the river, I admired the curve of the bridge. Even the bank I had scrambled down proved to be a rather damp dry-stone wall, green with moss and hart's tongue fern and crumbling away in places. With great satisfaction I waded into the copper-brown water, which pressed heavily against my gumboots. I walked slowly towards the bridge, and stood below it like a troll peering through the curtain of creepers, my den lit up by reflected ripples running up and down the walls.

Regretfully I left this enchanted place, and climbed a narrow path between tall young trees whose roots clutched firmly at the sloping bank, which was rapidly becoming a gorge. Some of the trees were dead, perhaps killed by zealous foresters, but all were swathed in moss and lichen, the greying hair of an age-old Green Lady. I was reminded first of Spanish moss in flooded Louisiana woodlands, then of Peruvian rain-forests, for the dripping branches formed homes for a variety of ferns that grew from the mossy wood. Emerging from this green ghost-forest, I came to a drier place, a grove of mature beeches. Suddenly my scalp froze, for I felt something looking at me! A cry escaped my lips, and I found myself gazing into an angry Druid face baring wooden teeth at me from the bole of the largest beech. Someone had carved a face from the living tree, the sawdust still fresh on the roots around. Angry eyes glared from below a furrowed brow, and the nose and grimacing mouth suggested primitive art at its most frightening. I placed an Irish coin in the mouth, and made a wish. Then I retraced my steps and confronted the tree again, pretending to be a scout from the Roman army, aware, as I examined their sacred grove, that the natives were hostile.

Clambering among the boulders, I admired the sheer stone wall which held back the trees growing downhill on the opposite bank. It was said locally to be a Roman wall, for the legions had camped nearby and later settled down to give such words as 'Pont' (bridge) to the Welsh language. As at Cilgerran, it was hard to tell where wild stones had been built upon tame, but every now and then the wall ended abruptly, as if to allow access to the water. Pressed by ash and beech, perhaps a section had fallen into the river, creating another waterfall in the gorge. I imagined a deer bounding down through one of these gaps, pursued by a roaring, skin-clad, bearded man holding a long spear poised for flight. Updating my imagination by centuries, I let the huntsman's horn sound gaily through the trees, as feather-hatted riders dressed in green and scarlet cantered out for the chase.

By now I had reached another bridge, almost as well hidden as the first, and I emerged by the river-bank in bright sunlight. Trout stood in mid-water, fanning their fins against the stream, and I could count their every speckle. As I walked carefully along the river-bed, the water an inch below my gumboot tops, the trout darted into crevices below the bank. A small gate opened on to the road, and I found myself near the Ebenezer Chapel. In the pub nearby, a lone farmworker with a caustic eye told me that the son of an English family living in the area had carved the Druid face while on holiday from public school. The boy must have had some acquaintance with ancient Celtic and pagan art.

Next time I took a walk through the woods, I found a silver coin in the Druid mouth, instead of my copper one. Someone else had carved a small cross into the tree above the face, to nullify the effects of the old gods. It seemed that I had played midwife to a new superstition in Old Wales.

Neo-Mods at Morecambe Every Easter, the heirs and descendants of the Mods of the 1960s attend a large rally at this Lancashire seaside resort (see p. 47) (Nigel Slater/*The Visitor*)

Hares   A carving in the church at Pennant Melangell, a tiny Welsh village, depicts St Melangell, the patron saint and protector of hares (top; see p. 161) (Tim Edye). The Christ Church and Farley Hill Beagles, however, are less kindly disposed towards hares, their quarry (centre; see p. 22) (Jim Meads); while it appears that in the Isle of Man, some still believe that the tailless Manx cat is the result of interbreeding between hares and domestic cats (left; see p. 127) (Sally Anne Thompson)

Midsummer, Stonehenge   In recent years the summer solstice at Stonehenge has attracted ever-larger numbers of visitors – druids, hippies, pop musicians and their audiences, sightseers – each intent on celebrating the event in their own way (see p. 95). In 1985 all such activities were prevented by the police, on the grounds that the pop festival and its crowds, the tepee village (above), and the intense activity among the stones themselves (below) were causing irreparable damage to this ancient and important site (Homer Sykes)

Appleby Horse Fair   Each year in June, thousands of gypsies come to Appleby in Westmorland for the horse fair (see p. 76). Dealers and owners wash and sometimes race their animals in the river (Homer Sykes)

Coracle Racing (opposite above)   In August each year, these primitive portable boats are raced on the River Teifi in Wales (Teifi Studios)

Up Helly-Aa (opposite below)   A replica of a Viking longship is dragged through the streets of Lerwick in the Shetland Islands, and then burnt, as a reminder of Viking invasions in the distant past (Homer Sykes)

Lewes, Guy Fawkes' Night   Since 1853 activities on 5 November in the
Sussex town have been controlled by bonfire societies. The Cliffe Society
always parades, then burns, an effigy of Pope Paul V, the pope at the time
of the Protestant martyrdoms in Lewes (see p. 175) *(Sussex Express)*

Horn Dancing Six horn carriers and a group of other folk characters, including a hobby horse, perform this dance to the accompaniment of accordion and triangle through the streets of Abbots Bromley, Staffordshire, on the first Sunday after 4 September (Homer Sykes)

A 'Mari Lwyd' Horse This horse, its head made from a horse's skull, is the only known Mari Lwyd left in public hands, though it no longer appears in the streets of its native Welsh town at Christmas (see p. 189) (Homer Sykes)

Tar-Barrel parade, Allendale, Northumberland The participants, 'guisers', run with burning barrels on their heads to a bonfire, which they light at midnight on New Year's Eve (Homer Sykes)

Along narrow lanes with steep banks, through a gentle countryside of cattle pastures and hedges, the bus had made its way from the main road near the Prices' farm to the cathedral city of St David's. Now I stood for a moment by the medieval gateway on the hilltop and gazed down at the great cathedral below, with jackdaws on its roof. As St David's is the smallest city in Britain, I soon left the last of the houses behind and walked along a narrow road through windswept fields to St Non's Well.

St Non, who gave her name to the absurd pug-nosed Labrador at the Prices' farm, was St David's mother. She came from Ireland, the land of saints, and gave birth to young David in this lonely place, denied shelter by the unfeeling pagans of the sixth century. A flash of lightning hit the spot where she had rested after her labour, and water bubbled out of the ground. Beside this holy well she had a chapel built, which can be seen to this day,

A signpost by the road showed the path to the well, where a modern Catholic shrine had been built, with steps down to a whitewashed grotto. There a simple, blue-clad figure of the Virgin stood in the shadows behind a clear pool, with a few coins as offerings, and some dead flowers in a faded garland. A retreat, for prayers and meditation, had been built nearby, and this must have played some part in the shrine's resurrection. I made a wish with an easier conscience this time, and before long a small, eager boy hopped excitedly along, followed by a heavy grandfather.

'Are you going to have a wish?' I asked him, and explained about the well.

'Is it really true?' he squeaked and ran to his grandfather to ask for a penny. However, the old man must have been Chapel, for he drew in his breath with shock when he saw Our Lady. 'We'll have no pagan customs in Holy Wales!' he announced firmly, and steered the boy away. Perhaps St Non had taken over from a goddess. The pagan survivals in Christianity do not disprove our religion, but merely show how old it is, drawing on many good things that went before.

Across the field from the holy well, the walls of St Non's Chapel stood humbly, the roof and door now vanished. All around it stood the faintly menacing stones of a Bronze Age circle. The western rim of the circle almost perched on the edge of the steep cliff where Wales ended and the dark-blue sea began. Here the air seemed so charged with Celtic magic that it almost crackled. A line of brown cliffs grew closer with every dip of the path that wound its way between tall bracken around St Non's Bay. Between grazing cattle I retraced my steps to the chapel, and saw, carved on a bare inner wall, a cross inside a circle. The person who carved that must have had the chapel itself in mind, for there was the Christian sign inside the pagan one.

Across the road yet another chapel could be seen, for the Catholics of the retreat had built a delightful miniature church on the same plan as that of St Non, to whom it was dedicated. Stained glass and decoration in the William Morris style replaced the bare broken walls across the way. St David and his mother would have been pleased, and perhaps they have told the retreaters so in dreams, for the long, gaunt, grey stone building overlooks the church and the waves beyond.

By an irony of fate, some modern-minded people would be more inclined to venerate the standing stones than the saints. Stone-worshippers often seem impelled to write 'teenage fiction', a category dreamed up by publishers and librarians. Real-life young people read both children's and adults' books, one kind overlapping the other. As every public library now has a 'teenage' shelf full of unread stories about stone circles and horned dancers, the authors can make a good living from municipal sales alone.

Another day I walked through twisting lanes from St David's to St Martin's Point, a lifeboat station in a lonely cove. One of the mothers of the two families already waiting there explained that if as many as ten people arrived, the lifeboatmen would take us out in a pleasure boat to see the seals. After a while another family drove up, and so we put to sea.

As we neared Ramsey Island the boat began to heave alarmingly, and we seemed to be climbing a jagged wall of water, a strong 'chase' or current to be surmounted. Seagulls, cormorants and guillemots were everywhere, but it was rather late in the year for puffins and razorbills. This was the season for seals, though, and soon I saw a great, whiskery animal, portly yet streamlined, charge through the wavelets. Its smooth grey fur was dappled with black, and its face wore a purposeful expression. A few more seals were in the water, but most lay on the stony beaches of the craggy island, and looked up to see us go by. Brown, half-fledged cormorants scrambled up rock buttresses patterned with orange lichen, their flat feet flapping and their flightless wings outspread. As we rounded a corner we came across a beach of half-grown seals, dark as sea-lions, who seemed wildly excited to see us. They flapped and rollocked down the slope, necks craning, eager to see what was going on.

That night, as I did justice to Mrs Price's delicious supper, I described what I had seen. Ted, Yvonne and Sharon were there, as well as Rosie and Tim, so I had a large audience.

'Did you see any of the little fluffy white baby seals?' asked Yvonne 'This is the time of year they have them.'

I had not, so Ted promised to take me to a seal beach.

Next day we set out in his old car, along with Yvonne and Sharon. The road climbed between sand dunes and soon revealed waves sparkling below a craggy shore. A strip of land, almost a causeway, led to a steep, rocky island. Here the seals lived, so we set out in single file to find them. Our first find was an elderly couple. Amateur archaeologists, they told us we were on a 'promontory fort' and that the remains of Iron Age huts had been found near the causeway. A wall had once existed, still visible in places, and the inhabitants had apparently driven their cattle on to the island when enemies approached, then barricaded themselves in, armed with spears, in readiness to sell their lives dearly. The couple were interested to hear about the seals, and here Ted came into his own and was soon talking about animals and birds with a poacher's expertise, impressing them no end.

Although he was a bit of a con-man, Ted knew his stuff, and soon we had clambered on to the island and were making our way to the sheer cliff edge. Far below, a few yards out to sea, a large grey seal was swimming round and round. We watched for a while and then noticed that what looked like a white duck seemed to be floating listlessly to and fro, sometimes gleaming with luminous green as ripples passed over it, then turning white once more. The seal seemed very solicitous about it.

'Ah, it's a dead baby one,' Yvonne whispered.

As yet the white shape had stayed just below the water, but now we saw the mother seal take it in her mouth, carry it to the surface and then down again. Suddenly it gave a kick with its flippers, a wriggle of joy, and began to glide round and round, exploring its new domain. Its mother had just taught it to swim! I had not realised the length of time a seal can stay under water, for the pup must have been drifting with the tide until it found out how to use its flippers. Now nothing could hold it, and it became a diving duck, instead of a dead duck – plunging, circling, zig-zagging and poking its head above the waves and then among the weeds on the bottom. Always its mother was at its side. Until that day, I had always supposed that seals never ventured into the water until they had lost their fluffy white baby coat.

Ted signalled to us to follow him, and we climbed a few yards over loose boulders until we were looking down over the other side of the island fort. Here a ridiculous sight met out eyes. A fat adolescent seal calf, in its grown-up costume of pale stomach fur and dark, mottled back fur, shuffled to and fro at the surf's edge, afraid to go in. A few yards out to sea, its mother's head bobbed invitingly; and she was clearly saying, 'Come in, the water's lovely!'

Now and again the panicky calf nearly decided to go in, but then a big wave would come along and he'd gallop up the beach again. His poor devoted mother looked more pleading than ever, but it was no use. Eventually we turned back to the first seal family, and found them snuggling together on the beach. Now that his fur was dry, the brave little white seal had acquired a yellowy tinge. Against our collective advice, the male archaeologist climbed precariously down a path that led to the shore, to take a photograph of the two seals. Both stayed where they were, the mother rearing her head and gaping at him with a mouth full of pointed teeth. He took his photograph and climbed safely back.

That night, with many a 'Well I never!' from Mrs Price, we told of our adventures. I expected Mr Price to tell one of his sea stories, but instead he fingered his grey beard, filled his pipe and told Sharon a yarn he had heard as a boy in a village just outside Merthyr.

'At one time there was an old hunchbacked, crippled peddler selling goods from a tray, village to village. How he had become a cripple was like this. As a young man he took a shortcut over the hills one day, when he found the entrance to a cave. Inside, he found his way barred by a large gong hanging from the ceiling. Behind it he saw a room where knights in armour, each with a sword sheathed by his side, lay on the ground, against the walls, fast asleep. They must have been there for hundreds of years. In the middle of the floor, surrounded by knights, he saw a great, glittering pile of gold and silver, rubies and emeralds! So the peddler edged carefully past the gong and filled his pockets. Then he flattened himself against the wall and squeezed back So he escaped with a lot of gold and jewels!

'The first thing he did was, he set himself up as a squire, with a big house and land. Then every night he held parties, with drinking and feasting and carrying on. After two years, his money was all spent. So back he went to the cave in the hill for more. But this time, he had a swag-belly on him from eating and drinking. He just squeezed past the gong on the way in, but on the way out, with his pockets full of loot, he brushed against it and it went 'boi-oing!' All the knights got up and pulled out their swords! One of them grabbed the peddler by the scruff of his neck, and they all took turns beating him with the flat of their swords. Then they kicked him out, penniless, a crippled hunchback to the end of his days. That shows what happens to those who are greedy.'

Dark Age Legends, and their Survival in Wales

Did you know that there is a patron saint of hares? Her name is St Melangell, known to her friends at Monacella. The friends she had were few in seventh-century Ireland when, as Princess Melangell, she fled her father's court, anxious to avoid an arranged marriage. She wished only to praise God, and made a vow of celibacy. Such vows were infuriating to parents in the Dark Ages, who saw them as straightforward rebelliousness. Melangell crossed the sea and hid from her outraged father, King Iowchel, in the most out-of-the-way place she could find – the farthest corner of a long, wild, dead-end Welsh valley. Hemmed in by mountains, she lived in an oak grove, praying by day and by night. Her only companions were the hares, which hopped around her, growing tame enough to be stroked and fondled by the beautiful young stranger. Rabbits, latter-day pilgrims to Wales, had not yet been introduced by the Normans.

One day in the year 604, Brochwell Ysgythrog, Prince of Powys, was out hunting in a seldom-visited tract of his domain. With horse and hounds and hunting-horn, he galloped through the wet, mossy forests and soon started a hare. Off went the hounds, with the hare bounding ahead of them, until the whole party burst into a clearing. There, before the astonished eyes of Brochwel, knelt a young lady in flowing garments, eyes downcast as she murmured her devotions. With a final leap, the exhausted hare sprang into a fold of Melangell's gown and huddled there, its ears folded along its back. Seeing this, and realising that they were on holy ground, the hounds recoiled whining, their tails between their legs. When Brochwel blew his horn, no sound came. Amazed, he alighted and asked the girl to tell her story.

So impressed was the prince that he granted Melangell the right to remain there, and asked her to found an abbey on the spot. She stayed in the valley until her death, thirty-seven years later, presiding over a community of nuns and over the creation of farmlands in the wilderness. Civilisation, in this beneficent form, did little harm to the hares, who were regarded as sacred to Melangell and were left untouched by the peasantry. As late as the eighteenth century, hares in this valley were known as Melangell's lambs. By then, the tiny village of Pennant Melangell had been built, dominated by its medieval church. If any stranger, unaware of the legend, unleashed his dogs on a hare, the horrified villagers would chant a prayer in Welsh: 'Duw a Melangell a'th gadwo!' ('God and Melangell preserve thee!'). With allies such as these, the hare would invariably escape, and justice would be done to Melangell.

Having long ago decided that the hare and the rabbit were my totem animals, I made a vow of my own to vist Pennant Melangell and pay homage to the saint. On a cold, windy October morning I set out from Bala, about sixteen miles away and struck up into the hills. Below me, Lake Bala shone like unpolished steel. A herd of grey cows and calves were being driven along the waterside path by a van, a sheepdog and a jaunty youth with a stick. A little higher up, the curved banks of the Dee came into view, vanishing here and there beneath flooded fields as the wind whipped water from the lake and overloaded the river. A little further still, upon high, open, bracken-covered ridges, I battled against columns of rain and hail advancing one behind the other, to my own and the local sheep's dismay. Gratefully I accepted a lift from a passing dormobile, then dried myself out in front of the fire at the Llangynog New Inn, where I dined royally on venison. At a cottage near the post office, I obtained the Pennant Melangell church key. This enormous iron key made quite a bulge in my plastic bag.

A long, twisty lane set off into the lost valley towards Melangell's resting place, and I set off after it. Beech hedges, carefully laid and hand-trimmed, bounded my path. Occasionally I had to wade through icy waters, when the lane mistook itself for a brook. 'Pennant' is supposed to mean 'head of the stream' in Welsh, not 'bed of the stream'! Fields and sessile oak gave way on either side to dark, grotesque mountains, rearing up like gigantic boulders and barring out the world. After some time I reached the village, which consisted of two cottages and a long, low church. Other dwellings had been pulled down when the farming population left to make way for

English weekenders. Few services were held in the old church now. Oil lamps hung from the ceiling, and there was even an oil lamp chandelier. Outside, the valley ended abruptly in a mountain wall with a white waterfall cascading over the top. I saw no hares, but game is still protected here, for cock pheasants ran about like chickens. A snow-white pheasant, seen against dramatic rocks and storm-twisted trees, made a pleasing picture.

Dusk was drawing on, and as I searched among the oak-wood carving in the church for the figure of a hare, two more visitors arrived – Cedric and Joyce. Cedric, a gentle, white-haired man, proved to be a vicar from Norfolk, who had been loaned a weekend cottage at Llangynog. With a gasp of joy he found a Book of Common Prayer in Welsh, with 'Ein Tad' instead of 'Our Father', out of which fluttered an ink drawing of hounds pursuing a hare. Together we discovered two stone figures, a knight with a shield and his lady by his side. A large tusk-like bone was laid across them, which Cedric said was a clavicle. It was labelled 'Giant's Bone'. There were faded paintings on the walls, and a rather forbidding Ten Commandments. Then we went outside and made our way to Melangell's shrine, a separate room, musty and cold, built on to one end of the church. Here a white stone tomb, carved with Celtic patterns, hid the dust of the Irish princess. Somewhere in the dank woods outside was the rocky ledge where the saint used to sleep – a hardier soul than I. Cedric and Joyce proved a happy encounter, and soon I was tucking into a toasted teacake in their fary-tale cottage, where Joyce was teaching herself to use a spinning wheel. Later they drove me back to the White Lion Hotel at Bala, where a doughtier traveller, George Borrow, had once stayed.

My infatuation, and identification, with hares and rabbits began when my mother read me the *Brer Rabbit* stories of Uncle Remus, when I was very small. She followed up this success with *Kalulu the Hare* stories collected in Northern Rhodesia by a noble-hearted district officer, Frank Worthington. When the Walt Disney film *Song of the South* came out, I became a total and ecstatic devotee. At one moment, Uncle Remus is talking to a little boy in a dull 'real film'. Then all at once, with a cry of 'Zippety doodah!' he steps into a brightly coloured heavenly cartoon world, where Brer Rabbit bounces towards him along a criss-cross fence beside a red dirt road alive with Southern animals. Miraculously, the rabbit's feet exactly fit the tops of the wooden posts. The film changed my life, drew my allegiance from Russia to the American South, and made me, at the age of six, see myself as a timid, helpless animal in a predatory world, able to succeed only by my wits and my sense of mischief. I hoped one day to see a pioneer-style fence like the one in the film, and practised jumping until that day should come.

Until I was about twelve years old I could not abide to see cruelty in a cartoon, and so had to be taken from any news-theatre that featured non-Disney films. My favourite Disney cartoonist, Jack Hannah, devised a pair of chipmunks who became my Brer Rabbit substitutes in between showings of *Song of the South*. Finally, when I was able to watch Warner Brother cartoons on my own, I discovered the incomparable Bugs Bunny, a hare at his suavest and most successful when produced by Chuck Jones. A new, adult phase of my life had begun.

These reminiscences from the Golden Age of news-theatres, which ended twenty years ago, seem a good occasion on which to speculate on the March hare, whose antics may have inspired belief in a god of craziness. With the natives of Southern Africa, the Celts and Saxons may have been able to perceive the figure of a hare in the shadows of the full moon – another link with madness. A jester's cap and bells may have begun as a hare-skin 'mad-cap', complete with ears, the badge of a holy fool or zany entertainer. Witches were once supposed to take the form of hares, and as late as the 1930s, a Cornish landlady threw out two startled holidaymakers who had told her of meeting a wild hare that sat on top of a stone wall and allowed itself to be stroked. Evidently they had been dealing with the devil!

Someone else who had dealings with the devil was the mother of Merlin the magician. According to Welsh legend, a Carmarthenshire lass dreamed of a midnight visit from a demon, and gave birth to a flesh-and-blood child nine months afterwards. A precocious boy, young Merlin was taunted by his playfellows for having no earthly father. One day these taunts were overheard by the soldiers of King Vortigern, who seized Merlin and took him to the top of a hill near Beddgelert, North Wales. Vortigern had survived the treachery of Hengist and Horsa and their Saxon hordes on the Night of the Long Knives. A footling, vacillating monarch, he had retreated with his fellow-Briton to wild Wales. There he decided to build a lookout tower on a hill that is now called Dinas Emrys. It was an ideal spot, for far below, the River Glaslyn broadened into a lake, and the Saxon war vessels might be seen from a distance. Dense oak forests no doubt made a tower essential, but to the Celtic Ethelred's dismay it kept falling over!

Vortigern had been shocked when he learned that the Saxons (or English) were pagans. But now he too had recourse to the old gods, and summoned local magicians who seem to have been Druids, although Britons (or Welsh) were nominally Christian. At all events, the solution the wise men offered was very druidical, for they all declared that a human sacrifice must be made in the tower's foundations. Just such an ancient sacrifice came to light at Chanctonbury Ring in Sussex. However, the tower at Dinas Emrys demanded the blood of a boy with no earthly father – hence young Merlin's presence there.

With the irritating precocity of any twelve-year-old know-all, Merlin calmly declared that the tower could not stand because it was built on top of an underground spring. While Vortigern's men dug the hill up to see if the boy was right, Merlin prophesied mightily, telling of events past and future with all the flamboyance of Taliesin and other prophet-bards. Alarmed, Vortigern ordered the lad to be released.

When a bubbling pool of water was revealed, Merlin urged everyone to stare into it and see a vision. The red dragon of Wales was fighting the white dragon of England, and finally chased it back over the border. In some versions of the tale the red dragon was helped, when all seemed lost, by an ally in the form of a bear. The bear, named 'Arth' in Welsh (perhaps after its cry), was a symbol of Arthur, the Once and Future King. Identification with a half-forgotten bear-god may have helped to change the king's name from the original Arturius. King Arthur, if he existed, would have worn Roman armour. He appears in old chronicles as 'the Bear', though in a confusion with the Celtic god Bran, he can also be symbolised by a raven. Merlin, at all events, remained adviser to King Vortigern, then to Uther Pendragon, and finally, when white-bearded, to King Arthur himself.

In the earliest version of this story, the boy magician is not Merlin, but Ambrose, or Emrys. That crafty Welsh historian Geoffrey de Monmouth altered legends at will, in his attempt to build up an Arthurian saga. He put Merlin into the tale, where the wizard has been ever since. Arthur may never have lived, outside the realm of imagination, but Vortigern was a real person who reigned in the fifth century. The legend must be partly true, for signs of Dark Age building work can still be seen on top of Dinas Emrys, or Fortress Ambrose.

It was another cold autumn day when I set out from Beddgelert to have a look at Dinas Emrys. I found the river easily enough, and followed it a little way out of town. Soon I came to a bridge that was being mended with great energy by a cheerful group of men, one of whom wore a slouch hat and bushy grey sidewhiskers. A foxy-faced individual, he was busily filling a bucket from the river, carrying the water to the cement mixer, and then going back for more. Every time he filled the bucket, he jumped out on to some boulders in mid-stream, and swept the water up with a histrionic gesture. All the men nodded 'Good afternoon' to me, and I asked if they knew of Dinas Emrys, 'where a king built a tower in the olden days'.

'Aye, keep on along the river, ya? When you reach another bridge, you'll see Dinas Emrys overhanging the road. There were some scholars there not long ago, looking for treasure, I suppose.'

It began to drizzle lightly as I stood below the craggy face of the hill. A raven from Arthurian legend flapped above me. There seemed no obvious way up from the road, so I enquired at a farm, where a determined-looking woman was shovelling manure, despite the rain. I asked for permission to cross her land and climb Dinas Emrys.

'Are you a historian?' she asked.

'Sort of,' I replied dubiously, and she showed me the way with care. Like Africans, the Welsh respect education. Soon I was scrambling among mossy boulders in enchanted woods of wind-bowed oak and ash, and running through fairy dells and bowers. Dinas Emrys could be seen from the first hill I climbed, and soon I was pulling myself up its steep path by catching hold of saplings. In the middle of the wood, below the hilltop, I found myself standing in the defensive moat, a wide circle of leaf mould around the tower. Iron Age Celts were here before their Romanised descendants. Stepping carefully among the rocks I reached the summit, which protruded from the trees much, I suppose, as in Vortigern's day. Below, I could see Llyn Dinas, a great widening of the river. In Wales, a lake is a llyn, in Scotland a loch and in Ireland a lough. According to legend, a water monster once lived here. Very soon, I found evidence of Vortigern's watch-towers. On a piece of cleared land, neatly tidied up by the last party of archaeologists, was the oblong stone foundation of a tower. At once I stepped into it and revelled in Celtic mystery. The fragments of well-built wall around me dated from the twelfth century but doubtless the tower of that day was merely a rebuilding of Merlin's original design, intended once more as a Welsh lookout post against the Normans and English.

I could see tumbled among the bracken in a very damp gulley, overgrown by trees, the uncanny grey stones of the fallen towers or perhaps of the wall surrounding a pool or cistern that had stood there in the fifth and sixth centuries. When I had finished admiring this proof that legends, like towers, have some foundation, it occurred to me that my bus would leave Beddgelert in twenty minutes. In order to catch it,

166

I took the desperate measure of climbing down the rocky face of the hill to the main road below. I descended very quickly, half-sliding, crouching on my heels, catching hold of trees and shrubs and swinging to right and left. At the bottom I climbed over the wire fence on to the road and caught the white minibus back to Caernarvon. There was not a mark on my suit, collar or tie, and no one would have supposed that I hadn't spent the whole afternoon in a tea shop.

'They say that Arthur chased the Saxons over the brow of a hill near here, and he thought he'd put them to flight. But when he climbed over the hill, he found the Saxons had hidden just beneath the rim, and they sprang out and killed him.'

I heard this novel description of the death of Arthur from Captain Livingstone-Learmonth, known to his friends as Sandy. Squire, scholar, sportsman and naturalist, the Cap'n was one of the old breed, a gruffly good-humoured Scotsman from Hampshire who had long made North Wales his own. Few men knew the principality so well or loved it more dearly than Sandy, who spoke Welsh fluently and told me a new tale of Old Wales every time I called on him. As I write these lines in 1984, in an oak-panelled room with views over the Welsh hills, it is less than two weeks since I received the news of Sandy's death. Something of his appearance can be gathered from the genial waxwork of a port-drinking Edwardian colonel in the Royal Welch Fusiliers Museum at Caernarvon Castle. Sandy helped to design this museum, and the courthouse where he was chief magistrate for many years can be seen from the castle ramparts. However, harking back a year or two, I have left Sandy in mid-conversation.

'Prince Caradoc was a great scourge of the Saxons in his day, the seventh century. He made a pass at St Winifred, they tell me, and when she rejected him, he drew his sword and cut her head off! Not very gentlemanly of him. Luckily St Beuno was passing by, and he stuck Winifred's head on again, as good as new. No shortage of saints in those days. To punish Caradoc, St Beuno turned the prince into a pool of water, which overwhelmed the Saxons and drowned some of 'em. So Prince Caradoc killed Saxons to the last. Years later, the locals had to be prevented from sacrificing oxen to Beuno in pagan style.'

Sandy broke off to hit a fly, expertly, with a long-handled swatter. Carefully he put the dead insect into a bottle, later to feed it to his beloved goldfish and cross-bred rudd, who lived in a pond on the hillside overlooking the Glaslyn estuary. Then he went on to tell me some more recent gossip.

'Did you know they're shoring up the mountain again, where it overlooks the village? There was a feller here a few years back who was an atheist, never believed in God. One day he took up a loose floorboard in his house, and found a slate floor underneath. The house was older than he thought. He ripped up more floorboards and found some silver spoons tucked away. So he ran outside to have them valued, and down came the mountain in an avalanche and smashed his house to pieces. That gave him something to think about. The council tried to get the neighbours to move into caravans while the cliff was being shored up. But they wouldn't go, as they said that others would steal out of their houses. Probably would, too. The real reason was that they had no title deeds to their homes, and were afraid of losing them. Cottages had been empty and people had simply moved in.'

Our talk turned to legal matters, and he told me of a local man in Victorian days who tried to sue his neighbour. His solicitor gave him a sealed note to take to the other man's lawyer. But on the way, the man opened the letter and read, 'Here are two fat geese for the plucking. One for you and one for me.' Hastily the man dropped his case. In our day of increased humbug, solicitors would probably not be so open with each other, or with themselves. The Cap'n went on to tell me a yarn or two about a Welsh squire of a century ago, a man whose antics amused him enormously, the aptly named Love Jones Parry.

'Old Love Jones Parry used to practise the *droit de seigneur*. Whenever one of the village girls had a baby, his agent would come and tell him about it – "Mary Jones has just had a fine baby boy." Each time, old Love Jones would say "Put twenty pounds in the child's account straight away." Twenty pounds was a lot of money in those days, so the squire was wonderfully popular.

'One day he was practising the *droit de seigneur* in a hayfield with one of the local wenches, when a scyther carelessly cut his leg off. Nothing daunted, old Parry had a cork leg made, and carried on as before. Just after the Crimean War, Queen Victoria was in these parts and she happened to call at Love Jones Parry's place. Out he came to greet her on his cork leg.

"How did you lose your leg?" Victoria asked him.

"In the field, ma'am,"' he replied.

"Equerry, my sword!" Victoria cried, deeply moved. "Kneel. Now arise, Sir Love Jones Parry!" So ever after, he was Sir Love Jones Parry, his reward for strictly keeping to the truth.'

Captain Learmonth always told the truth, for was he not a descendant of True Thomas, or Thomas the Rhymer? This early Learmonth was the poet celebrated in Scotish balladry for his affair with the Queen of the Fairies. The Russian author Lermontov was merely a Russified Learmonth, and Dinah Livingstone-Learmonth, the Marxist poet of Camden Town, is also a cousin of Sandy's.

As for Sir Love Jones Parry, he is no mere legend. In Bangor Museum there is a medal struck to commemorate the victory of Sir Love Jones Parry (Con.) over the Hon. George Douglas-Pennant in their contest for the Caernarvonshire seat at the general election of 1868.

The winding River Teme divides Radnorshire from Shropshire. Offa's Dyke, the Saxon border, crosses the Teme valley at Knighton, a Welsh market town built on a steep hill. A tall clock tower stands at the head of the main street, and behind it a lane called the Narrows mounts still higher, between old whitewashed shops. Old inhabitants mourn the cobblestones of the Narrows, now replaced by tarmac down which the wild young rapscallions of Knighton whizz on their BMX bikes.

I had been told by one of the locals that the castle at Knucklas, a nearby village, was the birthplace of Queen Guinevere. So one October day, when the rowans blazed with scarlet berries, I climbed the Narrows and then took the lane up Garth Hill, high above the town, with views across the valley to the hills beyond. The eighth-century dyke, dug to hamper Welsh cattle raiders, crossed the hills just below the dense, overhanging oaks of Kinsley Wood. In the midst of this forest stood a black patch of conifers, amongst which an inspired Forestry Commission foreman had planted the letters ER in bright shrubs, to commemorate the coronation of 1953. The two letters dominated Knighton. Behind the hill, on another plantation, he had done the same thing on a larger scale, each letter seeming half a mile in height in autumnal red against coniferous blue–black.

Below the patriotic hill the river lazily looped its way between fields and hedges, nature's contrast to the straight railway line beside it. Every field had its sentinel heron. Here and there a magisterial raven stood apart from the crows. Buzzards and kestrels were common, and the hillside facing me was dotted with vivid Herefordshire cattle, red and white. Sheep were everywhere, to be sold at the 'gradings', or butchers' auctions, held in Knighton every Thursday. I reached the top of Garth Hill, marked by a radio aerial and the noisy kennels of the hunt, then trotted rapidly down the other side, between well kept hedges. The care and love given to hedges along the border is remarkable; every local tree is pressed into hedgerow service, be it oak, beech or holly. Hedge-cutting machines have not yet arrived here.

'Farmers here won't stand for too much change,' I had been told, as an explanation of the council's unusual sanity.

Now walking rapidly up the hill towards me was a vigorous old man in a cloth cap, the normal headwear in these parts. He was Ted Dugan, who had once worked for the council. His love for Radnorshire was all the greater because he had spent part of his youth among 'the South Walians', and had worked down an Aberfan coal-mine at the age of fourteen, earning half a crown a day. It was a cold, bright day, but I was glad to stand and talk to Ted and tell him how much I enjoyed the sight of the trim hedges that curved over the tops of the high banks of sunken lanes. Now and again a round hole and a trail of earth on either side of the path showed where a badger had established a right of way. Ted had been a hedger in his time, and he told me how unlucky it was to burn the mountain ash (or rowan) branches when laying a hedge.

'I'll just tell you what do 'appen, I was pleating a hedge along wi' a young feller, and he set light and began to burn the mountain ash branches! "Don't you never do that!" I warned him, but he just laughed. Next day he ran up to me white-faced! A wall had fallen down be'ind 'is garden and killed most of his chickens. "That'll teach 'e to burn the mountain ash!" I says.

'Talking of chickens, it's a most unlucky thing to own a crowing hen. Someone gave me a hen once. I put her in a shed and she began to crow! "You'd better get rid of that hen," my next-door neighbour said, but I took no notice. And by gum, the very next day a lorry trailer broke loose, rolled downhill and injured my son! That isn't no tale, that isn't! I said, "That hen's got to go".

'Now you see that farm over yur, that's near a place called Craig-y-don. On the hill there, above the Knucklas Road, there's a rock called the Devil's Chair. You can't see it from the road since the Forestry came. But I always yeard that the Devil sat in his chair at Craig-y-don and threw a great big stone to knock the steeple off the church at Beguildy. His aim fell short, and the stone stuck in the middle of a field at Beguildy, where I've seen it myself. Nobody takes it from there, they ploughs round it. Of course if that'd been an ordinary stone, the farmer would've dug it up years ago. So that must be true.'

I told Mr Dugan I was writing a book, and asked him if it was true that Queen Guinevere had spent her formative years at Knucklas Castle, where her wedding to Arthur was supposed to have taken place. He recalled that a gold torque, an arm- or neck-band, had been ploughed up near Castle Hill. Furthermore, a broken iron sword had been found in a henhouse nearby, and had been taken to the chairman of the local

170

history society. 'I never heard of King Arthur's wife staying at Knucklas Castle,' he admitted thoughtfully. 'They do say that *giants* reigned there. But don't put that in your book until you've checked the facts.'

However, if Ted Dugan said that it was so, that was good enough for me. Bidding him a grateful 'Good day', I walked smartly on my way. Guinevere, a big girl, was supposedly the daughter of Cogfran Gawr, the giant king of Knucklas Castle, so everything fitted in nicely. Perhaps the 'torque' was really her wedding ring, lost by a nervous best man on the way to the ceremony.

Crossing the lane at the foot of the Garth, I ascended the next hill and so found myself high up in a wild country where cattle grazed freely, or crouched like deer with their heads just emerging from the bracken. Then I turned down a steep lane between hedges alive with songbirds, chaffinches and yellow-hammers, and found myself looking down at Knucklas. An immense grey Victorian railway viaduct, with grim Gothic towers at each end, bestrode the valley and almost seemed a part of Castle Hill itself. Guinevere's reputed birthplace – a flat-topped hill, eerie in Iron Age mystery – was clearly visible from above. Its broken ramparts reared up to meet me as I desended the impossibly steep lane known as the Cuckoo's Nest, and stepped into the border village of Knucklas.

At the post office shop I asked about the castle, and was told that a narrow road wound its way almost to the top of the hill. So the local rabbits were surprised to see me stumping about the grassy knolls around the former hill fort, later the medieval castle of the powerful Mortimer family. A deep hollow with a jagged earthwork rim may once have been the hall where the Dark Age princess had played. It seemed hard to visualise royal luxury in this spot, and my mind turned instead to visions of grim stone walls, thatched roofs, wooden palisades and sharpened stakes in ditches. But when I looked around at the views across the valley I could see where giants or glaciers had once been, knocking the corners off mountains as they went. Clouds sailed slowly above the hills, each sweeping down only to rise again and cast long shadows over the hedge-patterned valley. Every hilltop seemed haunted by prehistoric or Dark Age man. King Caractacus is supposed to have held his court near here. Sharpened flints found in a non-flint-bearing land show that prehistoric man had here engaged in trade from the earliest of times.

Leaving Knucklas, I took a gentle, winding lane back to Knighton on the Shropshire side of the river, following the road under the hills where Old King Offa dug his dyke. Suddenly I heard a loud bellow, ending in a sawmill whine, that proved to have been uttered by a magnificent Aberdeen Angus bull with enormous horns. As we were separated by both a hedge and an electric fence, I gazed into his eyes to see if he would turn away, as animals did when stared at by Mowgli in *The Jungle Book*. Eyes like polished black buttons stared distantly through me and across the lane, where Hereford cows were grazing. So in the end, it was I who turned away. Black calves raced around the field like lambs, jumping and whisking their tails, but their father paid them no heed.

Kinsley Wood, which looms over Knighton, is a great place for tawny owls. I had heard them calling below me when walking on the hill-top at dusk, but I did not expect to see one now, when the sun's setting rays turned the greenest trees black before a glow of gold and scarlet. Yet there was a big round owl perched on a branch, being pestered by a chirping blue-tit. Eventually the owl flew away on silent wings, still pursued by the angry tit. The leaves were on the turn, and the ash trees, yellow–green, seemed spring like.

I crossed a stile by a white cottage and walked back into town by the banks of the Teme, sheep moving away as I passed. There had been heavy rain the day before, and the waters hurtled along beside me. While looking out for kingfishers, which sometimes swooped in twin flashes of blue above the current, I saw what appeared to be a fat blackbird perched importantly on a wooden post in the middle of the shallow river. The bird turned towards me, showing a brilliant white breast, and I saw it was a dipper. Then it flew up in a breeze over the hurrying waters – which no doubt bore more insects than usual – whirled round abruptly in mid-air with a fanning of wings, dived towards the river and slipped beneath the waves without a splash.

It seemed as extraordinary a thing to do as if it had been its relative the robin flying underwater. A dipper, though built like any garden bird, can hold its breath and run along the bed of a river, snatching water-beetles. It makes its nest behind waterfalls. After some time, I saw it bob to the surface and float for a while like a sea-bird, reminding me of a little auk I had known at Ilfracombe. Then it flew to the opposite bank, wings whirring a foot above the water like a guillemot.

Orange lights came on around the clock tower as I walked into Knighton.

Next morning there was an important calf auction, and farmers and stockmen walked around Knighton in caps, brown overalls called 'slops' over thick jackets and waistcoats, and tall boots. This, together with a long ash stick with a fork at the top, was the unofficial uniform of a farming man. Compared to the grim farmers of Pembrokeshire and the harassed ones I had met in Sussex, these men seemed almost uniformly genial.

A stream joins the Teme at Knighton, disappearing under the main street and emerging by the iron rungs of the cattle market. As I crossed the bridge, I saw my old friend the dipper fly out of the water to perch on a stone near the tunnel.

In the market, stocky, adolescent and rather oafish calves, Herefords and muddy-white Charolais, were tightly penned in, admired by all as their owners anxiously groomed them. One farmer and his wife were particularly busy combing tails, sponging flanks and sprinkling knob-bly calves with a watering-can. They were helped by their two eager sons of ten and twelve and a teenage daughter, all correctly clad in the farmers' uniform except for the girl's hat. This belonged on Frank Sinatra. The youngest boy, tired of trying to water them from the railings, jumped on to the tight mass of calf backs and, climbing from beast to beast, peppered them with water from a shiny pouch of the kind once used for carrying shot for a flintlock rifle. Soon they were the cleanest calves in the market.

'Oh, drat the animal!' the farmer cried, as a tail swished across his eyes.

'What language! cried his wife, shocked. 'Good thing there's no parsons yurr!'

'Sorry, Mother,' he replied.

'Blast', I learned, was a terrible swearword in the Shropshire–Wales countryside. A young man told me that stronger language had first been heard among young people ten years before, but he believed that such swearwords had not existed at all until then. Meanwhile, lads with buckets and brushes were slapping paste on the calves and sticking labels on them. The auction was soon to begin. In a pen of his own, a magnificent white Charolais bull stamped and chafed, a ring in his nose and a rope bridle around his muzzle. Everyone began to hurry into the auction barn as an old man in a cap and brown overalls vigorously rang an old handbell. He walked up and down the pens, giving an extra loud peal outside the tea-room, with its warnings of Warbles disease on the walls.

Knighton was a place of bells, and I would not have been surprised to learn that a Celtic bell cult flourished there in early Christendom. Bell-ringers practised in the parish church three nights a week, and a Town Crier rang a bell to announce important local news. This Crier,

173

who was also the Mayor, came of four generations of hereditary Crying stock, unlike other, gimmicky, Tourist Board-appointed Criers. Main attraction at the Baptist Church harvest concert had been the Clun handbell-ringers who, spurred on by their fervent conductor, had played a selection of classical airs, ending with a beautiful version of 'The Bells of Aberdovey'.

Now the farmers' jollity was replaced by tight-lipped, pop-eyed intensity, as herd after herd was driven into the ring to be sold. I climbed the ladder to the topmost wooden stand, and stood elbow to elbow with the farmers. The sale proceeded as rapidly as the bearded auctioneer could sing and the bellringer could drive the cattle in and out again. Those who got in the way of the calves had to jump up on to the railings. Galleries were packed, and the intent farmers reminded me of horse-race-goers, their livelihood a gamble. Rapping the handle of his stick to announce a sale, the auctioneer introduced the heifers and steer calves, (beef cattle sold for breeding). 'HUP two ninety-five, HUP two ninety-five, sold and away for three hundred pounds if you're done!'

That night, as I climbed up the Narrows to the chip shop in the rain, I could hear the unsold calves mooing in their pens far below. On my way back I had a look at them, packed into concrete-floored pens with no room to move and standing beneath bright lights that revealed the drizzling rain. The old bell-ringer, still in his cap and brown overalls, was tossing them bundles of greenish hay with a pitchfork. All night long, as I lay comfortably in bed, I could hear them lowing and moaning. Their unhappy sounds seemed to ring through the town like bells.

174

Guy Fawkes' Day in Lewes, and a Gypsy Funeral

'Yeh, I was arrested on November the fifth in Lewes last year, for selling balloons at the war memorial when they was holding a service. I didn't know nothing about that, I just saw a crowd of people, so I walks into them shouting "Balloons!" I tells the magistrate that, and he lets me off with a talking-to.'

The speaker was a raffish young man in a lumber-jacket and Teddy Boy haircut; the place was Brighton, home of the spivs.

'It's helium balloons I sell,' he continued, 'blown up from a cylinder, and they flies straight up. If you put the helium in your mouth, you talk just like Donald Duck. You ought to try it! We used to use hydrogen, but it blew up. There was this old man, nice feller, went out with me one day an' got blown up. Talk about laugh! He looked a proper sight, swearing away and coughing, with no eyebrows! "I went through two wars and never got blown up once till now," he says.'

Surrounded by the Sussex Downs, which press against its ancient streets like glaciers, Lewes, the county town of East Sussex, proudly dreams the year away from November to November. For although both the castle and the priory are in ruins, the spirit of the town is active and vigorous, and manifests itself in bonfire societies. Outsiders sometimes talk of firework night in Lewes, but, although there are fireworks aplenty, they are only incidental to Lewes' Glorious Fifth. On that night, the Martyrs' Memorial on a hill outside the town is lit up in brilliant colours, that no one might forget the terrible times of Queen Mary's reign when Protestants were locked up in the vaults of the Star Inn (now the Town Hall) before being burned at the stake. Seventeen martyrs perished in this manner between 1555 and 1557. The young

175

toughs of Lewes do not go to church in any numbers, but they tend to have a ribald view of the Pope. Many of them belong to the Cliffe Bonfire Society, the only one which burns the Pope of Mary's day (Paul V) in effigy.

From the train window, as I rattled from Brighton to Lewes on 5 November, I could see a bonfire on the crest of a bare Down, evoking beacon fires and the pagan rites of ancient times. For it is easy to read a pre-Christian significance into the boisterous goings-on at Lewes, whether you choose the Norse gods of the Saxons or the older deities of the Celts. Borough Bonfire Society dress up as Zulus, their blackened faces perhaps recalling older rituals. Black is the colour of fertility, and chimney-sweeps once preserved many old customs in their May Day processions. Other Lewes societies – all taken very seriously – are the Commercial Square Pioneers (Red Indians), the South Street Juveniles (Siamese), the Waterloo (Genghis Khan and his merry men) and, most interesting of all, the Cliffe, who are Vikings in horned helmets. Some might say that these are followers of Cernunnos the horned god. Most historians agree that, in spirit, Guy Fawkes' Day is simply Hallowtide put forward a few days.

Before taking my place in the High Street to watch the processions go by, I wandered alone for a while among the ruins of Lewes Priory. There, in the half-light, the old walls stood sadly in jagged lumps of masonry, and seemed to groan in sorrow. Instead of being tidied up into a Department of the Environment park and rendered meaningless, they had been fenced off and left alone, stuck there between a road and a railway line. Nettles and weeds grew from the remains of the Norman arches, and the heaps of builders' sand and tumbled stones suggested that they were still being pillaged by the town. These were living ruins, telling the tragic Reformation story better than any guidebook could do. Although I was moved by the old stones, there was something attractive about a town of vigorous Protestants (or so they appeared to be) who had values so different from today's vacuous dreams of progress, tolerance and tourism. An Orange Lodge of sorts flourishes at Lewes, linked to the Jireh Chapel, and Ian Paisley has been seen here on at least one occasion.

By eight o'clock at night the pavements of Lewes were packed with sightseers, while others hung out of windows along the High Street. That afternoon parties had taken place all over town, and much mulled wine and roast turkey had been consumed. My friends and I, mulled wine lapping about inside us, stood on the kerb, gazing expectantly up the road.

GUY FAWKES' DAY IN LEWES, A GYPSY FUNERAL

To the sound of many silver bands, the South Street Juveniles led the way, dressed in superb Siamese temple costumes, burning torches held aloft as they marched. Despite their names, which suggests a Glasgow gang, they were of all ages, and held banners with slogans such as 'We Burn to Remember'. Indian princesses, cowboys and clowns followed, as outlying villages, each with its society standard, joined in, glad to be associated with mighty Lewes. 'We Burn for Good' read Crowborough's slogan. Burning tar barrels on wheelbarrows, and flames from the oil-rag torches, lit up the ancient High Street and its narrow, compressed Tudor houses with their Georgian fronts. Abandoned torches flickered by the roadside, and marchers stooped to re-light their staves.

Here came the Borough Zulus, some with feather head-dresses six feet high, arms, legs and faces blacked up, with white tribal patterns around the eyes and mouth. One man wore a badger skull among the feathers. Throughout the year they had laboured at their costumes, and each year the plumes rose higher. Some costumes were handed down from father to son, though constantly added to, and others changed hands for considerable sums. Borough's Guy Fawkes followed, one of many – a sinister black-clad conspirator about twenty feet tall. Next came Tudors, Normans, Cavaliers and even a few white-robed Druids, including a baby Druid with an ivy garland in a push chair; then princesses in wimples, Spaniards with halberds or ruffled flamenco dresses, and living replicas of Egyptian mummy-cases. Mongol warriors in grey wolf fur and bronze helmets swaggered past, some of them women with pencilled-on moustaches. A troop of red-coated soldiers were led by a beautifully groomed white regimental goat. Rumours that the goat would be barbecued afterwards upset the tender-hearted in the crowd. A Scottish pipe band, a new arrival, brought forth enormous cheers. As the last of the two-mile procession swung by, torches aloft, the whole town followed in its wake.

Hurrying along, I glimpsed cobbled alleys, or 'twittens', between the High Street shops, and once gained a sudden view of the castle towers, flood-lit in silver against the wintry sky. Further down the hill we could see the Cliffe Bonfire Society parade, which took no part in the general procession, scorning it as a pantomime. The organisers of Cliffe are serious anti-Papists, and they have on their side all the wild boys of the town. Daredevil toughness and swagger typify Cliffe, who are named after the chalk cliff which looms over the oldest part of Lewes. It is tempting to regard the Cliffe-dwellers as the original inhabitants of the town, not far removed from the neolithic flint-miners who dug caves with pick-axes formed from the antlers of the deer they hunted. Indeed, one of the Cliffe members carried a staff with antlers on the top, though most of them were Vikings dressed in shaggy furs, armour and helmets with real horns. More run-of-the-mill Cliffe followers dressed as smugglers in striped jerseys and caps of scarlet wool. Some of their banners, showing Protestant martyrs, were in the finest Orange tradition. Most were frightening, with skulls and crossbones grinning above slogans such as 'Faithful unto Death' and 'No Popery', reminiscent of the leather jacket decorations of motorbike boys.

Cheers greeted the Pope, an effigy of a dotty old man with streaming grey hair, carried on a throne. Oblivious of his fate, he raised a plaster arm to bless the crowds. Close on his heels came a gigantic Michael Foot, grinning fatuously as his head poked out of an enormous cannon, his CND tie flapping. Behind him a thirty-foot figure in a top hat, representing the political Establishment, prepared to fire him into space. It was hard to tell if the massive, brightly-painted tableau was for or against the Labour leader, and most of the spectators seemed rather puzzled. Foot's sleepily squinting eyes, and the similarity between the top-hatted giant and John Bull, suggests that warlike Cliffe had no time for pacifists. In 1982, the year of the Falkland War, Cliffe's Galtieri dummy bore the slogan 'Never Let a Dago By'.

Young men, with many chirpy girlfriends, surged behind the Cliffe parade, and I took leave of my friends and joined the throng. Flaming crosses and 'Enemies of bonfire' – lifelike effigies of local figures who protested against Pope-burning, their heads on stakes – were particularly gruesome. (A few years ago the local Catholic priest was caricatured in this manner.)

Up a hill and through a council estate the Cliffe followers tramped in their thousands, many of them singing as they marched. Older couples, deterred by the distance and the barbaric atmosphere, turned back while they could, for the crowd bore all in its wake, and buses and cars stood immobile, trapped among the Vikings. Girls from the council houses sat on the high grass banks above the horde, swigging from bottles and chanting bawdy songs. 'Seagulls! Seagulls!' roared one gang of youths in our midst, supporters of Brighton and Hove Albion, who use a seagull emblem.

Nearly everyone seemed to know a terrace chant; two skinheads gave Hitler salutes and cried 'Seagulls!' and 'Sieg Heil!' in a blend of old barbarism and new. One or two marchers wore Nazi SS uniform with replica pistols, but this appeared to be merely fancy dress bravado. French students, many of them girls, pressed along with the rest of us.

The atmosphere remained jovial until we reached the bottle-neck entrance to a disused chalk-pit, where everyone got stuck.

Ahead, leaping flames could be seen and events of great moment appeared to be taking place beyond our reach. Ducking and wriggling, I made for a rope barrier. Ignoring the officials, I slipped under it and ran the gauntlet of fiery torches and blazing tar barrels, that at one point seemed to form a wall of flame in my path. 'Where do you think you're going!' asked a stern man in the dress of a Beer Barrel Captain. 'Get back on the other side of the rope!'

A kindly pirate raised a rope for me as I ran blindly ahead, and by great good fortune I found I had reached the centre of the rally, just below a tar barrel bonfire. A steep wooden bank separated me from a platform on which four middle-aged men dressed as bishops stood addressing the crowd. I pulled myself up towards them by clutching at young trees swaying under the weight of teenage boys perched upon their branches. No one could hear what the bishops were saying, and the crowd began to heckle them.

The whole chalk-pit was packed from rim to rim with young people. 'Burn the Pope! Burn the Pope!' they cried in unison.

'I am your Bishop,' I heard from the platform, but then the 'clergy' gave up all pretence of a sermon and themselves began to clap and roar, 'Burn the Pope!' It was a very British occasion, similar to a royal jubilee or a last night at the Proms, as no one could tell how serious or how satirical they were being. There was something frightening about the oafish hilarity of it all, yet the shouting faces seemed to glow only with cold or drink, not with evil. Few of them were tipsy, but a cider keg was being passed around to ease throats strained by the shouting. 'Save the Pope!', a small group struck up on their own. Some boys in military clothes were jeered at good-humouredly, with cries of 'You're in the Army now! You're not be'ind the plough!'

On the far rim of the quarry, in the roped-off area, I suddenly became aware of the Pope effigy, lit up on its throne. Something may have happed to it since the town parade, for it seemed to closely resemble the present Pope. Faggots were lit, and as the chanting reached its climax, the Pope went up in flames, to a roar of triumph. His Holiness proved to be stuffed with fireworks, and rockets roared over our heads as if launched by a Papist army, only to explode in stars. Golden rain, green fire and Roman candles flew from the embers, and finally the Pope exploded with a tremendous bang. Somewhere in the darkness a band played 'Rule Britannia', which seemed to solemnify the occasion for a moment. But not for long, as Michael Foot was next for the torch.

Coloured stars exploded over our heads, and through an ever-changing mist, now green, now red, Foot's silhouette stood out bravely to the end. As clouds of spark-filled smoke heralded his demise, the hidden band played a funeral rhythm on drums, quiet and ominous. Most of the youngsters seemed content to sit huddled together on the hillside, watching the fires go out, but I caught a glimpse of burning torches amongst the trees and followed the Cliffe-ites back to town – Vikings, pirates and blazing tar barrels. Somewhere near the River Ouse I lost sight of them, only to confront the torches of the South Street Juveniles marching straight towards me. Rapidly changing my allegiance, I accompanied them to a spot where the torches and tar barrels were being heaped up and soused with water, while a band played the national anthem. It was now almost midnight, but food-and drink-vendors were everywhere. An old Negro was selling chestnuts, and private parties were being held in old terraced cottages.

Later, as the clock chimed midnight, I ventured out into South Street and was surprised to see the Cliffe Bonfire Society still marching. The crowds still looked alert and happy, and were forming a ring around yet another impromptu fire. Torches, tar barrels and flaming skulls were thrown triumphantly in a heap, and to the sound of bagpipes young men leaped across the flames. Whether Norse paganism or modern daredevilry, this ritual was extremely popular. Tough young men in windcheaters held their arms outspread as they jumped, while those in pirate costume seemed to dance across, sometimes hand in hand. Finally, as the fire began to die, lines of young men charged across it. It looked very dangerous as the tongues of flame shot upwards. Everyone grinned broadly as they jumped, and held hands, swaying to the tune of Auld Lang Syne.

Just then a fire-engine appeared, to cries of 'Shame!' Now, as any folklorist could tell you, came the most interesting part of the ceremony. The hose, swiftly unreeled, clearly represented Nidhug the world serpent that coils round the roots of the great ash Yggdrasil. As such it was attacked by several burly young men, who seized it from the fireman and tried to use it for a tug of war. Ignoring him, they struggled to and fro. In the end the fireman's token cries of protest were heeded – not least because the water had now been turned on. So the Cliffe fire was quenched at last, until next year.

Everyone started for home, and I followed a group of Elizabethan ladies and gentlemen whose burning torches lit my weary way along winding streets and cobbled alleys.

We stood at the doorway of a grey Norman church in East Sussex, looking along a narrow lane that wound its way between brown autumn hedges. 'They're not coming yet,' a policeman remarked.

Apart from the two policemen, there were five of us: two churchwardens, a red-nosed vicar with a greying Beatle hairstyle, the local gypsy patroness and myself. I had been summoned to this tiny village by the patroness, a jolly middle-aged woman who had bullied the local council into going ahead with plans to open a gypsy site. She had befriended the Chapman's, a gypsy family whose head was Jobey, a patriarch in his fifties. Jobey and his wife Mary had held the purse-strings for their clan, for gypsies hand their wages to clan leaders as fast as they earn them, receiving regular pocket-money in return. Jobey it was who had become reconciled to living on an official site as a registered gypsy. He had held his tribe together for the formidable licensing ceremony insisted on by the council, and had bitten his lip and kept his temper as everyone 'signed' the document with their mark. Few travelling gypsies can read or write. Now the Chapman children would go to school, to the great excitement of their parents.

Though not an important clan by Romany standards, the family was a popular one, and had offshoots as far away as Scotland. A large attendance was expected for Jobey's funeral. Only a few weeks earlier, his two grown-up sons had driven their battered old car straight into a lorry. Gypsies had invaded the hospital afterwards, and sat in the chapel day after day waiting for news of the young men's progress. One died and the other would for ever be bedridden. A small outdoor fire had always burned on the gypsy site, but now several larger bonfires were lit, and men huddled round them night after night, talking and drinking. It was too much for Jobey, who lost interest in life and was now about to follow his son to Hastings cemetery.

While we were waiting at the church, the gypsies back at the unlovely council site, with its high prison fences of wire netting, were parading solemnly through Jobey's caravan. They were paying their respects at the open coffin.

We sat down in the empty church and stared at the stained glass window.

'I am the Resurrection and the Life!' the vicar intoned from behind us. Four men in black walked in with Jobey on their shoulders.

Behind them poured a motley throng in drab brown and grey, the blond children staring about in bright-eyed impudence. Old Mary, the widow, was held up at either side by her two able-bodied sons, one of whom would probably be taking Jobey's place as chief. Within minutes the whole church was filled. As the service continued, I studied the unusual congregation. My first impression, as they swept in behind the coffin, was that the church was being invaded by East Enders. The skinhead look has long been fashionable among gypsies, as I had noticed at Appleby. Before that, Teddy Boy hairstyles were all the rage, and are still seen among the middle-aged.. The features of the rough diamonds I saw around me suggested Canning Town, East Ham and the pubs of Mile End Road. Some of the straggle-haired women and weatherbeaten men resembled poor Irish from some forgotten Dublin rookery, and a few looked like pinch-faced Indians with black piercing eyes. Every now and then, the rule against marrying outsiders is relaxed, only to close again as a new element is absorbed. Blond children often turn dark in adulthood.

Among long-settled East Enders, in the land beyond the River Lea, it is very common to meet 'true Cockneys', who boast of a gypsy grandfather. It is now impossible to tell if gypsies are East Enders or vice versa. The fierce family-centred brashness of East Ham serves nowadays to keep coloured immigrants at bay. This insistence on 'the purity of the race' is the essence of Romany, and may have been brought to London by bare-knuckle gypsy prizefighters who settled down there. At Appleby I had heard rural gypsies speak of 'Pakis' with contempt, unaware that they themselves were probably descended from travelling Indian musicians and dancers.

'When I went down to see Mary . . .' – a strange voice broke into my reverie. At first I thought the speaker, an evangelist named Fitzsimon, was quoting a modern version of the Bible. Then I realised that he knew nearly everyone in the Chapman family by name, and was referring to the unhappy widow. He was a great improvement on the vicar, who seemed to view the mourners with some trepidation. The evangelist's lapses of grammar ('we was all greatly distressed . . .') disturbed his audience not at all. They gazed at him raptly, swelling with pleasure whenever a family name was mentioned but never losing their air of solemnity. One young man, whose bristly blond hairstyle seemed a compromise between Teddy Boy and skinhead, stared with mouth agape as he concentrated on every word.

Both the gypsy patroness and I were curious about the gypsy view of the after-life. No ancient gypsy religion appears to have survived into modern times. Fitzsimon spoke of Jobey and other Chapmans as having 'received Jesus into their lives', but I doubt if they could have done so in the usual Chapel–temperance manner and still have remained gypsies, and popular ones at that. As far as I can tell, most gypsies have the same half-ribald, half-believing attitude to Christianity as most council-estate dwellers. They go to church on family occasions and tell their children, 'Nan has gone to live with Jesus', veering between vague faith and mild scepticism. Ghost stories are often told and believed, around Romany fires, but I do not think that Heaven, Hell or reincarnation are often discussed.

'One thing about travellers, the family is very important,' the evangelist continued. 'You all want to be together as a family. That's why it's so upsetting when you lose someone. But if you follow the Christian way, no family can be disunited, for you all shall meet again in Heaven, where Jobey and the others are waiting to see you. "In My Father's house are many mansions."'

At this the congregation looked dismayed, for most of them had a horror of council bungalows, let alone heavenly manor houses.

'Of course, you don't like mansions', the preacher amended hastily. "In My Father's house are many trailers . . ."' Flattered, the audience leaned forward, serious to the last. A glamorous woman in blue appeared, the preacher's wife, and they sang 'Abide with Me' as a duet.

The coffin was carried outside again and placed in a flower-covered hearse, with the word 'Dad' written in blooms on the roof. As the coffin was driven to Hastings cemetery, a fair distance away, the mourners followed in a long line of cars. This was why the police had been called out, and officers appeared now and again along the way to see that all went well. The gypsy patroness and I followed last of all, sixty brightly coloured vehicles moving along in front of us. Most of the Chapmans were tree-loppers and drive-tarmackers, but had left their usual battered vans and lorries behind out of respect.

'Don't you think the fence around the gypsy site makes it look rather like a concentration camp?' I asked my hostess.

'Well, the Chapmans like it, as they're afraid of an invasion by Irish tinkers. That seems to be their chief fear. They had hoped there would be a telephone on the site. "Oh ma'am, suppose the Irish come in the night, how will we tell you?" Jobey asked me. You see, the council have the right to evict gypsies whenever they like, providing there is a gypsy site to send them to. But over here they were evicting them before the site was ready! When it actually *was* ready, the council told them, "No bonfires and no animals". Of course the Chapmans let out a great wail and nearly left then and there, but as I'm on the council myself, the matter was straightened out.'

The original idea behind the Caravan Site Act of 1968 might have been to make gypsies stay in one place. However, Jobey got round that by declaring that his clan would pay rent whether their trailers were there or not, so that they could travel across Kent and Sussex and still come back whenever they wanted to. Since hop-picking has been mechanised, the Chapmans have had a hard time finding work. They breed fighting cocks as a sideline, and one of the first things that Jobey asked when he moved in was where the local cock fights took place. A permanent address meant that they could now draw dole. Despite the many advantages of council sites, I regard the municipalising of gypsies with horror, and would sooner put Shelley's skylark in a cage.

We sped past the imposing towers of Battle Abbey, through countryside dotted with smaller red owers – disused oast-houses or 'kilns' as they are known in East Sussex. Hastings cemetery, laid out on a hillside, was a cold and windy spot. Taking short cuts across the lawns, the mourners swarmed down the hill to Jobey's open grave, where they formed a large circle. From afar we could hear the wails of poor Mary, as she was restrained from jumping into the deep clay pit to join her husband. Clods of earth were tossed into the pit. Someone grinned, and although most of the crowd was solemn, an expectant festival atmosphere began to take over. Several families thanked my friend for coming along, deep gratitude in their eyes. Wild-looking women told her of their tribulations when housed by the council, and how happy they had felt when they finally took to the roads again.

'I'm back on a camp site now,' a genial, grey-haired man with a protruding tooth told us. 'After being blamed for everything that went wrong, with the council round every day, I was that glad to get out from under a roof, you wouldn't believe! The only way is to be among your own kind, far from house people.' All the same, I thought I saw a regretful look steal over his amiably crumpled features. I later learned that he had blocked the street outside his house with broken cars, so perhaps his neighbours had some cause to complain.

Just then a lorry arrived, laden with wreaths and large floral images of men and women, each about two feet high, which were set around the grave. Several cat-sized flower-horses pulled ploughs; shepherds of many colours tended yellow, red and white sheep; and floral effigies of Jobey's favourite possessions were placed in a row. These included a bed, an armchair and a television set with 'Dallas' inscribed on a screen of petals. Perhaps some gypsies really *are* Egyptians, the last of the pharaohs, and expect to find their belongings waiting in the next world, the television already tuned to their favourite programme. Here may lie a valuable clue to the faith of a gypsy. 'George won't be lonely now his father's there,' one of the Chapmans remarked, for Jobey was buried together with his son.

The man with the big tooth once worked for the same farmer as I had done, years before. We knew some travellers in common, and he grew quite talkative, telling me about the nearby firm of florists who were expert in making wreaths and models to gypsy instructions. Afterwards, my hostess drove me back to her house for tea. I was delighted to find that she was a lady of the manor, living in panelled rooms, with priest holes and all the Elizabethan trimmings. Great hounds loped around me as I ate my cake. Perhaps there will be a gypsy clan named after her one day, for long ago gypsies put themselves under noble protection, taking the surnames of their patrons, such as Lovell, Berners or Stanley. To this day they *talk* like aristocrats, saying things like, 'She married a Lee from Warninghurst,' or 'He's one of the Suffolk Smiths, I believe.' Caravans mean as much as coronets where breeding and blood are concerned.

In Spain, the nobility, where they survive, are the chief patrons of gypsy flamenco musicians. Like calls to like across the social divide. Of late, the custom of caravan-burning after a death in a gypsy family has been modified to allow the widow a place to live. I was told of a funeral where the car, instead of the trailer, was to be sacrificed to the flames. Unfortunately the owner had sold it just before he died, so his relatives were apparently scouring Sussex for the car, in order to buy it and burn it.

Terry Fitzsimon, evangelist to the gypsies, lives with his wife and family in a smart trailer home, so improved as to be unpullable, behind a hedge in a lane near Norman's Bay, Pevensey. With some difficulty I trailed him to earth, and he made me very welcome. Although he looks like a gypsy, he was an ordinary baker's roundsman before he felt the divine call to preach to the Romany.

'I bought this trailer and the land it's on from the Chapman family,' he told me. 'There are quite a few Christian gypsies now. In France, the Christian gypsy movement is really booming. Nobody fears the gypsies of France any more, they're so well behaved. Some of them come over here and help me in the Lord's work. I remember, near Cambridge, some teenage boys came to stare at the gypsies we were witnessing to, and tried to break the meeting up. They set fire to our gospel tent that had been consecrated by the French gypsies. All the gypsies formed a circle and prayed to God to forgive the boys. Before they knew the Lord, they would have half-murdered those lads, I can tell you! I've seen some terrible fights in my time.'

'Gypsies burn car tyres to get the wires out, and one fight I saw started because of this. Someone accused the tyre-burner of letting the smoke spoil a caravan. The first man couldn't take that, not with his woman around, so they began to fight. Everyone on the site joined in, taking sides. There was nothing I could do. The police turned up and stood watching while the two families beat the daylights out of each other with sticks and clubs. Afterwards one or two were arrested.'

'Their lives are steeped in fortune-telling,' Fitzsimon sadly told me. 'It's not nonsense at all, it panders to the forces of evil. God forbids fortune-telling, and anyone who does it must repent before they can know the Lord. If all the gypsies could be made to stay on official sites, the task of evangelising them would be that much easier. Some of them seem to have got Catholic ideas, perhaps from Irish tinkers. They seem to expect me to produce candles or a picture of the Virgin Mary! We are experimenting with simple Christian books using Romany words. There's a few Romany words you hear cropping up in conversation: "kushti" means "good", "rokkered" means "told", "jelling" means "going" and "nixes" means "nothing".'

I had to be jelling – I mean going – so I shook hands with Terry Fitzsimon and went on my way. Although I admired him for what he was doing, and realised that a more sophisticated man might not care for such work or be so good at it, I felt a pang of regret for the gypsy missionary who never was. Arrayed in bright vestments, he would have pulled down the devil's sign, 'Council Gypsy Site', and led his flock triumphantly into a Golden Age of caravans ablaze with candles and filled with ornamental figures of the Virgin Mary and her Infant Son. Again the darkness of November would have been brightened with a light more powerful than a bonfire.

Christmas Festivities in Radnorshire

Logs burned in the fireplace, nestling comfortably in their ashes, and I too nestled, in my cozy chair in the Prices' front room in Pembrokeshire. Cawl soup and slapover pie inside me, I browsed sleepily through a bound volume of *Strand* magazines. Mr Price gravely filled his pipe for a last smoke before crossing the cobbled stableyard, where ducks and hens pecked around, to work at his beloved lathe. Everything in the room seemed to be made of wood, from the handle of the harpoon above the chimney beam to the stock of the flintlock duck gun that leaned in a corner by the Welsh dresser, its muzzle nearly touching the ceiling. The fireplace was an exception, though wooden models or pipes reposed on the many slate-lined recesses among the rough grey stones.

Outside, wind and rain whipped across the small window-panes and the trees looked bare and grim. It would soon be Christmas.

'How did I come to choose this farm?' Mr Price echoed my question.

'I started on the beach with an oar on my shoulder and walked inland until someone said, "What's that?" Then I knew I was free of the sea and could settle down. I'm pulling your leg, Porridge, that's an old sailor's yarn. I was reading the *Nautical Magazine* a few years ago, and I saw an advert for a girl's caul. That's nothing to do with soup – it means the veil of skin sometimes taken from a newborn baby's face and sold as a charm against drowning. I was surprised an officers' magazine should have an advert like that. Sailors believe a lot of funny things – it's "bad joss" to have this or the other aboard. One ship I was on had a Chinese cook. Lin Pan, his name was. He cooked sharks better than I've ever tasted before, yet many of the men wouldn't eat them in case the shark had eaten a sailor at some time.'

'I've heard that in the Royal Navy, corned beef is sometimes known as "Hannah Lane".' I interrupted. 'A girl called Hannah Lane disappeared, and later her ring was found in a tin of corned beef.'

'I can't help what those Royal Navy people eat! As for sharks, Lin Pan would have baited hooks trailing from the ship at all times, with bells on. "A shark can't die till sundown," we would say. The shark's body, lying on the deck, would have spasms every so often, even though it appeared to be dead. At Rio de Janeiro we saw enormous stingrays leaping out of the sea. That was a beautiful city! We went ashore and walked on mosaic pavements, all different colours. We found a bar and had a good time, and on the way back to the ship we saw a marvellous big door, covered in patterns, set in the wall of some rich man's garden. "Open Sesame!" I said, and lo and behold, it *did* open, automatically. That surprised us all. The men thought I could do magic, but I was as surprised as any of them.

We had a mutiny on that ship in the end, it was so wet. I remember when I signed on, I turned up at the docks in Cardiff, looking for the right ship. When I found her, she looked a queer, old-fashioned thing. "What's she like?" I asked an old feller in oilskins who was coming ashore. "Wet," he replied.

'The pump on deck had a tall handle and as we sailed, it swayed from side to side. The mate could see this all day long from the bridge, and it drove him mad! Finally he offered a ten-bob reward for anyone who could remove it. Many tried to pull the handle off, but all failed. Finally a great Neanderthal feller with a bull-neck, a man we all avoided, pulled it out with a great heave and claimed the reward. By then the mate had changed his mind, as ten bob was a lot in those days. So in a rage this fellow banged the handle in again harder than ever, and it jammed so fast they had to take it off with a crane in the end.

'Our engineer was eighty-nine years old, and we carried him on board on a stretcher. He had a ticket – that was the great thing, as we couldn't sail without a ticketed man. It wasn't legal. As we took the poor old feller to his cabin, he feebly asked if he could see the engine. So we carried him to the door and let him have a look. He stayed ill in bed for the whole voyage, and when we were home again, he asked if he could see the engine once more. Back in Cardiff, Lin Pan the cook was a deacon in a church in Bute Street, and greatly respected. On board the ship he would boast of having had a thousand women in ports all over the world. A great character!'

Thinking of Cardiff set Mr Price reminiscing about Christmas back in the valleys, among terraced streets with rows of neighbours, instead of in a rambling stone-and-oak farmhouse in the woods at the end of nowhere.

'On Christmas night, men used to go round with a horse skull on a stick,' he recalled. 'It was covered in ribbons, and when you pulled a string, its jaws would snap. Mari Lwyd, it was called. They would ask riddles at the door, and if you couldn't answer, you had to ask them in and give them all a drink. Haven't seen that for ages, mind. The last time I saw a Mari Lwyd, it was a New Year's Eve, as they varied the day from town to town.'

'I'll tell you a strange custom they have round yere!' broke in his son Davey, who had just come in from the farmyard. 'There's a face carved on a tree in the woods, and if you put a coin in its mouth or in its eyes, you can make a wish!'

Next morning I had to go. 'That's the chap who married Hannah!' Mrs Price exclaimed, meaning 'That's the ticket!', when she saw I was packed and ready. Briskly, she tied a shawl over her head and trotted to the car, an air of 'do or die' about her, born of hard work and a Christian spirit. Stooping so as to look me in the face, Mr Price emerged from he workshop door in his overalls, and extended an enormous hand.

'Goodbye, Porridge,' he said roguishly. 'I'll look forward to seeing you again, the year after next.'

'Ready?' asked Mrs Price. I climbed into the car, Davey opened the farm gate and we clattered out into the lane and towards the coach station in town. I turned and saw the two men waving and Non wagging her tail.

Thursday is market day in Knighton, Radnorshire, on the border between Wales and England. On the first Thursday in December the Christmas auction is held. Here fatstock are sold from the 'Smithfield', as all livestock markets are known in the county. All along the border with Wales, Shropshire and Herefordshire, every fair-sized town has its Smithfield. I was shown one behind a cottage on an isolated hilltop near Radnor Forest, where cattle and sheep were bought and sold by farmers who lived far from any other human settlement.

A firm of auctioneers, McCartney's give free beer and whisky to farmers who have been their regular customers. So a holiday mood grips Knighton on Christmas auction day, and the streets are full of farmers. A barrel of beer is placed on the counter of the market café, surrounded by six bottles of whisky. First come, first served is the order of the day, and some rugged old men turn up very early indeed, to wait outside as housewives do at the January sales in London.

By the time I got to Knighton the revelries had moved to The Jockey, the town's oldest and most jovial pub. Drovers, farmers and butchers packed both the bars on this occasion, for the auctioneer was inside somewhere, still treating others and himself. Harvey, the Scottish landlord, stood in the middle of the dark, almost subterranean public bar, playing reels on the bagpipes. Crowded though the place was, a circle had been cleared around him, and big, gnarled, booted men stood clapping and stamping. A girl in a red jersey squealed in mock-displeasure as a burly, slouch-hatted man grabbed her for a kiss.

Back at 'the auction fields', Clun Forest sheep stood disconsolately in their pens, a bead of blood by the hole punched in each right ear, the mark of the butcher. (Knightonians still referred to 'fields', even though modern regulations ensured that the Smithfield was now a Smith-concrete floor.) Drovers today do not herd cattle or sheep for days along green lanes. That ended with the railway age, when special market-day trains were introduced to bring the livestock to town from Llandrindod Wells. More recently came the 'giant stock lorry age' and the trains were discontinued. However, there is still a use for drovers, who are expert in driving cattle from the hills, into the lanes and up the ramps of the stock-lorries. At the market, the drovers guide the beasts to the pens and the auction ring. One well-known drover in Knighton used to be called, before the vet, to see an ailing cow.

'Don't talk to me about bells!' a Knightonian remarked to me, when I said that the town should be famous for its chimes. 'The bells were supposed to be rung during the war if there was an invasion. One night I saw a girl home from a dance, and walked back to town in the dark along the road below Kinsley. A man was walking towards me. When he reached me, I said "Good night", but there was no one there! He vanished; there was no side-road or path there, under the rock face of the wood. At that moment, all the bells rang out! I ran home and woke my parents, but they hadn't heard any bells. Nor had anyone else. It was only me. The old people knew there were strange things going on at times. There was a path by a wood where no one was supposed to go, I never learned why.'

I asked if the path had been called Green Lady, but he thought not. In Britain it is safe to ascribe almost any custom to a pagan cause, for animist religion encompasses everything possible and impossible. Every human act, in the forest pagan mind, serves a dual purpose. There is the visible, practical purpose, and the invisible one, of serving, glorifying and propitiating a god. Pagan gods can be immoral, and some resemble devils. If only we, who know the God of Love, the God whose birth is Christmas, could think about Him as often as pagan animists in African forests invoke their uncanny, invisible friends! I know of a farmer from the hills above Knighton who has a hereditary belief in the Men of the Trees, so we do not need to search as far as Africa for the beliefs of our ancestors. A yew tree stands beside many a Radnorshire farm, planted for luck, they say.

On the third Saturday in December, Father Christmas comes to Knighton. With an expectant crowd of parents, children and sightseers, I waited at the Cenotaph war memorial, near a tall unlit Christmas tree, while the Knighton Town Silver Band played a selection of carols. The band consisted of ten adults and a great many red-nosed, bobble-capped children. My three-year-old nephew ran up and down the flat top of a low wall in great excitement. Across the road, Derek Price, the Mayor and hereditary Town Crier, seemed just as anxious for Father Christmas's appearance as were the children. He wore his Crying regalia, a beadle's cocked hat, a scarlet cloak trimmed with fur, white lace sleeves, black knee-breeches and buckled shoes. Over this, his silver chain of mayoral office hung impressively. The 'Teme Spirit', members of the local drama society, added a further Dickensian touch, for they wore their *Christmas Carol* stage costumes, the ladies in gowns and bonnets.

Suddenly the Town Crier rang his bell, and Father Christmas appeared in all his whiskers from out of the carriage driveway of the Norton Arms Hotel. Holding his sack of balloons and lollipops, he sat comfortably in a trim little brown and yellow governess cart, pulled by a tiny grey donkey. Leading this animal strode Big John Thornton, an Irishman from County Meath, whose accordion-playing in The Jockey is much admired. Donkey, cart and contents stopped at the tree, and the children rushed to stroke the ears and nose of Big John's gentle pet. Father Christmas handed out his gifts, and my little nephew accepted his two lollipops in wide-eyed wonderment. Meanwhile, another group of Knighton hand-bell ringers, adults and children, launched into 'Jingle Bells' and 'Little Donkey'. They bore a placard with the ominous sign KGB, but hastened to assure me that the letters stood for nothing more dramatic than the Knighton Guild of Bell-ringers. Their bell-ringing rival, the Town Crier, then announced that the Knighton lights were about to go on. He pressed a switch, illuminating not only the Christmas tree with the big star at the top, but also the fairy lanterns strung up and down the town, across the main street and above the entrance to the Narrows. As suddenly as he appeared, Santa was gone. I asked Derek Price, the Town Crier, to tell me something of his craft.

'Our family have been Town Criers in Knighton going back two hundred years. This costume I'm wearing was made in 1961. It's an exact copy of the old robes handed down from my grandfather. They're a bit tattered and torn by now. There are only seven other Town Criers in the country, where the office has been properly handed down. Llandrindod Wells appointed a Crier for the first time, not long ago, and I was called on to pick the right candidate. I'm a builder by trade, with two sons and a daughter to carry the Crying tradition on. I'd be really pleased if my daughter became the next Town Crier in Knighton.'

I have never yet spent Christmas away from home, but this year I stayed at an old coaching inn, the Red Lion at Epworth, on 6 January. This is the date of Old Christmas Day, before the Gregorian calendar was introduced in the eighteenth century. A place apart, Epworth and the surrounding villages are neither in Lincolnshire nor Humberside, as shown on maps ancient and modern, but on the Isle of Axholme. Red-coated singers, the Boggins, serenade every pub on the Isle for the week prior to Old Christmas Day. On that day the village of Haxey holds its winter feast.

Now is the time to invoke Janus, the god of endings and beginnings. He is also the god of January, and his worshippers may turn to the beginning of this book and read on.

'No one will turn up at school today, they'll all go over to Haxey,' my landlord's son told me. The landlord, an affable sportsman with a lurcher barking in a pen behind the house, shook my hand and bade me welcome. That night I looked from my window over the cobbled market square hung with fairy-lights. A tall spruce tree in a large tub dominated the square, its lights winking on and off. Cloth-capped revellers were slowly returning to their homes from the bar downstairs and from the Polar Bear down the hill. This snug little place was all a pub should be, the public bar consisting of one long stout domino table where several games played concurrently, cloth-capped old boys crowding elbow to elbow. Women and travelling salesmen sat in leather armchairs in the saloon.

I climbed into bed and fell asleep on the night that for centuries had been Christmas. As I slept, a delightful sound intruded on my dreams. I awoke and listened with sleepy pleasure to a party taking place in the next room. Five jolly girls could be heard singing and talking. When they sang, I was at once reminded of angels. I couldn't quite recognise the carols, which seemed to be mixed with country dance songs of the seventeenth century – 'fol de rol fa lol'. One song appeared to be a version of 'Deck the Halls with Boughs of Holly.'

Leaving the mystery until the morning, I fell asleep to the sound of light feet dancing and girlish laughter.

CHRISTMAS FESTIVITIES IN RADNORSHIRE

In the morning I was the only one at breakfast, which didn't surprise me because I had forgotten all about the wonderful singing. Only as I caught the bus near Wesley's old house did I remember the night before. Had I been dreaming after all? Or had five sisters once lived at the Red Lion in the days before the calendar changed, girls who stayed up late on Christmas night for games and singing, having such a good time that Heaven itself could not prevent them from re-enacting it every year?

THE END

The Old Mansion House
Knighton
Radnorshire
Christmas 1984.

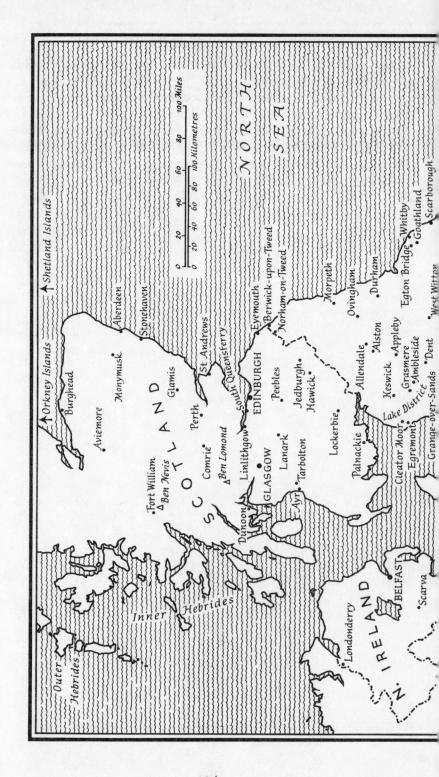

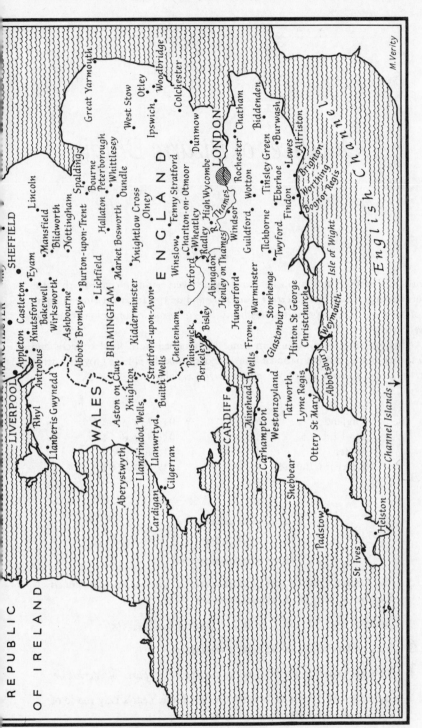

Location Map

A Gazetteer of Bizarre Britain

Whilst the author and publisher have made every effort to ensure that the information given in this gazetteer is accurate and up to date at the time of going to press, they can accept no responsibility for any errors or omissions that may have occurred.

Additional information can sometimes be obtained from local councils and newspaper offices, but the national Tourist Boards may be able to provide further details. Their London telephone numbers are as follows:

England	(01) 730 3488
Scotland	(01) 930 8661
Wales	(01) 409 0969
Northern Ireland	(01) 439 0601

JANUARY

1 Ba' Games (early form of rugby said to have been introduced by the Vikings), *Kirkwall, Orkney*

   Needle and Thread Ceremony *Queen's College, Oxford*

6 Haxey Hood Game *Haxey, Lincolnshire*

7 Plough Stots Services *Goathland and other parts of Yorkshire*

11 Burning the Clavie (a bonfire on Old New Year's Day made of casks split up) *Burghead, Morayshire*

196

12 Straw Bear Festival *Whittlesey, Cambridgeshire*

17 Wassailling Orchatds *Carhampton, Somerset*

25 Burns' Suppers *All over Scotland, especially Ayr*

29 Up Helly-Aa *Lerwick, Shetland*

FEBRUARY

2 Callants' Ba' (or Jethart Ba') *Jedburgh, Roxburghshire*

Forty Shilling Day *Wotton, Surrey*

Carlow Bread Dole *Woodbridge, Suffolk*

3 Cradle-Rocking Ceremony *Blidworth, Nottinghamshire*

4 Hurling the Silver Ball *St. Ives, Cornwall*

7 Cruft's Dog Show *Earl's Court, London*

14 Blessing the Salmon-Net Fisheries *Norham-on-Tweed*

15 St Andrew's Festival *St Andrews, Fife*

19 Pancake Race *Olney, Bucks*

Royal Shrovetide Football Match *Ashbourne, Derbyshire*

Skipping Festival *Scarborough*

MARCH

1 Whuppity Stourie (re-enacts escape of English soldiers from Wallace's men) *Lanark*

7 Maids Money Diced For (maidservants roll the die to win a sum of money) *Guildford, Surrey*

16 National Shire Horse Show *Peterborough, Cambridgeshire*

21 Spring Equinox Druid Ceremony *Parliament Hill Fields, London*

25 Tichborne Dole (a measure of flour) *Tichborne, Hampshire*

29 Edinburgh Folk Festival *Edinburgh*

31 Oranges and Lemons Ceremony (schoolchildren visit RAF church of St Clement Danes and receive orange and lemon) *St Clement Danes, London*

APRIL

5 Pace Egg Play *Upper Calder Valley, Yorkshire*

British Marble Championships *Tinsley Green, Sussex*

6 National Scooter Club Ralley (Mods) *Morecambe*

7 Hot-Air Balloon Day *Holker Hall, Cark-in-Cartmel, Grange-over-Sands*

Clipping the Church (parishioners hold hands and form a ring around church) *Radley, Oxfordshire*

8 Biddenden Dole (bread and cheese) *Biddenden, Kent*

Bottle-Kicking and Hare Pie Scramble (a scramble for pies, loaves and ale, dating from 1770) *Hallaton, Leicestershire*

Running Auction *Bourne, Lincolnshire*

Harness Horse Parade *Regent's Park, London*

9 Candle Auction (every 3rd year) *Tatworth, Somerset*

10 Northumbrian Gathering (northern games) *Morpeth, Northumberland*

16 Tuttimen Hocktide Ceremony *Hungerford, Berkshire*

20 International Clown Convention *Bognor Regis, Sussex*

21 London Marathon *Greenwich to Westminster*

23 Order of the Garter Parade *Windsor, Berkshire*

St George's Day Court, (sixteenth-century custom) *Lichfield, Staffordshire*

27 Rare Breeds Sheep Show *Otley, nr Ipswich, Suffolk*

28 The Tyburn Walk (in memory of Roman Catholic martyrs) *Old Bailey to Tyburn Court, London*

MAY

1 Singing on Magdalen Tower (6 a.m.) *Oxford*

Hobby Horse Day *Padstow, Cornwall*

Hobby Horse Day *Minehead, Somerset*

Chimney Sweeps' Procession *Rochester, Kent*

Garland Dressing Day *Charlton-on-Otmoor, Oxford*

2 Shetland Folk Festival *Shetland*

4 Knutsford Royal May Day *Cheshire*

Flower Parade *Spalding, Lincolnshire*

5 Hame Farin (for Shetland exiles) *Shetland*

6 Well-Dressing *Newborough, Burton-upon-Trent, Staffordshire*

8 Furry Dance (Celtic *feur* = festival) *Helston, Cornwall*

12 Blessing of the Water *Mudford Quay, Christchurch, Dorset*

13 Garland Day *Abbotsbury, Dorset*

15 Planting the Penny Hedge *Whitby, Yorkshire*

16 Well-Dressing *Wirksworth, Derbyshire*

19 Chatsworth Angling Fair *Bakewell, Derbyshire*

21 Lilies and Roses Ceremony *Tower of London*

Mayoral Weigh-in *High Wycombe, Bucks*

25 Canal Rally *Union Canal, Linlithgow*

26 Cheese Rolling Ceremony *Cheltenham, Gloucester*

27 Dunmow Flitch Trial (for matrimonial bliss) *Dunmow, Essex*

28 Blessing the Wells *Bisley, Gloucestershire*

29 Castleton Garland Day *Derbyshire*

Arbor Tree Day *Aston on Clun, Shropshire*

Founders Day (Chelsea Pensioners) *Royal Hospital, Chelsea, London*

29 Neville's Cross Commemoration *Durham Cathedral*

JUNE

6 Lanimer Day: Riding of the Marches *Lanark*

Common Riding *Hawick, Borders*

9 The Edinburgh Gathering *Edinburgh, Lothian*

12 Appleby Gypsy Horse Fair *Appleby, Cumbria*

15 Goose Fair *Ovingham, Northumberland*

16 Royal Highland Agricultural Show *Ingliston, Edinburgh*

Beltane Festival *Peebles*

21 St Magnus Festival *Kirkwall, Stromness*

Summer Solstice, Druids at Stonehenge (cancelled 1985)

Midsummer Climb of Ben Lomond *Dunbartonshire*

22 Drovers' Walk *Llanwrtyd, Powys*

Mock Mayor of Ock Street *Abingdon, Oxfordshire*

23 Anglo-Saxon Skirmish *West Stow, Suffolk*

24 Knollys Rose Ceremony *Mansion House, London*

Midsummer Bonfire *Tarbolton, Ayrshire*

Peace and Good Neighbourhood Dinner *Kidderminster, Worcester*

29 Mind–Body–Spirit Festival *Olympia, London*

JULY

4 Henley Royal Regatta *Henley on Thames, Oxfordshire*

5 Bawming the Thorn *Appleton Thorn, Cheshire*

5 Tynwald Ceremonies *Isle of Man*

6 'Sealed Knot' Re-enactment of Battle of Sedgemoor *Westonzoyland, Somerset*

7 Monmouth Rebellion Vintage Car Rally (follows route of the Rebellion) *Lyme Regis to Wells, Somerset*

8 Lincoln Minster Mystery Plays *Lincoln Minster, Lincoln*

11 Church of the God of Prophecy Convention *Brighton*

12 Orange Parades *Liverpool, Belfast, Glasgow*

13 Miners' Gala *Durham, and Mansfield, Nottinghamshire*

The Sham Fight *Scarva, County Down*

Festival of Childhood *Lake District*

Keswick Evangelical Convention *Keswick, Lake District*

18 Art in Action *Waterperry House, nr Wheatley, Oxfordshire*

20 Eyemouth Herring Festival *Eyemouth*

22 Royal Welsh Show *Llanelwedd, Builth Wells, Powys*

24 Miracles at Glastonbury *Glastonbury, Somerset*

Cutty Sark Tall Ships Race *Chatham, Kent*

25 Knillian Games (1986 and every 5 years) *St Ives, Cornwall*

·Jehovah's Witnesses Convention *Twickenham, London*

Horn Fair *Eberhoe, West Sussex*

27 World Flounder Tramping Championship *Palnackie, Kirkcudbright*

29 Swan Upping *River Thames, London to Henley*

AUGUST

---

1 Doggett's Coat and Badge Race *London*

Scottish National Sheep Dog Trials *Monymusk, Aberdeenshire*

3 Royal National Eisteddfod of Wales *Rhyl, Clwyd*

4 National Raft Race *Great Yarmouth*

Hot-Air Balloon Race *Grange-over-Sands, Cumbria*

6 Old Gooseberry Show *Egton Bridge*

Rushbearing *Ambleside and Grasmere*

8 Battle of Flowers *Jersey, Channel Islands*

9 Adam Sedgewick Festival (nineteenth-century geologist) *Dent, Cumbria*

10 Liverpool Carnival *Toxteth, Liverpool*

Burry Man's Parade *South Queensferry, West Lothian*

15 Our Lady's Day *Bogside, Londonderry*

Putcher Fishing (raising of salmon baskets) *Berkeley, Gloucestershire*

19 Croquet Tournament *Fettes College, Edinburgh*

22 Grasmere Sports (fell racing, hound-trailing) *Grasmere, Cumbria*

24 Burning Bartle *West Witton, Yorkshire*

Coracle Sports *Cilgerran, nr Cardigan*

25 International Teddy Bear Reunion *Warminster, Wiltshire*

Plague Memorial Service *Eyam, Derbyshire*

26 Country Music Festival *Peterborough*

Notting Hill Carnival *London*

31 Cowal Highland Games *Dunoon, Argyll*

SEPTEMBER

1 Intrepid Birdman and Nothe Fayre *Weymouth, Dorset*

5 Pilgrimage to Replica of Grotto of Lourdes *Cleator Moor, Cumbria*

Psylocobin Festival *Aberystwyth*

6 Viking Sea Angling Festival *Lerwick, Shetland*

7 Victorian Festival *Llandrindod Wells, Powys*

Race up Ben Nevis *Ben Nevis, nr Fort William*

English Vineyard Wine Festival *Alfriston, East Sussex*

Barnet Horse Fair *London*

8 Grand Contest of Arms, Battle of Bosworth *Bosworth Field, Sutton Cheney, Market Bosworth, Leicestershire*

9 Abbots Bromley Horn Dance *Abbots Bromley, Staffordshire*

St Giles' Fair *Oxford*

12 International Sheep Dog Trials *Lockerbie, Dumfries and Galloway*

14 Findon Sheep Fair *Sussex*

18 Frome Cheese Show *Frome, Somerset*

21 Egremont Crab Fair *Egremont, Cumbria*

22 Clipping the Church *Painswick, Gloucester*

27 British National Ploughing Championship *Glamis, Forfar*

29 Bare-Back Horse ride: 'Oda' *Hebrides*

Tramway (Centenary Day in 1985) *Blackpool, Lancashire*

end Running the Walls Race *Berwick-upon-Tweed, Northumberland*

OCTOBER

3 Nottingham Goose Fair *Nottingham*

5 Alston Leek Club Show *Alston, Cumbria*

7 Bellringers' Feast *Twyford, Hampshire*

11 National Gaelic Mod (singing and music) *Fort William*

12 Mop Fair *Stratford-upon-Avon, Warwickshire*

13 World Conker Championships *Ashton, nr Oundle, Peterborough*

20 Oyster Feast *Colchester, Essex*

21 Aberdeen Angus Bull Sales *Perth*

26 All Scotland Accordian and Fiddle Festival *Perth*

27 Snowdonia Marathon *Llanberis Gwynedd*

31 Punkie Night *Hinton St George, Somerset*

NOVEMBER

2 Soul-Caking Play *Antrobus, Cheshire*

3 Veteran Car Run *London to Brighton*

5 Turning the Devil's Boulder *Shebbear, Devon*

Burning of 'Pop' or Pope *Orkney*

Carrying Burning Tar-Barrels *Ottery St Mary*

Bonfire Societies *Lewes*

9 Clapham and Patching Firework Display *nr Worthing, Sussex*

Lord Mayor's Procession and Show *London*

10 Orange Parade *Liverpool*

11 Firing the Penny Poppers *Fenny Stratford, Buckinghamshire*

Wroth Silver Paid (a sort of rent) *Knightlow Cross, Warwickshire*

Scotland's Whisky Festival *Aviemore, Highlands*

23 Feast of St Clement *Burwash*

30 Racing Pigeons Old Comrades Show *London*

DECEMBER

2 Smithfield Cattle Show *Earl's Court, London*

6 St Nicholas Festival *Aberdeen*

12 Christmas Lights Switched On (1985 is Diamond Jubilee of Regent Street, Assoc.) *London*

Boar's Head Ceremony *Queen's College, Oxford*

24 Tolling the Devil's Knell *Dewsbury, Yorkshire*

26 Boxing Day Meet *Knighton, Powys*

Whaddon Chase Hounds Meet *Winslow, Buckinghamshire*

31 Tar-Barrel Fire Ceremony *Allendale, Northumberland*

Flambeaux Procession *Comrie, Perth*

Fireball Parade *Stonehaven, Grampian*

Index

Sands, Bobby, 118
Sandy (Captain Livingstone-Learmonth), 167–9
Sandy Row, Belfast, 103–4, 107
Scottish tinkers, 82–3
seals, 158–60
Sealyham Estate, 154
Seven Dials Anglican Church, Brighton, 16
Shankhill Road, Belfast, 105
Sharington, Sir William, 91
Sharon, 11, 13, 68, 69, 158
Shepherd, J.A., 78
Shula, 94, 95
Silbury Hill, 91
Skillycorn, Mr, 126–7
Smith (gypsy family), 82
Snaefell, 127–8
South Street Juveniles, Lewes, 177, 180
Sprott, Miss Molly, 83
Stacksteads Band, Bacup, 43
Stanton Fitzwarren, 92
Star Inn, Lewes (now Town Hall), 175
Steve (the exorcised), 57
Stonehenge, 35, 96–100: Druids at, 96–9; pop festival, 96
Stukely, William, 99
Swindon, 92: Old Town, 88

Ted (friend of Prices), 11, 13, 34, 67–8, 158–60
Teifi, River, 31, 132, 135–7
Telfer, Mabel, 63, 64, 65, 66
Teme, River, 169, 172
Tepee Valley, nr Aberystwyth, 148–50
Thornton, Big John, 191
Tim (farmhand to Prices), 8, 9, 10, 11, 12, 36, 67, 158
Toland, John of Londonderry, 99
Tynwald Hill, 128

UFOs, 141: Society, 14–15
Uffington, 87: Castle, 87; White Horse, 87
Ulster Protestants, 115–16
Ulster Volunteer Force (UVF), 104, 122

Vale of White Horse hunt, 94
Veal, Mr Ray and Colin, 60–1
Vermuyden, 1
Victoria, Queen, 168
Victoria Working Men's Club, Rossendale, 46
Vineyard, Abingdon, 7
'Voice of the Yob, The', 19
Vortigern, King, 164–5

Wakeman of Ripon, 29
Wallingford, 83–4
Walsh, Mr, 111, 112
Wantage, 85–6
Watt (evangelical architect of Knutsford), 64–5
Wayland's Smithy, 87
Westwoodside, 2
'White Gloves', 26–7
White Hart, Appleby, 76
White Horse of Uffington, 87
White Lady, 40
White Lion Hotel, Bala, 163
Wicca, 143
Williams, Tracey, 134
Williams-Ellis, Sir Clough, 111–12
Williamson, Paula, 62, 63
wire-weaving, 17–19
Wistman's Wood, 41
Wolf's castle, Pembrokeshire, 154
Woolpit, Suffolk, 139–42

Yvonne (friend of Prices), 11, 13, 34, 67–8, 158–9